I0887018

Transatlantic Women Travelers, 1688–1843

TRANSITS:
LITERATURE, THOUGHT & CULTURE, 1650–1850

Series Editors
Kathryn Parker, University of Wisconsin—La Crosse
Miriam Wallace, New College of Florida

A long running and landmark series in long eighteenth-century studies, *Transits* includes monographs and edited volumes that are timely, transformative in their approach, and global in their engagement with arts, literature, culture, and history. Books in the series have engaged with visual arts, environment, politics, material culture, travel, theater and performance, embodiment, writing and book history, sexuality, gender, disability, race, and colonialism from Britain and Europe to the Americas, the Far East, and the Middle East. Proposals should offer critical examination of artifacts and events, modes of being and forms of knowledge, material culture, or cultural practices. Works that make provocative connections across time, space, geography, or intellectual history, or that develop new modes of critical imagining are particularly welcome.

Recent titles in the *Transits* series:

Transatlantic Women Travelers, 1688–1843
Misty Krueger, ed.

Laurence Sterne's "A Sentimental Journey": A Legacy to the World
W. B. Gerard and M-C. Newbould, eds.

Hemispheres and Stratospheres: The Idea and Experience of Distance in the International Enlightenment
Kevin L. Cope, ed.

Rewriting Crusoe: The Robinsonade across Languages, Cultures, and Media
Jakub Lipski, ed.

Narrative Mourning: Death and Its Relics in the Eighteenth-Century British Novel
Kathleen M. Oliver

Lothario's Corpse: Libertine Drama and the Long-Running Restoration, 1700–1832
Daniel Gustafson

Romantic Automata: Exhibitions, Figures, Organisms
Michael Demson and Christopher R. Clason, eds.

Beside the Bard: Scottish Lowland Poetry in the Age of Burns
George S. Christian

The Novel Stage: Narrative Form from the Restoration to Jane Austen
Marcie Frank

The Imprisoned Traveler: Joseph Forsyth and Napoleon's Italy
Keith Crook

Fire on the Water: Sailors, Slaves, and Insurrection in Early American Literature, 1789–1886
Lenora Warren

Community and Solitude: New Essays on Johnson's Circle
Anthony W. Lee, ed.

The Global Wordsworth: Romanticism Out of Place
Katherine Bergren

For a full list of *Transits* titles, please visit our website: www.bucknelluniversitypress.org.

Transatlantic Women Travelers, 1688–1843

Edited by

MISTY KRUEGER

Bucknell University | University Press
LEWISBURG, PENNSYLVANIA

Library of Congress Cataloging-in-Publication Data
Names: Krueger, Misty, editor.
Title: Transatlantic women travelers, 1688–1843 / edited by Misty Krueger.
Description: Lewisburg: Bucknell University Press, 2021. | Series: Transits: literature, thought & culture 1650–1850 | Includes bibliographical references and index.
Identifiers: LCCN 2020027638 | ISBN 9781684482962 (paperback) | ISBN 9781684482979 (hardcover) | ISBN 9781684482986 (epub) | ISBN 9781684482993 (mobi) | ISBN 9781684483006 (pdf)
Subjects: LCSH: Travelers' writings, English—History and criticism. | English prose literature—Women authors—History and criticism. | English prose literature—17th century—History and criticism. | English prose literature—18th century—History and criticism. | English prose literature—19th century—History and criticism. | Travel in literature. | Women literature. | Women travelers in literature. | Women travelers—History.
Classification: LCC PR756.T72 T725 2021 | DDC 820.9/9287—dc23
LC record available at https://lccn.loc.gov/2020027638

A British Cataloging-in-Publication record for this book is available from the British Library.

This collection copyright © 2021 by Bucknell University Press

Individual chapters copyright © 2021 in the names of their authors

All rights reserved

No part of this book may be reproduced or utilized in any form or by any means, electronic or mechanical, or by any information storage and retrieval system, without written permission from the publisher. Please contact Bucknell University Press, Hildreth-Mirza Hall, Bucknell University, Lewisburg, PA 17837-2005. The only exception to this prohibition is "fair use" as defined by U.S. copyright law.

∞ The paper used in this publication meets the requirements of the American National Standard for Information Sciences—Permanence of Paper for Printed Library Materials, ANSI Z39.48-1992.

www.bucknelluniversitypress.org

Distributed worldwide by Rutgers University Press

Manufactured in the United States of America

This book is dedicated to both the students who enjoy learning about eighteenth- and nineteenth-century women's transatlantic travels, and the scholars who love writing about them.

CONTENTS

Transatlantic Women Travelers, 1688–1843

INTRODUCTION

Tracing the Lives of Transatlantic Women Travelers

Misty Krueger

Across numerous genres in the seventeenth through nineteenth centuries we find abundant examples of real and imagined women's Atlantic crossings, as well as their encounters in unfamiliar situations and locales. Their stories, some told in first-person accounts by actual women travelers and some fictionally narrated by other authors, illustrate lengthy, harrowing travel by sea and land and note the variety of people and experiences women faced en route to and upon reaching their destinations. These texts show the resilience of women who willingly, forcibly, or some version between these two conditions sailed across all directions of the Atlantic. Take as an example Lady Maria Nugent, who made the transatlantic journey multiple times (from America to England, England to Jamaica, and Jamaica to England) with her family—first her English loyalist parents and then her husband (the lieutenant governor and commander-in-chief of Jamaica) and their children. She kept a journal of her voyage to and residence in Jamaica from 1801 to 1805, and in it she not only documents her own experience, but also reflects on the treatment of enslaved people. Women's transatlantic journeys are portrayed not only in genres where we expect to find them, such as memoirs, travelogues, letters, and tales focused on their travels, but also in what might seem to be unlikely texts, such as novels having very little to do with travel, much less a transatlantic passage. Even Jane Austen ventured to write in her 1817 unfinished novel, *Sanditon*, of a transatlantic female traveler. Similar to the Jamaican heiress in the 1808 novel *The Woman of Colour* who ventures to England due to the stipulations of her inheritance, Austen's Miss Lambe—a biracial seventeen-year-old heiress—makes the trip from the Caribbean to England to inhabit a seaside village. Miss Lambe is the only character of color we find in an Austen novel and one of the two women in Austen's oeuvre (the other being *Persuasion*'s Mrs. Croft) who travel by sea to start a new life.

In reading the many accounts of women's travels, we learn that the reasons for their transatlantic seafaring in this time period were as multifarious as their experiences when they arrived at their points of disembarkation. Some depictions of women's transatlantic movements point to travel as a means of escapism, full of exploring new places, finding adventure, and socially or economically transforming women's lives. In some cases, accounts of transatlantic travel depict migrations of countless women in their roles as wives, daughters, sisters, and mothers venturing to start a new life far from home (often at the bequest of a male family member). They also serve as a record of women forced to leave their homelands with the sole purpose of being enslaved. These women's experiences show that although travel and transformation can represent liberation, they can also signify devastating loss. They indicate that the freedoms afforded to some women travelers in this era, especially those of white European descent, were the result of imperialism, colonization, and Black women's trauma. While certainly we find in transatlantic stories the transformative power of travel in terms of women's observations and examples of personal autonomy, we would be remiss not to recognize that this independence is contingent upon the involuntary migration of other women.

This collection of essays, *Transatlantic Women Travelers, 1688–1843*, sets out to explore the variety and vexed depictions of women's travels across the Atlantic, paying particular attention to who represents women's travels, what they represent, and what we can learn from accounts about real women's lived experiences and imagined portrayals of seafaring women in this time period. This volume aims to increase the study of transatlanticism focused not only on women who lived around the margins of the Atlantic Ocean, or even those whose works were published across the sea, but also on women who traveled this ocean and, for better or worse, found a new life in the Atlantic world.

TRACING TRANSATLANTIC WOMEN'S ROUTES, NETWORKS, AND PUBLICATIONS

There is great historical and literary value in what Brigitte Bailey calls "the mapping of women's routes, networks, and publications."[1] *Transatlantic Women Travelers, 1688–1843* takes up this charge by tracing women's transatlantic journeys, their roles in and observations of communities outside of their homelands, and how women represented themselves (as well as the people and places they encountered) or were represented by others in the long eighteenth and early nineteenth centuries. In large part this collection is a study of *images* of transatlantic women travelers, some historical and others fictionalized, rather than purely a recording of women's historical "routes, networks, and publications." This collection puts into conversation texts written by women that document their own experiences, men that represent women in the Atlantic world, and women and men who figuratively characterize women who traveled transatlantically. The outcome amounts to a "mapping" of long eighteenth- and early to mid-nineteenth-century transatlantic women travelers as writers, artists, critics, renegades, spiritual leaders, explorers, settlers, colonists, wives, daughters, enslaved people, and more.

In examining women who crossed the Atlantic (in any time period, but especially in the long eighteenth and early nineteenth centuries), we must consider why and to where women traveled, how their travels have been depicted, and the significance of these travels. Was this travel forced or voluntary? Were these women trepanned or exiled? Were they exploring to record their observations or relocating to establish new lives? To where did these women travel, and with whom did they meet en route to and upon landing at their destinations so far from and, often, unlike their homelands? We have to ask what women's transatlantic travels show us in particular about eighteenth- and nineteenth-century women's experiences. What do women encounter by sea and once they settle on land? How do they break boundaries in undergoing transatlantic travels? What do accounts show us about women's autonomy, mobility, and critical observation? What can we learn from the woman's gaze about travel and people in what Mary Louise Pratt calls "contact zones"?[2] Further, we must consider who depicted women's travels: women, men, gender unknown travel writers, writers of fiction (often presented as fact), or historians? What do these portrayals reveal about gender and genre?

On the whole, the essays in *Transatlantic Women Travelers, 1688–1843* answer such questions and show that the study of transatlantic women travelers, whether historical or fictional, lies at the intersections of gender, sexuality, race, adaptability, movement, mobility, and reconstruction. By engaging in what Heidi Slettedahl Macpherson refers to as the "performance of travelling gender," women travelers faced expectations of femininity and passivity associated with their sex while they also "tailor[ed]" and even "invent[ed]" a version of gendered selves suitable for their travel identities.[3] Sometimes women presented themselves as feminine, masculine, or androgynous to maximize their travel potential, as in the case of women who traveled in male disguise or under the guise of another race or ethnicity. Sometimes they mastered a hybrid gender performance through disguise, as in the case of *The Female American*'s Unca Eliza Winkfield, or the famed pirates Anne Bonny and Mary Read, in order to sustain themselves.[4] The fact that these women are aware of themselves as objects always being watched underlies this performance, and the fact that travel itself is "an enterprise requiring a certain degree of camouflage," as Ivette Romero-Cesareo states, means that, for women, this facade may require them to blend in with men on ship or land, to protect themselves, or simply to allow themselves to enjoy what Adriana Méndez Rodenas calls "the liberating experience of travel."[5] Narratives involving masquerade indicate the dangers associated with female bodies as well as the power of disguise to allow women to enter spaces typically defined as masculine—certainly intended for men—and to thrive. Such performances reinforce the root of the prefix "trans-" in transatlantic travel representing a move "across" and "beyond" boundaries, as Macpherson defines it.[6]

Portrayals of women's transatlantic travels point to what Méndez Rodenas terms an "ethnographic gaze" that is implicitly connected to "the gendered nature of their travels."[7] We find in women travelers' experiences what Susan C. Imbarrato calls in *Traveling Women* "a keen, eyewitness view" directly correlated with gender, race, and class, yet one also that allows women to observe other women and empathize with or critique them.[8] The role of what I call sight-as-insight is crucial to this study. Women internalize and reflect upon what they see; then they share this view with others. Also important to this activity is a gendered self-awareness. More so than men, women are aware of their positions as seen objects, but as the essays in this collection will show, many transatlantic women travelers who wrote on their experiences, even when pseudo-fictionally, move into the subject position of seeing. In *Imperial Eyes*, Pratt explains this problem when she writes of Anna Maria Falconbridge, who traveled from England to Africa: "As a woman she is not to see but be seen, or at least she is not to be seen seeing."[9] Such an axiom rings true for the women examined in this collection. A woman, as Pratt has suggested, must engage in "reciprocal seeing" or "vision" if she is to become an agent, but of course, this "seeing violates norms of conduct for her gender."[10] However, Falconbridge and other women travelers knew that "the imperative of reciprocity extends to knowledge and culture."[11] When women travelers embrace this imperative, they find themselves serving as what Imbarrato calls an "information conduit."[12] This conduit shows us not only their own experiences, but also other women's situations too. Thus, women travelers' accounts of their own travels come to provide a lens on women's lives generally that should be seen through and interpreted by the woman's gaze.

However, not all essays in this collection address women travel writers; many of the essays address either women who might have traveled transatlantically—at least their authorial voices (even when the author is anonymous) claim they have done so—or women characters who imaginatively symbolize transatlantic travelers. In these situations, we must ask ourselves what writers are trying to convey about the woman's gaze and voice. What is it that the woman traveler reveals about gender, race, ethnicity, cultures, colonialism, and imperialism? Melissa Adams-Campbell identifies "literary-historical" writing (stories about historical women) as a kind of reframing of women: in the case of authors portraying other women's transatlantic travels, they are attempting to "imaginatively reconstruct" the very idea of women as individuals and even "political agents" who crossed the Atlantic, sometimes on multiple occasions.[13]

Regardless of authorship, in representations of these travelers we tend to find what Lizabeth Paravisini-Gebert and Ivette Romero-Cesareo term "voices of contestation."[14] An integral part of this discourse is found in the woman traveler's "ability . . . to revise and reimagine the world, to question and destabilize" reality, as Yaël Rachel Schlick reminds us.[15] Likewise, Clarinda Donato affirms in her work on travel writer Flora Tristan the importance of the transatlantic woman traveler's imagination, interrogation of people and ideas, and transmission of information:

> Questioning takes place through the prism of transatlantic space, where [women] are forced to call into question and reorder almost every category of their lives and, in particular, their relationships with men and women, and the geographical and cultural determinants of their sexuality, whether in their countries of origin, in transit while traveling, or as restructured (or not) in the new environment. [They must] extrapolate universal observations about the status of women in general from their internal trajectories; moreover, [they] are forced to redefine themselves in the absence of the legal and moral codes that had previously conferred identity upon them.[16]

We should appreciate this concept of "transatlantic space" as a metaphor for adventure, renewal, and appraisal. We must not forget, however, the junction of the literal and the symbolic, for without physical movement there cannot be mobility. As essays in this volume demonstrate, women travelers crossed not only the ocean, but hemispheres, not only land to sea and sea to land, but social spheres. "Mobility" is not synonymous with "travel," Peter Adey and Ingrid Horrocks confirm, for mobility is metaphorical, performative, and affective.[17] It is "an orientation to oneself, to others and to the world," Adey argues, and "a way of having a relation to, engaging with and understanding the world *analytically*."[18] In her work on eighteenth-century women wanderers, Horrocks clarifies that through mobility "a person becomes isolated from an assumed community and is subjected to repeated encounters with strangers."[19] Often mobility is thought to signal freedom, but sometimes, as Horrocks recalls, it is "associated with, and reinscribes, social and economic inequalities."[20] Viewed positively or negatively, mobility exists in opposition to something or someone else: to separate oneself from or to transcend something or someone. Mobility is crucial to the traveler's experience and her ability to reflect on it.

Gender matters, for historically women's mobility has been impeded by a "lack of choice" and a "heightened sense of exposure."[21] Men have traditionally been more mobile and women more stationary—men, Odysseuses and women, Penelopes.[22] Unlike women who "have been cast as the ones left behind in male narratives of adventure and quest, assuming the role of patient Penelopes awaiting their heroes' returns rather than questioning themselves," transatlantic women travelers well into the twentieth century, Macpherson reminds us, have taken "leading roles in women's narratives of discovery, travel and escape."[23] In many cases, transatlantic travel offered women "opportunity for adventure and advancement" and a "metaphor for personal transformation," as Imbarrato notes.[24] The potential for this transformation is realized through what Macpherson labels "reconstruction: of place and location (both figurative and real), of identity and of genre."[25] Even when presented fictionally, this reconstruction can be read as an autobiographical act that includes a woman's appropriation of her surroundings and the social roles at her disposal to carve out a space for herself in her new environment, even when the odds are stacked against her.

While oftentimes eighteenth- and early nineteenth-century depictions of (predominantly white) European, British, and American women's travels frame their experiences as harrowing and life threatening to titillate readers or to dissuade women from traveling, not all accounts share such perspectives. As Sarah Crabtree explains, conventional descriptions impressed upon "readers the dangers of women at sea in spite of the courage and triumph of female passengers."[26] At times, *Transatlantic Women Travelers, 1688–1843* takes the latter view in focusing on women's abilities to adapt as they embark on a seafaring course and relocate in unfamiliar territory. Essays in this collection illustrate that even when transatlantic women find themselves in adverse circumstances far from home, isolated from family and friends, they find ways to cope with their conditions and even flourish in their new environs. Upon examining the transatlantic women travelers featured in this collection, most who travel voluntarily, one thing becomes clear: the "transformative power of travel" reveals itself through "the sea changes wrought to individual women's lives as a result of their journeys."[27] Regardless of the cause of the journey, travel changes the traveler. Crossing the Atlantic is certainly a rite of passage.

(PSEUDO)HISTORICAL AND FICTIVE PERSPECTIVES ON TRANSATLANTIC WOMEN TRAVELERS

Although Susan Manning and Susan Lamb argue that transatlantic women are "all metaphor" or "figurative," this collection argues for a literal-figurative hybrid perspective on eighteenth- and nineteenth-century transatlantic women travelers.[28]

It examines women's travels across and around the perimeter of the Atlantic as lived experiences that have historical and literary bearings on the Atlantic world. This study also broaches the idea of transatlantic women's travels from a pseudohistorical and fictive perspective to illustrate how authors depicted women's travels, and to consider images that painted pictures of their travels. The volume's grouping of essays demonstrates how literary representations of women's transatlantic travel mirror the acts of observation and vocalization present in historical accounts of women's encounters at sea and abroad, rather than merely the trope of the suffering, abandoned, captured transatlantic woman. Hence, *Transatlantic Women Travelers, 1688–1843* is a study of images of women, some of lived women from their own writings and some narrated by others, depicting actual women and imagined ones, but certainly speaking to physical and sociological issues transatlantic women travelers faced in this time period.

The division of essays into two parts might seem to demonstrate a distinct difference between historical and fictional, but the writers and texts analyzed in this collection actually reveal a gradient rather than a rigid boundary between fact and fiction. The contributors to this volume thus grapple with the issues of the historical and the fictional as they explore depictions of transatlantic women travelers. As with the fuzzy line between the historical and the fictional, the contributors blur the line between historical and contemporary language when it helps us better see women's groundbreaking travel. Essays in this collection are mindful of the debate regarding presentism in studying historical materials (as examples, regarding discussions of silences and gaps, and of women of color's and white women's stories). While it is compelling and productive to use feminist and Marxist language to talk about eighteenth- and nineteenth-century women, the scholarship in this volume employs terminology that represents women geographically and culturally *in their time* as well as theoretically through our own twenty-first-century understandings of gender, race, and class. At times, gender-specific language regarding "femininity" describes details historically associated with sex, though terms such as "agency" or "empowerment" are also used to emphasize women's sense of independence. Essays focused on racial and ethnic individuals and groups, such as Shelby Johnson's, choose signifiers, such as "African" or "Black" when appropriate, to denote the differences between races, places, and cultures, but also to affirm significance. In this volume, the terms "Black" and "Indigenous" will be used as proper nouns and therefore capitalized. The essays in this book are mindful of the political ramifications of language that reinforces Eurocentric perspectives, such as those involving the enslavement of people. For instance, in shifting from "slave" to "enslaved person/people," scholarship affirms the status of people as individuals who exist in their own right first and have enslavement forced upon them. Likewise, in moving from place-oriented terms like "periphery" or "New World," language in these essays displaces the view of Europe as the center and Africa, the Americas, and the Caribbean as space to colonize. Lastly, terms regarding the geographical and geological overlap with gender and identity categories. For instance, Pam Perkins uses the phrase "outport women" rather than "working-class women" to describe Newfoundland women. Some scholars focus on the relationship between ecology and illustrations of material items, such as flora and fauna, and people.

Part 1 of the volume highlights issues of what Macpherson labels the "performance of travelling gender" in regard to accounts of historical, or pseudohistorical, women—some written by women, and some by men. The women featured in this section, whether as writers or figures under observation, play two significant and complementary roles: as critics of institutions that control, even enslave, women and as creators of knowledge of the Atlantic, its colonies, and its peoples. These women function as transatlantic information conduits shaping representations of the Atlantic world by offering testimonies of women's mobility, adaptability, and reconstruction.

To begin, Diana Epelbaum examines German-born entomologist and artist Maria Sibylla Merian's (and her twenty-one-year-old daughter's) 1699 travel to Surinam and the images Merian brought back with her to Amsterdam. Merian's 1705 folio-sized text, *The Metamorphosis of the Insects of Surinam*, not only signifies Merian's mobility, but also represents a European scientist-artist's view of culture and clime generally not recorded and publicized by a woman. As Epelbaum explains, Merian's travels and *The Metamorphosis* are metonymic for the production and circulation of transatlantic knowledge; they mark both the exemplarity of a woman naturalist's preservationist, "proto-ecologic sensibility" and her observations of not only the flora and fauna, but also colonialism and enslavement. As examples from *The Metamorphosis* reveal, Merian's drawings and descriptions anthropomorphize her ecological subjects in a way that also critiques gendered contests for power in contact zones.

Approximately one hundred years after Merian's renderings of Surinam, Anna Maria Falconbridge's 1794 *Two Voyages to Sierra Leone* provided readers with another European woman's ecologically minded, (anti)colonialist gaze. As Shelby Johnson's essay notes, Falconbridge's epistolary travel narrative uses female interlocutors' perspectives to evaluate male colonists' motives, "slow violence" (which occurs over time and in some ways is immediately and directly unseeable), and failures in sustaining livability in their settlements. Falconbridge's "sympathetic vision" reflects a "politico-climatic" critique of unethical population relocation and the resulting distress upon the people the British claimed to assist. Johnson situates Falconbridge's text among late eighteenth-century debates on Black resettlement and specifically links the author's sympathetic voice to gender and reparative justice. The essay closes by putting Falconbridge's narrative into conversation with Black Nova Scotian emigrant Susana Smith as a way to speak directly to women's views on "thresholds of livability" in the African colony. In doing so, Johnson reminds us of the relationship between somatic experience and the ways a woman can "write [her]self into visibility."

Grace A. Gomashie's essay puts into conversation two mid-nineteenth-century women's travels and world views. In her study of Flora Tristan and Frances "Fanny" Erskine Inglis Calderón de la Barca, Gomashie recounts not only each social explorer's travels—Tristan's from Europe to South America and back, and Calderón's from Europe to the United States of America to Mexico and then back to Europe—but also each woman's eyewitness accounts of the women they met in Latin American contact zones. Collectively, Tristan's 1838 *Peregrinations of a Pariah* and Calderón's 1843 *Life in Mexico during a Residence of Two Years in That Country* offer readers a feminist perspective on women's rights—including those of each author's. While both women's relationships with men serve as the impetus for their travels, their travelogues prompt us to look at their relationships with and views on women, particularly regarding oppression, sympathy, and empathy. In the end, these women's journeys come to represent much more than their own travels and acclimations; they interpret and give voice to the women they meet.

Women's transatlantic travel and the people, cultures, and environments encountered as a result of this travel are not always documented by women travel writers in this period. In many cases, men provide written accounts of the women they meet in their travels and the women they live with in communities far from "home." Such is the case in Pam Perkins's essay on Newfoundland, which addresses the roles of transient women in early nineteenth-century settler colonial cultures. Even though most descriptions of Newfoundland are written by males and only include "glimpses" of women, it is vital to explore these snapshots, as Perkins does, in her examination of Sir Thomas Cochrane's journal and letters detailing his interactions with St. John's women. Perkins indicates that the women Cochrane hailed as the "daughters of Terra Nova," such as Anne Aplin, represent relocated and reconstructed British femininity and culture, as well as the domestic pillars holding up St. John's new society. Perkins also addresses the few surviving writings by women who made the trek to Newfoundland. In Mary Elizabeth Brenton's letters, for instance, we hear an echo of Maria Sibylla Merian, for Brenton corresponded with botanist Sir William Jackson Hooker about plants in Newfoundland; also like Merian, Brenton and most of the Englishwomen who traveled to Newfoundland returned to the comforts of home. This trajectory appears in contrast to Perkins's closing account of the "unfeminine" outport women who remained in Newfoundland.

Ula Lukszo Klein's essay on "busty" buccaneers gives us another view on unfeminine laboring-class women recorded by men in her examination of the early eighteenth-century female pirates Anne Bonny and Mary Read, who traveled from Britain to the Caribbean, masqueraded as men, and fought for personal freedoms, love, and glory. Klein's essay considers how these transatlantic travelers engaged in gender subversion, achieved "independence of movement" and "outlaw mobility," and to this day symbolize autonomy and fluidity in a space not meant for women to have much, if any, subjectivity. In addition to gender, an examination of Bonny and Read must take into account their class and race, Klein reminds us, for their lower-class origins and whiteness in part determined their freedoms. Although we might think of Bonny and Read as actual transatlantic women travelers, in Klein's view we cannot forget that their tales recorded in Captain Charles Johnson's 1724 *A General History of the . . . Pyrates* and their collective story represent various tropes of eighteenth-century British women, such as the cross-dresser, the criminal, or the lower-class woman. We must recall the tenuous line between Bonny and Read as historical travelers and textual representations hailed as Others, self-exiles who leave their homelands and land itself to gain independence, and as quasi characters objectified as gendered and sexualized deviants who textually come to speak for social mores censuring women's rights to act upon same-sex desires and enact female masculinity.

Part 2 of *Transatlantic Women Travelers, 1688–1843* explores women who mirror and expand upon images of actual transatlantic travelers, such as those featured in this volume. The first essay, Jennifer Golightly's examination of Samuel Jackson Pratt's 1780 *Emma Corbett*, provides an interesting counterpart to Klein's on the importance of cross-dressing in eighteenth-century women's transatlantic travel. Like the accounts of Bonny and Read, who used disguise to allow them unrestricted passage from England across the western Atlantic, Pratt's epistolary novel draws on cross-dressing as a trope for women's deviance and autonomy, and a tool with which women can navigate a liminal transatlantic space. Unlike the female pirates, though, who are exposed publicly as being women and begrudgingly use their female bodies to plead for their lives, Emma Corbett freely shifts between embodying the positions of woman and man (in this role twice: one, at sea, is British and one, on land, is Native American). These gendered performances lead Emma to successfully save her husband and eventually return to her preferred roles as daughter, sister, and wife, each of which is built on femininity and sensibility. Ultimately, Golightly's essay points to Emma's sensibility not only as a lasting marker of womanliness, but also as an ability to assert feminine power over men at home in England and in America, thus positioning sentiment as a tool for embodying the suffering caused by war and mediating political boundaries. In this rendering of transatlantic space, we must recognize not only Emma's gender performance by sea and on land, but also the impact of a woman to cultivate affective bonds—rather than patriotic and personal strife—between women and men, between men, and across national identities.

Disguise, feminine performance, and the renegotiation of national and cultural differences also play crucial roles in Unca Eliza Winkfield's 1767 *The Female American*, even though in this novel physical disguise allows the narrator to assume the role of a god rather than mere man. In Unca Eliza's history we find what Alexis McQuigge calls a "fantasy of female empowerment" inherited from Unca Eliza's Native American matriarchal ancestors and appropriated throughout the novel. Although the actual author's identity cannot be verified as male, female, English, or American, McQuigge argues that the text clearly provides readers with an image of an eighteenth-century transatlantic woman's autonomy, adaptability, and self-construction as she travels by sea and land. These traits, McQuigge finds, should be read alongside those of Unca Eliza's mother and aunt, thus balancing our study of her bicultural background rather than focusing exclusively on her Englishness's correlation with her religious conversion of the Indigenous people she encounters. In turning to Unca Eliza's matriarchally derived authority, McQuigge offers a counterpoint to transatlantic Robinsonades focusing solely on European and American men's imperialist and colonial pursuits.

In turning from *The Female American* to *The Woman of Colour*, an epistolary novel published anonymously in 1808 that also focuses on the heroine's biraciality, we encounter another example of a woman's transatlantic travels framed as a kind of Robinsonade. However, Octavia Cox's essay on *The Woman of Colour* proposes that we examine this text as a "reverse-Robinsonade": a tale that reverses the trope of the white European discovering and civilizing an island culture. Instead, in the Jamaican-born protagonist, Olivia Fairfield, we find an "uncultured native" traveling to a supposedly civilized culture and exposing its inhabitants' incivility. This genre, Cox argues, provides readers with a "female transatlantic critic" who observes and speaks against both Englishmen and *women's* prejudices and hypocrisy regarding race and abolition. Alongside Falconbridge's critical outlook on the English and Tristan's and Calderón's discerning views of the institutional oppression of Latin American women, we find in Olivia an eyewitness, a political voice, and a conduit of social mores. However, as Cox argues, Olivia is not as progressive as we might imagine or want her to be; in many ways she is more conservative than radical.

Victoria Barnett-Woods's essay on the 1820 novel *Zelica, the Creole*, attributed to American author Leonora Sansay, also addresses how the voice of a mixed-race woman provides critical insight into interracial relations, colonialism, and warfare. In Barnett-Woods's argument, creole women represent cultural fluidity and nationalism in flux. Like many of the essays in *Transatlantic Women Travelers, 1688–1843*, Barnett-Woods's work highlights the contrast between men's penchant for conquest and violence and women's attention to "sorority and empowerment," as well as women gazing at women in attempts to better understand and even glorify them. Barnett-Woods's treatment of Zelica's relationship with Clara (one of the female characters from Sansay's 1808 epistolary novel set in Haiti, *Secret History*) leads us to see a "female creole collective" representative of women's transracial networks in transatlantic spaces. These networks rely on multiple kinds of mobility, gender mutability, and women's banding together to fight for women's rights. In a sense, creolization becomes analogous to women's transgressive positions in the circum-Atlantic world. The characters in Sansay's works come to "reflect the truth of people's lives"—possibly including Sansay's—as well as the "construction of early hemispheric American literary history," Barnett-Woods reminds us.

Like Barnett-Woods's analysis of *Zelica*'s revisionist treatment of creole women in Sansay's *Secret History*, Kathleen Morrissey's comparative essay on Aphra Behn's 1688 novella *Oroonoko* and Phebe Gibbes's 1789 novel *Hartly House, Calcutta* establishes a textual relationship between women characters and women writers, in this case across one hundred years and set in English colonies on opposite sides of the Atlantic. Morrissey makes a case for both works' generic similarities as women's colonial travel texts, and she examines Gibbes's debt to Behn's writing on colonial women by articulating a kind of transatlantic imagination first created by Behn and then used by women writers depicting women's travels to British colonies. This essay makes a case for studying imagined women's travel experiences, of which Behn may or may not have actually endured herself in Surinam, and of which Gibbes most likely did not in Calcutta. Ultimately, Morrissey's essay asks readers to consider transatlantic women's "convergence of feminine resistances," and Gibbes's eastern-reaching revision of western, transatlantic narrative. In doing so, we find in Gibbes's text many of the "colonial heroine's tropes" regarding women (such as objectification, "calculated employments of femininity," and agentive acts) established earlier in the period by Behn's novella. We also find two women writers using fictional travel writing not only to portray for their readers seemingly exotic cultures, but also to look back at England with a critical eye.

The collection begins with a woman's account of factual eyewitnessing in late seventeenth-century Surinam and her artistic depiction of it and closes with a woman's possible, but certainly fictional, portrayal of the colony. In coming full circle, this collection is mindful of the relationship between women's movement, contact with different cultures, and mobility. In a final example of reflection, Eve

Tavor Bannet's afterword speaks to the "historicity of female subjects" in this collection. Bannet points to the ways the essays "distribute" transatlantic women figures "along a spectrum between history and fiction in which there are no pure exemplars of either extreme." To that end, Bannet asks us to remember that all narratives, even those claiming to be true or based on a true story, blend fact and fiction—thus representing a *mixta genera*—and that transatlantic women travelers' tales, whether they are recorded by women or imagined by men, fall within the purview of generic and tropic multiplicity. This acknowledgment affords scholars and readers the choice of isolating which facets, such as genre or markers of travel, become the most salient for examinations of such historical and literary figures.

Scholars, such as Bannet, have identified the Atlantic world as a site of convergence, and this collection of essays situates women as key players in this interchange. Even though transatlantic travel can give way to transnationalism, it often bears the sign of empire. Transatlanticism can lead to the blending of nations, but it can also serve to erase nations already in existence. Despite cultural differences that might, and often do, tear people apart and lead to violence, transatlanticism represents communal experiences. It represents individual stories, as well as the merger and overlapping of stories. This collection exemplifies the latter as it brings together women who traveled by choice and those who traveled unwillingly. We find accounts of wanderers setting out to start new lives and women who have been transported. These are the stories of free women, enslaved women, wives, sisters, intellects, laborers, white women, women of color, biracial women, bicultural women, transnational women, and more, who co-exist literally and figuratively across and around the Atlantic and across genres. In its convergence of accounts of diverse women's travels, this collection aims to take an intersectional perspective as it resists a hegemonic feminist point of view. The volume makes an intervention in transatlantic studies not only through its resistance to a masculinized view of the Atlantic world, but also by putting into conversation stories of women of color and non-English-speaking women with stories of white British, American, and European women in the entire circum-Atlantic world. On the whole, the volume intercedes in transatlantic scholarship in its renegotiation of boundaries, ultimately in complicating the divide between historical and literary studies of the Atlantic world and addressing both historical and fictional accounts as legitimate representations of travel. By addressing the intersections of gender and race, the essays in this collection both introduce readers to lesser-known texts, such as letters and journal entries, by women of color and revitalize treatments of canonical works, such as literary travel narratives and novels. This collection is a compendium of women who travel, tell their stories, tell others' stories, and have their stories told.

WOMEN'S TRANSATLANTIC STUDIES: AN EMERGING FIELD

It might still come as a surprise to readers familiar with "canonical" long eighteenth- and early nineteenth-century literature and history to find that women's transatlantic travels are the stuff of narratives from this time period. In the 2012 collection of essays *Transatlantic Women: Nineteenth-Century American Women Writers and Great Britain*, Brigitte Bailey indicates that although transatlantic studies initially focused on men's travels and writings, in the first decade of the twenty-first century "a surge of scholarship on women writers and travelers" signaled "an important moment in what continues to be an emergent field, especially in the mapping of women's routes, networks, and publications."[29] Indeed, many transatlantic studies from the 1970s–1990s, as well as the first decade of the twenty-first century, concentrated on men and relegated women to the margins of a field vital to eighteenth- through twentieth-century historical and literary studies.[30] Since the turn of the twenty-first century, books and essays have addressed transatlantic women, but we have not necessarily seen the "surge" Bailey postulates. Foundational studies from the first two decades of the twenty-first century set the stage for closely examining eighteenth- and nineteenth-century transatlantic writers, characters, and publications; however, women still appeared on the sidelines of this scholarship. While Eve Tavor Bannet's *Transatlantic Stories and the History of Reading, 1720–1810: Migrant Fictions* includes a chapter on Penelope Aubin, and another on the publication in America of British-authored, women-centered novels, such as *Moll Flanders* and *Pamela*, most of the study analyzes men's travels and publications.[31] Bannet and Susan Manning's collection of sixteen essays, *Transatlantic Literary Studies, 1660–1830*, also takes a single-author, literary-publication approach to representing women in transatlantic studies.[32] In it, Lise Sorenson's chapter on Susanna Rowson follows suit with Bannet's work on Aubin in its concentration on women in captivity narratives.[33] Manning and Andrew Taylor's collection of forty-two essays, *Transatlantic Literary Studies: A Reader*, considers one woman traveler, Frances Erskine Inglis Calderón de la Barca.[34] Further, women are mentioned in Manning and Francis D. Cogliano's introduction to *The Atlantic Enlightenment*, but they do not figure prominently in the collection's essays.[35] Upon reading these books, and others, one might ask why there are not more women writers, characters, and travelers featured in eighteenth- and nineteenth-century transatlantic studies.

The study of transatlantic women "continues to be an emergent field," but there has been scholarship that moves women from the periphery to the center of analyses.[36] For instance, the introduction to Lisa L. Moore, Joanna Brooks, and Caroline Wigginton's *Transatlantic Feminisms in the Age of Revolutions* contextualizes women's transatlantic travel alongside feminist and historical revolutions; it also includes samples from approximately fifty women writers spanning the mid-seventeenth through early nineteenth centuries.[37] Toni Bowers and Tita Chico's collection of essays, *Atlantic Worlds in the Long Eighteenth Century: Seduction and Sentiment*, includes a handful of chapters addressing eighteenth-century transatlantic women, such as Susanna Rowson and Phillis Wheatley, even though they do not all focus on travel per se.[38] Unfortunately, few studies of eighteenth- and early nineteenth-century transatlanticism explore women's travels—fictional or nonfictional; most concentrate on textual transmission. This is the case in Bailey's latest work, *American Travel Literature, Gendered Aesthetics, and the Italian Tour, 1824–1862*, and Annika Bautz and Kathryn N. Gray's volume, *Transatlantic Literature and Transitivity, 1780–1850: Subjects, Texts, and Print Culture*.[39] Even though studies such as Elizabeth A. Bohls's *Women Travel Writers and the Language of Aesthetics, 1716–1818*, Susan Lamb's *Bringing Travel Home to England: Tourism, Gender, and Imaginative Literature in the Eighteenth Century*, Katrina O'Loughlin's *Women, Writing, and Travel in the Eighteenth Century*, and Ingrid Horrocks's *Women Wanderers and the Writing of Mobility, 1784–1814* all address women who travel, they focus on eighteenth-century tourism and depictions of European travel writing—quite a different version of travel as compared to ones undertaken across the Atlantic.[40]

There are studies that address women's transatlantic travel, though they do not focus solely on the long eighteenth and early nineteenth centuries. Paravisini-Gebert and Romero-Cesareo's collection, *Women at Sea: Travel Writing and the Margins of Caribbean Discourse*, explores women's sea travel to and within the Caribbean from the sixteenth through the twentieth centuries (two of the twelve essays examine long eighteenth-century women). The study begins with an important point: "the exploration of travel" in scholarship on "travel, travel literature, and gender" needs to "be expanded to include those traveling the social and economic periphery, the margins of colonial societies."[41] In *Women at Sea*, these marginalized figures are women whose experiences in the Caribbean are shaped by gender, race, and class. Most examinations of transatlantic women feature mid-nineteenth- through twentieth-century American and British women writers or American, British, and European travelers, and these analyses, like *Women at Sea*, tend to emphasize nationality and gender as a starting and often ending point for their considerations of literary characters, publications, politics, colonialism, and imperialism. Méndez Rodenas's *Transatlantic Travels in Nineteenth-Century Latin America: European Women Pilgrims* is one of the few studies to concentrate exclusively on nineteenth-century women's transatlantic travel as well as their post-travel experiences. *Transatlantic Women: Nineteenth-Century American Women Writers and Great Britain*, edited by Beth L. Lueck, Brigitte Bailey, and Lucinda L. Damon-Bach, makes a good case for studying mid- to late nineteenth-century American women writers and their travels to Britain. Nineteenth-century British and European women travel writers also figure prominently in Schlick's *Feminism and the Politics of Travel after the Enlightenment*, although only one of these writers, Flora Tristan, writes about crossing the Atlantic. Readers hoping to locate examples of long eighteenth- and early nineteenth-century transatlantic women's writings in Macpherson's *Transatlantic Women's Literature* will find only twentieth-century literature. Nevertheless, Macpherson's work reminds us of the importance of tracing women's depictions of Atlantic crossings, and it purposely cultivates a transnational approach that rejects the notion of transatlantic travel merely representing a linear, uni- or bidirectional route between Britain and America, and vice versa, as it calls attention to subjects who originate from and arrive at destinations circling the Atlantic. This approach is mirrored in *Transatlantic Women Travelers, 1688–1843.*

Like many eighteenth- and nineteenth-century circum-Atlantic women travelers, this introduction concludes by returning to a point of embarkation: the charge to register transatlantic "women's routes, networks, and publications" and transatlantic studies scholars' need to continue this work. In bringing together essays that examine women's routes across the Atlantic, *Transatlantic Women Travelers, 1688–1843* provides a map of women's travels with points marking the entire perimeter of the ocean: England, Europe, Africa, South America, islands in the Caribbean, Mexico, America/the United States, Newfoundland, and Ireland. While these sites are important to the study of women's travels, the experiences women encountered en route and upon landing speak to this study's goals—to trace accounts of women's encounters in environments foreign to them and with people seemingly unlike themselves, as well as women's malleability and resilience in situations that would test even occupational travelers. In recognizing traveling women's wills to endure and desires not only to record what they see, but also to give voice to traditionally underrepresented people (in many cases, women), we find a diverse, and sometimes unexpected, women's network and even sisterhood. Through publications of women's travel writing, which oftentimes depicts colonial encounters, we have the privilege of receiving women's self-representations; of interest to this collection, many essays show that these representations appear in tandem with depictions of the plights of women they meet and observe as potential mirrors of themselves. Even when the essays in this collection examine transatlantic women who were not actual but fictionalized travelers, we find writers (men, women, and in some cases gender unknown) focusing on similar issues illustrated in actual travelers' accounts: women must confront objectification through fluid gender performances; they must examine their surroundings and social institutions with a critical eye; they must not remain silent; and they must empower themselves and other women. Given the fact that for so long the Atlantic world has been thought of as a man's space built upon exploration and conquest, we cannot ignore the position of women's points of view and voices in shaping this world and their own lives. Their routes, networks, and publications have much to show readers about how transatlantic travel affected long eighteenth- and nineteenth-century women's experiences and why we must pay attention to it.

NOTES

1. Brigitte Bailey, "Introduction: Transatlantic Studies and American Women Writers," in *Transatlantic Women: Nineteenth-Century American Women Writers and Great Britain*, ed. Beth L. Lueck, Brigitte Bailey, and Lucinda L. Damon-Bach (Durham: University of New Hampshire Press, 2012), xiii.
2. Mary Louise Pratt, *Imperial Eyes: Travel Writing and Transculturation* (London: Routledge, 1992).
3. Heidi Slettedahl Macpherson, *Transatlantic Women's Literature* (Edinburgh: Edinburgh University Press, 2008), 81.
4. For a full treatment of Unca Eliza Winkfield's performance, see Kristianne Kalata Vaccaro, "'Recollection . . . Sets My Busy Imagination to Work': Transatlantic Self-Narration, Performance, and Reception in *The Female American*," *Eighteenth-Century Fiction* 20, no. 2 (Winter 2007–2008): 127–150.
5. Ivette Romero-Cesareo, "Women Adrift: Madwomen, Matriarchs, and the Caribbean," in *Women at Sea: Travel Writing and the Margins of Caribbean Discourse*, ed. Lizabeth Paravisini-Gebert and Ivette Romero-Cesareo (New York: Palgrave, 2001), 135; Adriana Méndez Rodenas, *Transatlantic Travels in Nineteenth-Century Latin America: European Women Pilgrims* (Lewisburg, PA: Bucknell University Press, 2014), 13.
6. Macpherson, *Transatlantic Women's Literature*, 6.
7. Méndez Rodenas, *Transatlantic Travels*, 11.
8. Susan C. Imbarrato, *Traveling Women: Narrative Visions of Early America* (Athens: Ohio University Press, 2006), 1.
9. Pratt, *Imperial Eyes*, 104.
10. Pratt, *Imperial Eyes*, 82–83, 104.
11. Pratt, *Imperial Eyes*, 83.
12. Imbarrato, *Traveling Women*, 1.
13. Melissa Adams-Campbell, "Writing Pocahontas: Romantic Women Writers and the Transatlantic Rescuing Indian Maiden," in *Transatlantic Literature and Transitivity, 1780–1850: Subjects, Texts, and Print Culture*, ed. Annika Bautz and Kathryn N. Gray (New York: Routledge, 2017), 70, 83.
14. Lizabeth Paravisini-Gebert and Ivette Romero-Cesareo, "Introduction: Traveling the Margins of Caribbean Discourse," in *Women at Sea: Travel Writing and the Margins of Caribbean Discourse*, ed. Lizabeth Paravisini-Gebert and Ivette Romero-Cesareo (New York: Palgrave, 2001), 2.
15. Yaël Rachel Schlick, *Feminism and the Politics of Travel after the Enlightenment* (Lewisburg, PA: Bucknell University Press, 2012), 3.

16. Clorinda Donato, "The Peregrinations of Two 'Péruviennes': Travel, Gender and Sexuality in the Transatlantic Crossings of Mme de Graffigny's Zilia and Flora Tristan," *Revista de Humanidades*, no. 27–28 (October 2010): 44.
17. Peter Adey, *Mobility* (London: Routledge, 2010), 14–15, 162; Ingrid Horrocks, *Women Wanderers and the Writing of Mobility, 1784–1814* (Cambridge: Cambridge University Press, 2017), 23–24.
18. Adey, *Mobility*, xvii–xviii.
19. Horrocks, *Women Wanderers*, 25.
20. Horrocks, *Women Wanderers*, 21.
21. Horrocks, *Women Wanderers*, 27.
22. Horrocks, *Women Wanderers*, 4.
23. Macpherson, *Transatlantic Women's Literature*, 2.
24. Imbarrato, *Traveling Women*, 1, 14.
25. Macpherson, *Transatlantic Women's Literature*, 6–7.
26. Sarah Crabtree, "Navigating Mobility: Gender, Class, and Space at Sea, 1760–1810," *Eighteenth-Century Studies* 48, no. 1 (Fall 2014): 97.
27. Méndez Rodenas, *Transatlantic Travels*, 11.
28. Susan Manning, "Characterless Women and Men: A Transatlantic Perspective," *Symbiosis: A Journal of Anglo-American Literary Relations* 10, no. 1 (April 2006): 27; Susan Lamb, *Bringing Travel Home to England: Tourism, Gender, and Imaginative Literature in the Eighteenth Century* (Newark: University of Delaware Press, 2009), 13.
29. Bailey, "Introduction: Transatlantic Studies," xiii.
30. One of the first scholarly monographs to treat transatlanticism offers such an example: Walter Allen, comp., *Transatlantic Crossing: American Visitors to Britain and British Visitors to America in the Nineteenth Century* (London: Heinemann, 1971). Other excellent studies on transatlanticism followed, but unfortunately they do not feature women. Many of these studies focus on literary figures, publishing, or periods, such as Romanticism. See Eve Tavor Bannet, *Transatlantic Stories and the History of Reading, 1720–1810: Migrant Fictions* (Cambridge: Cambridge University Press, 2011); Eve Tavor Bannet and Susan Manning, eds., *Transatlantic Literary Studies, 1660–1830* (Cambridge: Cambridge University Press, 2012); Susan Manning, *Poetics of Character: Transatlantic Encounters, 1700–1900* (Cambridge: Cambridge University Press, 2013); Susan Manning and Francis D. Cogliano, eds., *The Atlantic Enlightenment* (Burlington, VT: Ashgate, 2008); Susan Manning and Andrew Taylor, eds., *Transatlantic Literary Studies: A Reader* (Baltimore: Johns Hopkins University Press, 2007); Kevin Hutchings and Julia M. Wright, eds., *Transatlantic Literary Exchanges, 1790–1870* (Burlington, VT: Ashgate, 2011); Kevin Hutchings and John Miller, eds., *Transatlantic Literary Ecologies: Nature and Culture in the Nineteenth-Century Anglophone Atlantic World* (London: Routledge, 2017); Andrew Hemingway and Alan Wallach, eds., *Transatlantic Romanticism: British and American Art and Literature, 1790–1860* (Amherst: University of Massachusetts Press, 2015); Lance Newman, Joel Pace, and Chris Koenig-Woodyard, eds., *Transatlantic Romanticism: An Anthology of British, American, and Canadian Literature, 1767–1867* (New York: Pearson Longman, 2006); and Joselyn M. Almeida, *Reimagining the Transatlantic, 1780–1890* (London: Routledge, 2011), among others.
31. Bannet, *Transatlantic Stories*. Aubin has proved to be a popular representative in scholarship on transatlantic eighteenth-century women. In addition to Bannet's work, see Aparna Gollapudi, "Virtuous Voyages in Penelope Aubin's Fiction," *Studies in English Literature* 45, no. 3 (Summer 2005): 669–690; and Edward J. Kozaczka, "Penelope Aubin and Narratives of Empire," *Eighteenth-Century Fiction* 25, no. 1 (Fall 2012): 199–225.
32. Bannet and Manning, *Transatlantic Literary Studies*.

33. Lise Sorensen, "Susanna Rowson and the Transatlantic Captivity Narrative," in *Transatlantic Literary Studies, 1660–1830*, ed. Eve Tavor Bannet and Susan Manning (Cambridge: Cambridge University Press, 2012), 169–185.
34. Manning and Taylor, *Transatlantic Literary Studies*.
35. Manning and Cogliano, *The Atlantic Enlightenment*.
36. Important studies of women traveling within America are not included in this list because they do not focus on transatlanticism. For example, Pratt's *Imperial Eyes* offers many useful frameworks for understanding contact zones, travel writing, and transculturation, and the text addresses women travelers who crossed the Atlantic, but Pratt places her attention mostly on male travelers and writers. Imbarrato's *Traveling Women* addresses eighteenth- and nineteenth-century American women travelers, but these women are settlers who inhabit the frontier, rather than make a transatlantic voyage.
37. Lisa L. Moore, Joanna Brooks, and Caroline Wigginton, eds., *Transatlantic Feminisms in the Age of Revolutions* (Oxford: Oxford University Press, 2012).
38. Toni Bowers and Tita Chico, eds., *Atlantic Worlds in the Long Eighteenth Century: Seduction and Sentiment* (New York: Palgrave Macmillan, 2012).
39. See Brigitte Bailey, *American Travel Literature, Gendered Aesthetics, and the Italian Tour, 1824–1862* (Edinburgh: Edinburgh University Press, 2018); and Bautz and Gray, *Transatlantic Literature and Transitivity*.
40. See Elizabeth A. Bohls, *Women Travel Writers and the Language of Aesthetics, 1716–1818* (Cambridge: Cambridge University Press, 1995); Lamb, *Bringing Travel Home to England*; Horrocks, *Women Wanderers*; and Katrina O'Loughlin, *Women, Writing, and Travel in the Eighteenth Century* (Cambridge: Cambridge University Press, 2018). For another study focusing on eighteenth-century women and the Grand Tour, see also Brian Dolan, *Ladies of the Grand Tour: British Women in Pursuit of Enlightenment and Adventure in Eighteenth-Century Europe* (New York: HarperCollins, 2001).
41. Paravisini-Gebert and Romero-Cesareo, "Introduction: Traveling the Margins," 1.

Part One

(PSEUDO)HISTORICAL WOMEN'S TRAVELS

1

"LITTLE ATLAS"

Global Travel and Local Preservation in Maria Sibylla Merian's *The Metamorphosis of the Insects of Surinam*

Diana Epelbaum

IN 1699, AT THE AGE of fifty-two, and at a time when women's mobility was limited, German-born entomologist Maria Sibylla Merian, an engraver's daughter and artist's stepdaughter, traveled at her own expense and with one of her daughters, across the Atlantic to Surinam on a collecting expedition. For two years, Merian observed Surinamese insects in their natural habitats, purporting to compose her illustrations "from life," a critical practice that grounded her work in the New Science.[1] After returning to Amsterdam, Merian published *The Metamorphosis of the Insects of Surinam* (1705), a stunning volume of folio-sized plates and descriptive text that by all accounts—even for her male contemporaries—was an eminent contribution to the natural history genre. Merian's emphasis on the symbiotic relationships of insects, fauna, and flora in their local environments, with enlarged focus on the life cycles of insects, shifted the generic standard away from the classification of dead, decontextualized specimens.

Where comparable works of natural history depicted significantly fewer species, *The Metamorphosis* depicted approximately one hundred species of insects and fifty-three species of plants.[2] Where European insect books depicted plants in one stage—either flower or fruit—Merian compressed both flower and fruit into one plate, at once conserving space and heightening the aesthetic illusion of motion and transformation.[3] Although Merian could not identify food sources for all of the five dozen butterflies she depicted, insect interactions with their host plants were at the heart of her compositions.[4] After having published three flower books (1675, 1677, and 1680) and two caterpillar books (1679 and 1684), her artwork in *The Metamorphosis* was doubly extraordinary because it reimagined the role of natural history art as itself expanding the parameters of scientific knowledge.

In *Imperial Eyes: Travel Writing and Transculturation*, Mary Louise Pratt attends to the false dichotomy erected between conquest and specimen collecting by coining a term for naturalists professing innocence but very much in the service of European hegemonic empire: "anti-conqueror."[5] The global circulation of knowledges generated by explorer-naturalists rhetorically cast them as androgynous tools of empire, despite their highly gendered presence as male colonizers on site.[6] Merian's female body reconfigured this problematic trope; the difficulty of disabling gender barriers in order to travel transatlantically and collect specimens was mitigated by the power to move in colonial spaces without exciting perceptions of threat, without symbolically performing "conquest." In *The Metamorphosis*'s privileging of insect life cycles, imperialist and preservationist orientations complexly cohabitate in ways that are not overtly "anti-conquest" and that may be ascribed to gender difference, though I do not offer extended comparative readings of male natural histories in order to make the latter argument here.

Merian's work is certainly a departure from the work of her male counterparts in its co-present preservation ethos: alongside the undergirding colonialist strain in the work, the governing principle driving Merian's representations of Surinam's local ecologies is what Richard Grove calls "environmentalist" rather than "conservationist." In Grove's paradigm, "environmentalism" stipulates that nature should be preserved for its own sake, while "conservationism" functions as largely anthropocentric, concerned with how nature can be best preserved for human use.[7] The latter is largely the province of Merian's male contemporaries (like Hans Sloane), whose veneration of local ecologies is subsumed by their projects' imperial aims.[8] Merian's work, on the other hand, simultaneously reifies colonization and sustains an interest in habitat preservation that suggests an ambivalence for the colonial project. If Merian's own global travel is a metonym for knowledge circulation, then her plates themselves mirror the circularity of her voyage, exposing through the fluidity of their compositions the depth of her global *and* local investments. Merian's preservation ethic is ultimately rooted in the fertility of her ecosystems, a fertility in continual tension and causality with forces of consumption (and itself a widely circulated myth that justified exploitation in the Americas). This essay argues that in the broader context of colonial consumption, and especially in the threat of eviscerated local ecologies, Merian's fixation on Surinam's reproductive capacity reveals dueling instincts for local preservation and global circulation.

It was Merian's fortune to practice "science" at a time when knowledge production was not yet so rigidly circumscribed, codified into disciplines, or explicitly exclusionary of women. Susan Scott Parrish finds that "knowledge making about American nature took place across inchoate and, hence, permeable boundary lines"; in return, "empiricism . . . gave authority where political empire took it away."[9] That is to say, the New Science, in its early years, and out of necessity, gave leeway to colonial practitioners. The unintended effect of European demand for American specimens was a reluctant inclusion of "such a range of people in the colonies"—and even the odd woman—that a long tradition of voluminous transatlantic exchange was launched.[10] Remarkably, Merian operated both within and without these institutional railways, finally falling back on her independent scholarship and the private execution of her science to occupy spaces of both colonist supplier and European recipient of this exchange. Merian's magisterial tome made its way to the prestigious Royal Society of London, where the knowledge of colonial practitioners was evaluated and, if deemed worthy, ratified and circulated. Isaac Newton, then president, left this record from July 14, 1703: "Some new engraven Prints of Plants & Insects of Surinam by Madam Maria Sibylla Mariana Graffen, were shewn. Many persons present approv'd of the design, and promis'd to subscribe to it."[11] And he left this one from October 27, 1703: "Mr. Pettiver shewed some Materials & Draughts, for an History of Insects, by Sibylla Mariana Graffen, of which she intend's to print many Copies. Divers present said they would take of Copies of it, when printed in English or Latin."[12] The Royal Society's endorsement secured a place for Merian's volume in elite European libraries, perhaps encouraging Merian to proceed despite considerable difficulties in production.

The archival project of reading for Merian's interests is twofold, and inseparable from questions of genre. On the one hand, the archives show an active pursuit of institutional inclusion: Merian fully intended to produce an invaluable *scientific* natural history with transatlantic reach. On the other hand, the natural history's inherent hybridity, its blurring of "history," "science," and "narrative," evokes questions about how Merian's navigation of this hybridity, complicated by her gender, exposed her sensibilities and motivations. I closely read Merian's work for both what is present and what is absent, alluded to, inferred, barely there, or silent. What Merian chooses to depict "from life," what she embellishes, what she stages, what in her plates is proportional, what might not be, are all both literary and historical markers of her agency within a genre that was open in an institution that was prescriptive and exclusionary.

Undeniably, Merian's work was highly crafted and generically and institutionally aware. We can infer, for example, that *The Metamorphosis* only sparingly narrates her journey to, within, and from Surinam because de-centering the self was the mark of the disinterested scientist; perhaps, too, she did not wish to draw further attention to her gender, to the remarkable vision of the traveling woman. In a genre where peoples were curiosities alongside flora and fauna, Merian sometimes validated Indigenous knowledges in her descriptions, a generic practice that while not uncommon, registered her presence, corroborated her eyewitness accounting, and exposed the centrality of enslaved labor to European knowledge production.

Londa Schiebinger, for example, reads Merian's record of Amerindian and enslaved African voices in her description of the peacock flower's abortive properties as indicative of "colonial struggle"; in a sexual economy that consumed women and their children, Merian's mediation of fraught knowledge is itself reproductive.[13] We might also surmise that a deep interest in local ecologies could not be sustained without bare attention to these voices; neither could Merian have effectually recorded what Pratt calls the "contact zone," or the local spaces of transcultural, unbalanced, relational contact between those with and without power, without the occasional eruption of these voices.[14]

By rhetorically privileging on-the-ground "observations" over "conclusions," the preface to *The Metamorphosis* signals Merian's belief in Baconian eyewitnessing as the foundational mode of scientific inquiry, as central to the Royal Society's model of communal, revisable knowledge production. Merian tells her readers that she could "easily have extended [her] descriptions" to include conclusions drawn, but she writes, as a naturalist, "I am required to hold simply to what I observed, I am just giving *matter* to the reflections of others."[15] The matter she is lending to the scholarly debate is that which is observed "on the spot," "from life," "after nature": in other words, *new* matter, *privileged* matter from a firsthand observer-traveler-artist. René Descartes, with his publication of *Principles of Philosophy* in 1644, ignited discourses around "matter" that continued throughout the Enlightenment. He defined matter as "extension" and "motion," the implications of which are powerful for Merian's use of the term. Descartes explains that motion can only be defined as that which moves in comparison to that which is stationary (two moving objects are not in motion).[16] The substance, then, that Merian claims to be giving to "the reflections of others" is "extension," or lengthening, widening, and "motion," or movement—travel, if you will—in a field of knowledge (on Surinam, on metamorphosis) that has up until this moment stood still.

It was during the Age of Discovery, from roughly the early fifteenth into the early seventeenth century, that new knowledge was framed through "marvel," or "wonder," what Stephen Greenblatt calls "the decisive emotional and intellectual experience in the presence of radical difference."[17] This notion of difference persisted as discourses around the role of observation, and by extension of vision, lent themselves to "curiosity" as a dispositional mode of inquiry in the seventeenth and eighteenth centuries. Curiosity hinged on the practice of eyewitnessing, or beholding that which was different. Barbara M. Benedict calls eighteenth-century curiosity culture "transgressive": at first, communing with specimens implied "an involuntary slide between species," but eventually, the observer achieved distance through disinterestedness, or the construct of (cultural) superiority over the objects viewed. The collection of specimens and artifacts—itself an inversion of traditional hierarchies (human now in a position of power over nature)—became a method through which to elevate social status.[18] By the late seventeenth century, "curiosity receded from designating a quality of the external and became a quality of the observer. This is the period that marks a fresh shift in the weighting of the meaning of curiosity from objects to subjects."[19] The power imbalance culturally built into the subject-observer lens buoyed colonialist practices like collection, transplantation of specimens (including people), and naturalization, and implicated nature documentation in the imperialist project.

The idea of difference extended further, however. Merian's gender—the ultimate marker of difference, more so than that of colonial traveler—required merging with her scientific practice and generic production. Short of treating Merian as curiosity (although certainly this argument can be made), the community of virtuosos who ultimately granted her work provisional institutional acceptance deemed her exemplary. Merian's work was the first by a woman recorded in the Royal Society's minutes; notable in both entries for July 14, 1703, and October 27, 1703, is Newton's seamless integration of Merian's volume among curiosities, observations, and membership applications presented by male naturalists. Her anomalous presence in the Royal Society's journals alone attests to an exceptionalism no other woman—though many practiced natural history—earned in the eyes of the society. Jacobus Houbraken's well-known copperplate engraving of Merian after a portrait by Georg Gsell, circa 1717, shows her as an elderly woman in the godly endeavor of scientific study, suggesting again that age and elite artistic connections allayed the threat of her participation.[20] (See figure 1.1.) Cultural ruptures, including her gender and a divorce, were overshadowed by a rhetorical framing as exceptional, an unsteady category that she openly plays with in her preface to *The Metamorphosis*. There, she both enacts her own inclusion and draws attention to the extraordinary character of her work. First giving rhetorical deference to Jan Goedart, Jan Swammerdam, and others as predecessors who had already contradicted the widespread theory of spontaneous generation and including her own work alongside theirs—she "call[s] with [Thomas] Mouffet nocturnal Butterflies those who fly only at night"—Merian then tells her readers that she is literally painting her way into a new tradition; after all, hers is "the most beautiful work that had ever been painted in America."[21]

Carolus Linnaeus, Mark Catesby, and John Gabriel Stedman were among those who later engaged Merian's work, signaling institutional circulation, although Catesby, for example, did so without attribution.[22] For Stedman, Merian was "the Celebrated Miss Merian," in whose "Drawings I pledge my Honour to point out many Faults."[23] For Linnaeus, Merian was a fascination, as shown in my discussion below of the Surinam toad. The historical traces of Merian's inclusion, then,

Figure 1.1 Jacobus Houbraken's copperplate engraving of Maria Sibylla Merian, ca. 1717. Royal Collection Trust / © Her Majesty Queen Elizabeth II 2020, RCIN 670216.

are blemished with disregard like Catesby's, irony like Stedman's, and curiosity like Linnaeus's. Seizing upon the instability of Merian's legacy, nineteenth-century historians of science used the narrative of exceptionality to minimize Merian's contributions, thereby furthering her marginalization:

> The lady to whom the following notices refer, forms a signal exception. Not that she can lay claim to distinction as a scientific naturalist, nor can it be affirmed that her powers of observation or the capacity of her judgment were of the first order. But the extraordinary zeal she shewed in the study of that branch to which her attention was directed, the sacrifices and inconveniences to which she submitted in prosecuting it, the excellent delineation which she has made of many natural objects, and the mass of materials which she has thus provided to facilitate the labours of future inquirers, justly entitle her to an honourable place in a biographical series of those worthies who have exerted themselves to promote the study of nature, with which it has been our anxious endeavour to enrich the volumes of the Naturalist's Library.[24]

Because exemplarity justified women's work performing within certain generic parameters, while simultaneously accounting for gendered orientations, it granted only tentative, conditional inclusion and could then be harnessed to push women out of institutional bounds.

* * *

On June 18, 1701, Merian and her youngest daughter, twenty-one-year-old Dorothea Maria, "loaded with rolled vellum paintings, brandied butterflies, bottles with crocodiles and snakes, lizards' eggs, bulbs, chrysalises that had not yet opened, and many round boxes full of pressed insects for sale," as Natalie Zemon Davis puts it, set sail for home.[25] Merian had likely expected to stay several years longer, but malaria shortened her expedition. Perhaps this return voyage was laced with a certain disappointment; after all, conditions in Surinam had been treacherous and developing new methods of collection, observation, and recording suitable for the tropics affected her productivity.[26] In spite of these circumstances, we can imagine an exuberant mother and daughter escorting thousands of specimens and illustrations transatlantically for the final purpose of further examination, compilation, and publication. At her disposal was an unnamed Amerindian servant.[27]

It is harder to imagine what Merian might have felt en route to Surinam. Everything was at stake: she had sold off the great majority of her artwork; executed commissions; informed professional contacts, including collectors, scientists, artists, and publishers, of her plans; and shrewdly drafted a will.[28] We know little about what such a journey must have entailed, but we do know Merian's ship probably moved through the coastal towns on the English Channel, south to the Spanish and Portuguese coasts, toward Africa, into the Atlantic, with a final docking in South America after two months at sea. We know that her ship avoided pirate capture and fatal storms to land at Paramaribo, capital of Surinam, late in the summer of 1699.[29] Merian and her daughter searched for a suitable home, one with a vegetable plot, a water source, and, inspired by Dutch design, gauze-covered windows. It appears that Merian's son-in-law made use of his global network to help arrange plantation visits where she could scour for insects in the adjoining jungle.[30]

Within Surinam, Merian navigated thick forest and swampland that were largely prohibitive; attempts to travel and collect specimens in uncultivated zones outside the more developed Paramaribo required expert assistance, sometimes from Indigenous peoples, sometimes from enslaved Africans. In plate 36's textual description, Merian uncharacteristically complains that locals "mocked" her for "looking for something other than sugar."[31] To imagine the extreme difficulty Merian faced in collecting specimens, Redmond O'Hanlon, documentarian and explorer, asks us to envision a middle-aged woman in traditional eighteenth-century undergarments and skirts, bitten from head to toe for lack of protection, encountering, in the wet season at least, a scorpion under every eleventh leaf.[32] Nor did Merian escape disease, likely suffering from a benign form of malaria every few months, an illness that ultimately cut her trip short.

The Labadists, a small religious community outside of Friesland, Germany, to which Merian had retreated with her daughters, aging mother, and half brother Caspar Merian, from the years 1685 to 1691—probably to enact a final separation from her husband—had established a colony further upriver at La Providencia in 1683, which Merian visited from April to June 1700.[33] From the Labadists who had returned, and implicitly from those who had not returned, she may have been familiar with the hardships of the landscape and of settlement in the abstract. While living with the austere sect in Wiewert, Germany, Merian had become used to deprivation in diet and material comforts, which were strictly monitored.[34] For all she heard of Surinam, however, of its rich ecology, perhaps even of its incompatibility with the European constitution, Merian could not have truly been ready to live and work in Surinam as it was: in 1699, already the paradoxically stable locus and emblem of racial disturbance and revolution in the Americas until the Haitian Revolution at the turn of the next century.

The Spanish had laid claim to the land on the northeast coast of South America called Guiana, or, as the Portuguese referred to it, "the Wild Coast," in the early seventeenth century. Guiana's landscapes of thick forestland and rough rivers made for difficult terrain, and neither Spain nor Portugal was able to seize the colony. The French, Irish, Dutch, and English all made attempts to colonize.[35] Guiana was the stuff of legend, the El Dorado of Spanish lore. Sir Walter Raleigh's natural history, *The Discouerie of the Large, Rich, and Beuutiful Empyre of Guiana* (1596), propagated the legend, chronicling an impassable interior and two failed, treasure-seeking voyages.[36] It was not until the mid-seventeenth century that Francis Willoughby, who had already established a colony in Barbados, settled Guiana. The first three hundred settler colonials came in 1651–1652, and a decade later there were some five hundred riverside plantations comfortably scattered with Europeans and Caribs in peaceable relations.[37] Surinam was a small colony in comparison to Barbados, but it worked quickly to import enslaved Africans and export sugar, and continued to do so when it switched hands in 1667 and the Dutch occupied it.[38]

In her critical edition of *Oroonoko; or, The Royal Slave* (1688), Catherine Gallagher's image of one land mass eons ago connecting, like puzzle pieces, Guiana and Guinea, South America and Africa, is an apt one if we are to envision Guiana as an extension of Africa through the forced migration of its peoples, who then escaped their enslavement and continued living as West Africans in independent agrarian communities halfway across the world. "As if testimony to their primeval adjacency," Gallagher says, Guinea's and Guiana's topographies mirror each other, with immense forests and traversable rivers familiar landscape for Africans while wholly unnavigable to Europeans.[39] A crucial participant in the triangular trade's maniacal sugar production from the outset of its establishment as an English colony in 1651, Surinam rapidly became a hotbed of revolt and autonomous African settlement, a condition that endured for its early colonial history and further troubled the linear imperial narrative told and retold throughout the Atlantic triangle.

When Oroonoko, Aphra Behn's glorious West African prince, lands in the mid-1600s, "after a tedious Voyage . . . at the Mouth of the River of Surinam, a colony belonging to the King of England," he lands in a metaphorical no-place.[40] The eponymous hero of Behn's novella is sold in the "first lot" along with seventeen others—who were, incidentally, his subjects in Coramantien (Ghana)—into the precarious condition of slavery, for which Oroonoko's royal upbringing makes him uniquely unsuited. But we are told nothing of Surinam, its landscape, and its peoples in that first transcultural encounter between enslaved people and place. Instead, Surinam is a void to which enslaved men and women come to labor, then die. Behn compounds this sense of Surinam as site of unregenerative consumption and depletion with female insignificance: "But [Oroonoko's] Mis-fortune was, to fall in an obscure World, that afforded only a Female Pen to celebrate his Fame."[41] Later representations, like John Gabriel Stedman's *Narrative of a Five Years' Expedition against the Revolted Negroes of Surinam* (1796), portrayed Surinam as site of horror above beauty, emptiness above fecundity. For Stedman, Surinam is imagined in recycled and recirculated ideas of the tropics, and at the same time as a death trap.[42]

Merian's Surinam, however, reveals a reproductive capacity that neither Behn's nor Stedman's does. One illustrative example is Merian's "Surinam Toad," or *Pipa pipa*—plate 59 in her volume, and one of only two underwater compositions (including plate 56, the tree frog), as shown in figure 1.2.[43] Plate 59 evokes fertility to an almost parodic extreme. As the grotesque toad swims under the water's surface, with a toadlet tailing it, Merian exposes the toad's innards by omitting the exterior epidermis. Her text for plate 59 tells us that "the female carries its young on its back; because it has the Uterus along the back, and that's where it conceives & nourishes the embryos, until they have received life, then they open a passage through its skin, and they come out as an egg, one after another. Once I had taken note of this, I threw the mother in ethanol with its remaining little ones whose heads or bodies were already out. The Negroes eat these toads and find them delicate; they are a blackish brown, their front legs resemble those of Frogs, and those from behind those of Ducks."[44] In the image and accompanying textual description, the toad's "uterus" stretches across its back, and approximately fifty-five offspring, in various stages of development, sprout. The text, however, tells us that eggs emerge through a "passage" in the skin. Merian's plate depicts both eggs and toadlets, but no tadpoles, as the Surinam toad was "the first known example of a frog species without a free-swimming larval stage."[45] Though this plate does not represent insects, Merian follows her project's design by compressing the life cycle—here of the toad—into one image. The circularity of the larger composition is disturbed by the sharp edges of the shells and the toad's appendages, and, as in plate 1, the pairing of the grotesque and the beautiful emphasize the singularity of this habitat.

Merian's depiction of the Surinam toad began a century-long scientific debate and interest in this amphibian that occupied Linnaeus and others in the question of Surinam as a fertile and productive nexus of the larger West Indies, and consequently in the Americas as a site ripe for exploitation.[46] (See figure 1.3.) Though by most accounts Surinam was considered a Caribbean colony—in terms of its heavy and early participation in the triangular trade—naturalists understood Surinam to be a highly idiosyncratic, *South American* colony, one sharing some environmental features with others in the tropics, but ultimately set apart by its verdant forests. Merian's provocative plate represents a colony in miniature teeming with life. The Surinam toad symbolically promises the treasure of knowledge, its feverish reproduction mirroring the growth of the colonial enterprise, the growing rapidity of knowledge dissemination. In plate 59, then, Merian's lens is colonialist

Figure 1.2 Merian's "Surinam Toad," plate 59. New York Public Library, Rare Book Division, New York Public Library Digital Collections.

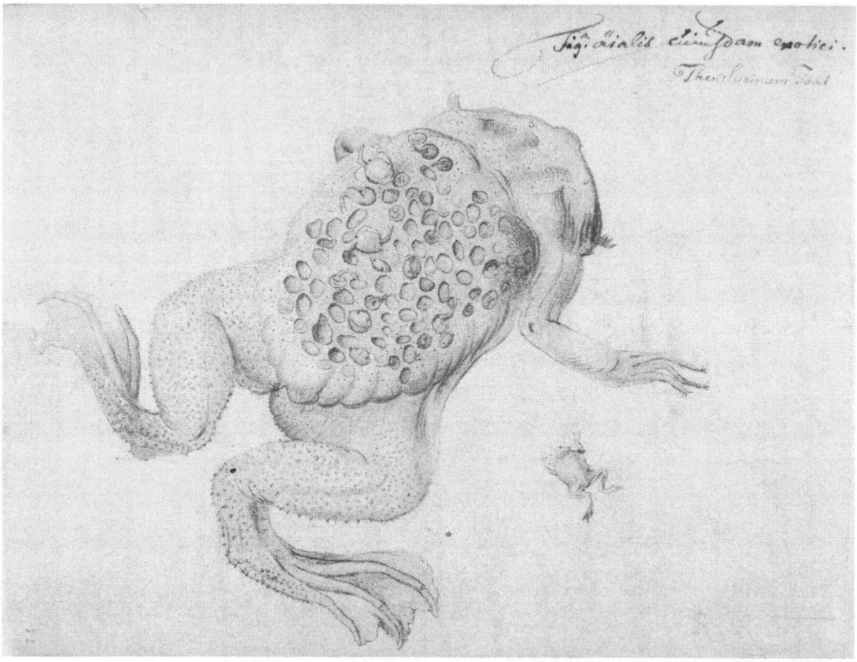

Figure 1.3 R.R., "The Surinam Toad," n.d. Royal Society, Classified Papers on Zoology, 1660–1724. CLP/15i/36.

even as she depicts a species in all its particularity whose existence is unknown outside Surinam—exemplifying how reproduction in the context of imperial consumption generates tension between colonial and preservationist impulses in the larger work.

Surinam's distinctive topography, its incessant pull on the tropics-preoccupied European imagination, and its relative stability as unstable epicenter of slave revolt in the larger West Indies over the course of the eighteenth century, when the genre of natural history and the slave trade exploded in tandem, begins to explain Merian's complicated orientation or the complex, sometimes contradictory messages of her plates and text. Surinam's rich cyclical history of settlement and rebellion and its resistance to a sweeping plantation economy (despite its economic status as such) is expressed in her contesting imperialist and ecosystemic lenses. In 1705, at the height of the influx of African slavery, Merian portrayed Surinam's natural habitats as untouched and harmonious, implying that Surinam would prove infinitely abundant and endure as a trove of scientific knowledge—very much a preservationist fantasy that bled into imperialist myths of the "New World." Naturally,

Surinam's landscape transformed over the course of the eighteenth century as enslaved Africans and Europeans arrived: by the mid- to late eighteenth century, Surinam's African to European ratio, 25:1, and in plantation zones sometimes 65:1, was the most severe of any West Indian colony, signifying an ongoing process of alteration to a deeply affected landscape.[47]

The sense, however, that the landscape would not be given over wholesale to white planters, that the disastrous effects wrought by Surinam's plantation economy on the environment could be slowed, served as a powerful fancy for Merian, who was invested in the localized insularity of her habitats and simultaneously in their global marketability. Although Merian's representations of Surinam's local ecologies traveled globally, the plates' internal motion and stasis, together, was preservationist: the habitat felt alive, active, and evolving, and at the same time still. Merian's evident desire to attend to and preserve the intricacy of biological ecosystems through art prompted Kay Etheridge to call Merian "the first ecologist."[48] In fact, "ecology," a fairly modern word traced to the late nineteenth century, has come to be aligned with land politics and efforts of conservation. Carolyn Merchant, in her important work *The Death of Nature: Women, Ecology, and the Scientific Revolution*, points to ecology as the model for the premodern universe; it was the rise of modern science and the advent of the Enlightenment that precipitated a transformation "when our cosmos ceased to be viewed as an organism and became instead a machine."[49] Though natural history propelled the "mechanistic model" forward, it was also the incipient genre of ecology. Laura Dassow Walls calls these confused beginnings "early ecologic discourses," while Dana Phillips calls the engagement with these discourses "points of view."[50] I like the terms "proto-ecologic orientation" and "proto-ecologic sensibility." In the context of launching early ecologic discourses and the "mechanistic model" simultaneously, the genre serves as its own fraught geographic site, its own "contact zone." Interconnecting contacts made transatlantically by scientists, explorers, travelers, writers, and illustrators through natural history saturated the world with observations, composing a system of synergetic knowledge production and exchange based in a proliferating globalism.

Where visible, ecology as biological, characterized by how organisms interact in their natural environments, is the basis of Merian's proto-ecologic sensibility. Merian's art and textual descriptions functionally classify the insects portrayed, and yet the universalizing instinct of classification—of finding commonalities among species—is contradicted by sustained attention to the vitality and particularity of the local habitat. This attention is a rhetorical move that eschews a *certain principle* of what came to characterize taxonomy: that is, the fixed in space, place, and time, and decontextualized specimen. Classification does not by any means preclude a holistic approach to natural processes, as exemplified in Merian's spider plate (plate 18; figure 1.6), which represents organic processes in a methodically executed tableau that identifies particular species and in its elisions invites questions and implications about a fuller local ecology.

The central tension in Merian's work is between symbiosis, reproduction, natural processes, and fecundity—all within a local ecology—and the project itself, or Merian's physical encroachment onto these habitats, her consumption of nature as traveling scientist. Merian certainly propagated the fantasy that the condition of rapidly expanding colonialism had not altered her independent ecosystems, but then again the meticulousness of her symbiotic tableaus might in fact reflect the urgency she felt in recording these local ecologies as they were before their irrevocable transformation. Plate 18 (figure 1.6) in particular registers nature's enigma of internally and externally motivated environmental dynamism by alluding to what is not eyewitnessed. If, after all, we are entreated to look upon the spiders as pictured (their size, shape, color, and movement), we are also meant to envision her spiders and ants in perpetual motion, performing other undocumented acts. Merian's plate staging simultaneously expands and limits our vision, highlights and understates the intervention—there may be changes, yes, but short of these habitats' externally forced destruction, which may or may not be on the horizon, these changes can be scientifically bound and imagined.[51]

"LITTLE ATLAS": CLOSELY READING FOR THE LIMITS OF MERIAN'S PRESERVATION ETHIC

In the very first plate of Merian's opulent *The Metamorphosis of the Insects of Surinam*, cockroaches hover over a prickly pineapple in bloom, as shown in figure 1.4. Beginning with the glorious pineapple sent a clear message to Merian's subscribers—this volume would be matchless, sumptuous. As readers, we are infected by the cockroaches' appetite for this sweet fruit, an exotic rarity that few but royalty had then seen or tasted; the beautiful description of the leaves as "long, outside, a light sea-green, and within, like a green prairie, with reddish edges and filled with enough sharp thorns" heightens our sensory experience of the plate.[52] Merian's cockroaches are an integral part of the composition, drawing our attention through their carefully directed antennas to the pineapple, steering the composition to the center by pulling to the right and balancing the left-leaning pineapple, and finally by enclosing, as though in an oval frame, the fruit itself. In the accompanying textual description, cockroaches are agents "gnawing," "casting seeds," "eating

Figure 1.4 Merian's plate 1. New York Public Library, Rare Book Division, New York Public Library Digital Collections.

through the hull," and "destroying"—and even possessive of a sense of humor—"if we touch the animal, it leaves the sac, to save itself and does so with levity."[53]

As with "Surinam Toad" in plate 59 (figure 1.2), and in all of her plates, Merian is centrally concerned here with reproduction. How the cockroaches "hatch," morph, slough off skin, inhabit or empty their "sacs," exit and enter private spaces, and of course raid and eat the pineapple is of prime fascination. In the case of the cockroaches, reproduction and consumption proliferate causally: in order to reproduce, they must first consume. Consumption is balanced by a parallel strain of sustainability, wherein Merian pairs the most attractive with the most repulsive in environmental interdependence. This pairing strategically highlights the beauty of the insects she so admired and suggests that if we look closely, what we see in God's handiwork is a mirror of human life. Beginning with the familiar and revered pineapple and relying on the "learned men who have spoken strongly on this fruit," Merian impresses Europe onto Surinam, reinforcing imperialist modes of knowledge production, and yet, her own science and marvelous, ecosystemically driven art proceeds to reject those modes by depicting the insects and plants in their local context, in habitat-specific interrelation.[54]

The language Merian employs to describe the cockroaches, their entries and departures, their relentless motion, reflects the workings of the natural history genre. The very way Merian frames this first plate—the revelation of the celebrated pineapple as it blooms, accompanied by two species of cockroaches, one metamorphosing—implies her own commitment to glorifying and revolutionizing the genre all in one. One way in which she does the latter is by complicating the provocative imperialist trope of feminized nature conquered and subsequently defiled. The cockroaches are on the verge of fulfilling their instinctual needs, here their love for "sweet things," the result of which, the devouring of the pineapple (not pictured), is a natural if invasive process. While the genre's own role in colonial conquest, and the observer-naturalist's, might be metaphorically represented here, the plate's function is to create the illusion of ecosystemic balance. The cockroaches and pineapple illustrate the unaltered continuance of environmental processes—with both consumption and reproduction at work—even as analogously, the naturalist's documentation of this scene is consumptive and its dissemination is reproductive. Harnessing the familiar imperialist emblem of the pineapple to frame a volume deeply invested in representations of local ecologies exemplifies the contradictory impulses of Merian's work: local relations, global circulation.

In plate 23, we are pulled further into a nuanced proto-ecologic fantasy. For instance, in figure 1.5, see the rounded edges of the butterfly wings, the banana, the lizard eggs, the curve of the lizard's tail, and the miniscule rounded tail of the

Figure 1.5 Merian's plate 23. New York Public Library, Rare Book Division, New York Public Library Digital Collections.

baby lizard on the edge of the round leaf. Moving counterclockwise, we perceive the life cycle of the butterfly starting in the middle of the frame and resting on the banana leaf and move to the chrysalis atop the banana, the side view of the butterfly, and then the frontal view of the flying butterfly. The lizard here again balances the composition, weighing it left, since we already have the rounded downward bellies of the banana, the oval stalk upon which the eggs sit, and the lizard for the downward pull, and the tensed cocoon, butterfly wings, and curved lizard tail for the upward pull. The lizard, though overlaid onto this habitat by Merian's own admission, appears at home here and does not interrupt the butterfly's life cycle. Instead, its rounded form and little eggs and tiny baby lizard create the impression of a perfectly balanced ecosystem, of a natural Elysium. Here, Merian employs both classificatory and holistic approaches, staging her lizard alongside the caterpillar, butterfly, and banana to complete or round out her composition. She creates order of two distinct natural processes—that of the metamorphosis of caterpillar into butterfly on the banana plant and the birth and death of the baby lizards—by marking similarity and difference, the work of classification, and bringing symbiotic order, the province of ecology, to these same events. The cross section of the banana plant disrupts the composition's holism, reminding the viewer of the scientist's intervention, of the observer as consumer or reproducer of knowledge; the performative staging of this habitat once again places local and global interests in tension. As Etheridge notes, Merian's addition of the little tropic vertebrate "add[ed] interest to her book," serving too as a "market testing strategy."[55] To maximize the global salability of the knowledge generated by this plate, Merian markets both the ecosystemic fantasy realized by the superimposition of the blue lizard and the scientific endeavor represented by the cross-sectioned banana specimen.

Plate 23 is remarkably fluid, and this fluidity is reflected in the incantatory rhythm of the accompanying text: "On the 20th of the same month, there emerged a beautiful Butterfly with two superior wings that under the light are a clear ocher color, and the two sides a beautiful blue; and the top of the whole Butterfly is a yellow, brown, white, and black stripe, and its name in Holland is Little Atlas."[56] The scenes Merian describes in the text for plate 23 both expand transatlantically and contract on the physical page. Merian locates the composition's brown caterpillar on the banana tree, the blue lizard in her Surinamese yard, and the hatched baby lizards on her transoceanic journey's ship. But the narrative spans across time too, for Merian tells us that it takes the brown caterpillar seventeen days to morph into a beautiful blue butterfly, and the blue lizard's eggs hatch and die en route home to Amsterdam. We are to ostensibly imagine Merian's daily return to the banana tree, but we are left without knowledge of the precise location of this banana tree: Has it been cultivated on some plantation Merian is visiting? Does it grow

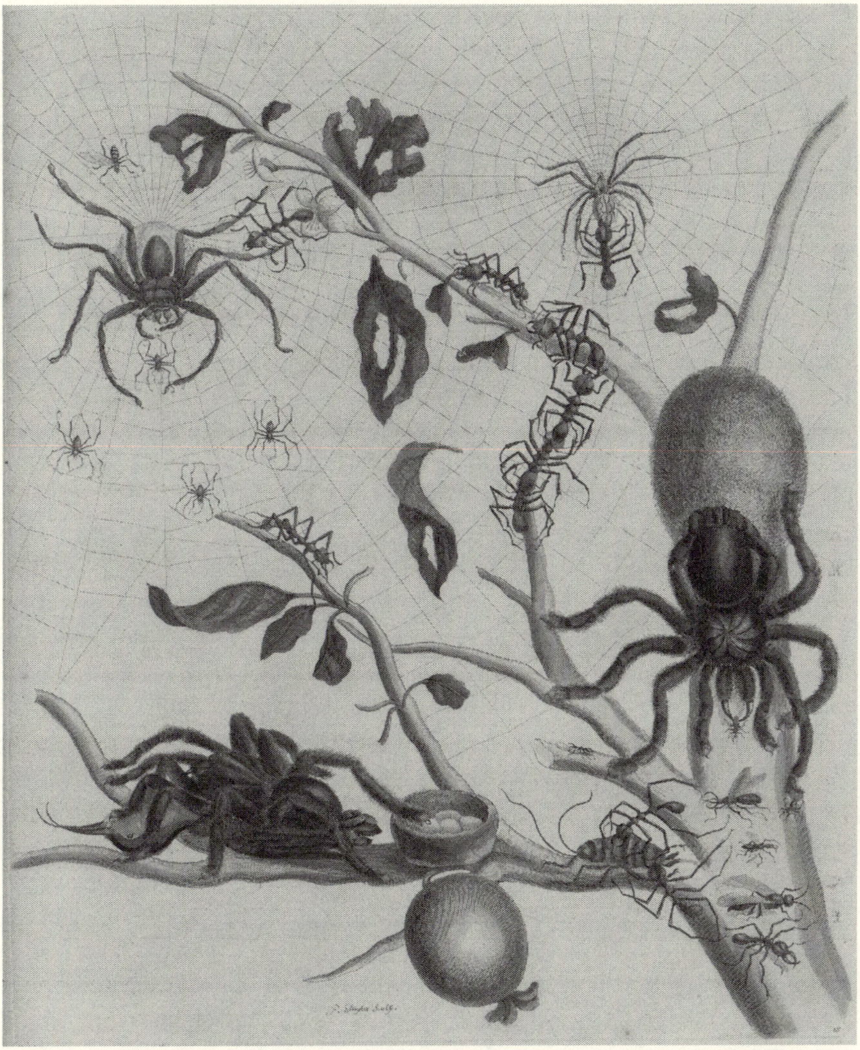

Figure 1.6 Merian's plate 18. New York Public Library, Rare Book Division, New York Public Library Digital Collections.

wild, and if so, where? The butterfly is aptly named "Little Atlas," for something about the blue lizard's attempted transatlantic journey has inspired Merian to pair these tiny world travelers in one plate.

In Merian's frequently reproduced and highly active plate 18 (see figure 1.6), this staging is apparent. Where hummingbirds typically lay two eggs, Merian depicts four; where leaf-cutting and army ants move in separate circles, here they are represented together; the extraordinary Goliath bird-eating tarantula, identified as the largest spider species in the world by Henry Walter Bates in his 1863 work *The Naturalist on the River Amazons*, is in the act of devouring a prostate, carefully positioned hummingbird.[57] The perfect guava fruit and the proportional egg-like abdomens and heads of the spiders are juxtaposed against crisp lines: the gangly limbs of the spiders and tree branches and falling, munched-on leaves. A great deal is happening here as the large spider on the right pinches a tiny ant, the spider on the left consumes that still exquisitely colorful dead hummingbird, marauding ants make a bridge from limb to limb of the tree, and a smaller spider captures an ant in its web. The composition itself is a complex web representing life and death at work and conveying Merian's sentiment that "the ants are always at war with the Spiders and Insects of this country."[58] The language of war, or here of predation, among Surinamese insects, is not bemoaned; rather, ants "armed with curved teeth" are a part of this web of life. The rounded, slightly oval guava fruits form an imperfect, left-tilted circular frame with the egg-shaped abdomens of the three larger spiders in the upper left, lower left, and middle right. The four tiny hummingbird eggs in the nest above the lower guava fruit complete this frame. The ant-wing color matches that of the guava fruit. The proportionality and magnification of this plate are astonishing: the upper left quadrant appears more distant, and as the webs the spiders have woven ripple out, so too does the plate zoom in on the two larger spiders, the guava fruit, the dead hummingbird, and the stalk of the tree. Processes of predation and death are integral to Merian's preservationist vision here; after all, this ecosystem is violently alive because it is unspoiled by human interference. In reading the perfect abundance of this plate, one might imagine that Merian rejected slavery and consumption as the definitive destructive forces of local ecologies in the Americas. Alternately, this plate's staging might be metaphorically read as a tacit acknowledgment of, if not resignation to, colonial consumption, revealing the illusory nature of Merian's preservationist vision.

Merian's textual description follows this same circular framework, beginning with the spiders, moving to the ants, then back to the spiders, and finally to the hummingbird. Her description of the ants echoes that of plate 1's cockroaches, entreating us to see her project as a unified representation of a larger, highly intricate network of life processes: "They come out from their caves in countless swarms. . . . [M]en are obliged to flee as they enter room by room by troupes."[59] Hummingbirds, for their part, are compared to marvel-inducing peacocks, and of prime importance is the mutually sustaining food reliance of insects on the plate, as well as of humans and animals outside the plate, including "Surinam hens," which eat ant eggs, and "priests," who, like spiders, relish the hummingbird for its meat. This involved ecosystem again bespeaks Merian's contesting orientations. Her comparison of the unfamiliar and the familiar, of the hummingbird and the peacock (well circulated in imperial natural history discourses), is a generic convention. Her complex integration of humans within this scene works on two planes: it both registers a colonial presence and suggests a profoundly transformative human-nature alliance that sees humans and spiders competing for one food source.

In line with male generic convention, Merian boldly asserts her right to publicly produce the new knowledge represented in this plate and description and to correct those "facts" that have been documented incorrectly by other naturalists: spiders "do not spin long Cocoons as some travelers would have us believe"; "the ignorant call these pupae eggs of ants, but they are wrong because the ant eggs are much smaller."[60] Her observations are keen and scientific, and yet her text, for this plate in particular, is highly narrative, embodying the genre's hybridity. Once more, her insects are sentient actors, for they make bridges, bite, make war, hibernate, attack, devour, terrify, and even manifest the illusion of winter. The ants dig underground caves "as well as men might do."[61] The use of anthropomorphism, analogy, and metaphor—techniques used by imperial naturalists that are employed descriptively—here plant the reader into this scene of predation in medias res. The reader/viewer experiences this scene as an observer (from the outside) and as a participant (from the inside). This dynamic tableau and its description render Merian too, as naturalist-illustrator, and alongside her reader, both invisible and invasive in the habitat.

Merian's overarching claim to illustrations "from life"—certainly the sentiment in this remarkable plate—also acknowledges multiple other levels of the naturalist's intrusion, from the practice of staging plates to that of basing foundational knowledge on human-flora-fauna analogy. At the same time, Merian's symbiotic focus, her "time-lapse of life cycles" as Etheridge calls it, and the giant folio-sized plates that allowed for a full observational and sensory experience of a plate like this one, literally and symbolically magnify what Phillips would call an ecologic point of view.[62] Plate 18 seems to say that nature should operate unimpeded, and yet the audience can "eyewitness" almost as nearly as the naturalist herself does, from home: the spiders Merian chronicles have already traveled globally even as the home viewer looks upon a dynamic ecosystem that ironically appears undisturbed.

Though de-centered in the larger work, Merian's gender comes into focus if we read the uneasy co-existence of local and global investments as a fraught performance of genre necessitated by her status as interloper. As a female naturalist working in the Americas, Merian enacted her own inclusion; by undertaking great personal risk as traveler, explorer, and scientist, she had hoped to emerge from the thick forests of Surinam institutionally sanctioned. Back home, her active correspondence with men in institutional circles forged the path for the volume's design, production, and publication. Indeed, what traveled globally in Merian's time and persists today was the narrative of her exemplarity as female naturalist, a marker of gender difference.

Plate 18, the most complex and frequently replicated of her images, exceptional even for *The Metamorphosis*, embodies this narrative. Remarkably, Merian engages the male tradition of sexualizing nature through the parted leaf lips of the oval guava fruit, as well as through the labial falling leaves, their lip shape if we turn the plate horizontally. The falling of these leaves toward the nest of hummingbird eggs is not accidental. Neither is it a coincidence that her ants are winged, or breeding. Reproduction, not death, is primary. Merian's preoccupation with Surinam's reproductive potential not only suggests a desire to privilege self-sustaining local ecologies, but also acknowledges the consumptive forces of empire, without which she could not have traveled, collected specimens, composed or circulated her natural history, and for which local reproduction, depicted in her art in all its beauty and brutality, might serve as a metaphor. Plate staging was but one conceit that evidenced this tension, heightening, as it did, the sense of realism for a European audience who wished to figuratively eyewitness. Where Merian's work is both preservationist and interventionist, both proto-ecologic and imperialist in sensibility, Merian, as a woman naturalist, strains to belong both somewhere and everywhere at once. Through her art she exposes the complexity of gendered relations to the environment in an age where nature study and conquest could not be disentangled.

NOTES

1. "From life," or "on the spot," was not an entirely accurate descriptor, of course. Only what was absolutely necessary was drawn on site. Though colors were a critical identifier, painting in the field was impossible, so all watercolor studies on vellum were made from transported specimens—either living or newly dead. Much relied on meticulous methods of preservation and record keeping, particularly in tracking larval metamorphoses. See Kay Etheridge, "The Biology of *Metamorphosis insectorum Surinamensium*," in *Metamorphosis insectorum Surinamensium*, by Maria Sibylla Merian, facsimile ed., ed. Marieke van Delft and Hans Mulder (Tielt, Belgium: Lannoo Publishers, 2016), 31.
2. Etheridge, "Biology of *Metamorphosis*," 31.
3. This artistic innovation further compromises the conceit, "from life."
4. Etheridge, "Biology of *Metamorphosis*," 31.
5. Mary Louise Pratt, *Imperial Eyes: Travel Writing and Transculturation* (London: Routledge, 1992), 7.
6. Pratt, *Imperial Eyes*, 33.

7. Grove locates the origins of conservationism and environmentalism in colonial dogma, with the tropics at the heart of imperial environmentalist discourses; he argues that these discourses circulated transatlantically as early as the fifteenth century and were concerned with the destruction wrought on fertile landscapes, concerns that were spurred by, and influenced, colonization projects. See Richard Grove, *Green Imperialism: Colonial Expansion, Tropical Island Edens, and the Origins of Environmentalism, 1600–1860* (Cambridge: Cambridge University Press, 1995).
8. Londa Schiebinger argues that Merian and Sloane each employed European collecting and naming practices, but that the case of the peacock flower, an abortifacient that both naturalists documented, demonstrates a gendered divergence. Merian's description of the peacock flower "located it within the colonial struggle," while Sloane "carried fully-formed notions concerning abortion with him to Jamaica . . . [that] mirrored those of the majority of his male medical colleagues in Europe." See Londa Schiebinger, *Plants and Empire: Colonial Bioprospecting in the Atlantic World* (Cambridge, MA: Harvard University Press, 2007), 108–112; quotation on 109.
9. Susan Scott Parrish, *American Curiosity: Cultures of Natural History in the Colonial British Atlantic World* (Chapel Hill: University of North Carolina Press, 2006), 22.
10. Parrish, *American Curiosity*, 15.
11. Isaac Newton, Minutes, Journal Book of the Royal Society, vol. 11 (1702–1714), July 14, 1703, 27–28, JBO/11, Royal Society of London.
12. Isaac Newton, Minutes, Journal Book of the Royal Society, vol. 11 (1702–1714), October 27, 1703, 32–33.
13. Schiebinger, *Plants and Empire*, 107–109, 132.
14. Pratt, *Imperial Eyes*, 7.
15. Maria Sibylla Merian, preface to *Dissertation sur la generation et les transformations des insectes de Surinam* (Paris: a la Haye, chez Pierre Gosse, 1726), emphasis added, New York Public Library, Rare Book Division, New York Public Library Digital Collections, accessed May 11, 2020, http://digitalcollections.nypl.org/items/f160db30-ad53-0135-88ba-0f6a25accce9. Unless otherwise noted, all translations are my own.
16. René Descartes, *Principles of Philosophy* (London: D. Reidel, 1983), 51.
17. Stephen Greenblatt, *Marvelous Possessions: The Wonder of the New World* (Chicago: University of Chicago Press, 1991), 14.
18. Barbara M. Benedict, *Curiosity: A Cultural History of Early Modern Inquiry* (Chicago: University of Chicago Press, 2001), 158.
19. Benedict, *Curiosity*, 158.
20. Jacobus Houbraken, after Georg Gsell, *Maria Sibilla Merian 1717*, RCIN 670216, Royal Collection Trust, London, accessed February 18, 2020, https://www.rct.uk/collection/search#/1/collection/670216/maria-sibilla-merian.
21. Merian, preface to *Dissertation*.
22. Kay Etheridge, "Maria Sibylla Merian: The First Ecologist?," in *Women and Science, 17th Century to Present: Pioneers, Activists and Protagonists*, ed. Donna Spalding Andréolle and Véronique Molinari (Newcastle upon Tyne: Cambridge Scholars Publishing, 2011), 46–47.
23. John Gabriel Stedman, *Narrative of a Five Years Expedition against the Revolted Negroes of Surinam, Transcribed for the First Time from the Original 1790 Manuscript*, ed. Richard Price and Sally Price (Baltimore: Johns Hopkins University Press, 1988), 9.
24. James Duncan, "A Memoir of Maria Sibilla Merian," in *Lives of Eminent Naturalists, with Engraved Portraits Accompanying Each* (Edinburgh: W. H. Lizars; London: S. Highley; and Dublin: W. Curry, 1840), 2:17.

25. Natalie Zemon Davis, *Women on the Margins: Three Seventeenth-Century Lives* (Cambridge, MA: Harvard University Press, 1995), 177.
26. Etheridge, "Biology of *Metamorphosis*," 31.
27. Ella Reitsma, "Maria Sibylla Merian: An Exceptional Woman," in *Metamorphosis insectorum Surinamensium*, by Maria Sibylla Merian, facsimile ed., ed. Marieke van Delft and Hans Mulder (Tielt, Belgium: Lannoo Publishers, 2016), 16.
28. "Like many male naturalists," Schiebinger reminds us, "Merian also joined commercial interests to her scientific voyage": her plans included specimen exchange and silkworm harvesting. Schiebinger, *Plants and Empire*, 34.
29. Kim Todd, *Chrysalis: Maria Sibylla Merian and the Secrets of Metamorphosis* (New York: Harcourt, 2007), 146–148.
30. Todd, *Chrysalis*, 156.
31. Patrick Lennon, "Translation Original Texts *Metamorphosis insectorum Surinamensium*," in *Metamorphosis insectorum Surinamensium*, by Maria Sibylla Merian, facsimile ed., ed. Marieke van Delft and Hans Mulder (Tielt, Belgium: Lannoo Publishers, 2016), "Plate 36," 183. Merian mentions an Amerindian servant digging up a plant by the root for transplantation to her garden and enslaved Africans hacking an opening for her in the jungle.
32. Redmond O'Hanlon, "Maria, the Jungle and Bird Eating Spiders" (presentation at the Maria Sibylla Merian Conference 2017, "Changing the Nature of Art and Science: Intersections with Maria Sibylla Merian," Amsterdam, June 4–7, 2017).
33. Reitsma, "Maria Sibylla Merian," 15–16.
34. She did manage to raise caterpillars and record observations, if only very little, as well as paint seventeen works in her time at Waltha Castle, as per Todd, *Chrysalis*, 107.
35. Catherine Gallagher, "The Caribbean in the Triangular Trade," in *Oroonoko; or, The Royal Slave*, by Aphra Behn, ed. Catherine Gallagher with Simon Stern (Boston: Bedford/St. Martin's Press, 2000), 328–329.
36. Sir Walter Raleigh, *The Discouerie of the Large, Rich, and Beuutiful Empyre of Guiana, with a Relation of the Great and Golden Citie of Manoa (Which the Spanyards Call El Dorado), and of the Prouinces of Emeria, Arromaia, Amapaia, and other Countries, with Their Riuers Adioyning. Performed in the Year 1595* (London: Robert Robinson, 1596).
37. Gallagher, "Caribbean," 329.
38. For a summary of Surinam's early colonial history, see Gallagher, "Caribbean," 326–334.
39. Gallagher, "Caribbean," 326, 331.
40. Aphra Behn, *Oroonoko; or, The Royal Slave*, ed. Catherine Gallagher with Simon Stern (Boston: Bedford/St. Martin's Press, 2000), 66.
41. Behn, *Oroonoko*, 69.
42. Stedman, *Narrative of a Five Years Expedition*.
43. Merian, *Dissertation*, plate 59.
44. Merian, *Dissertation*, 59.
45. Etheridge, "Biology of *Metamorphosis*," 36.
46. The image of the Surinam toad was reproduced again and again throughout the eighteenth century, and Merian was credited with its origination. The following citations are two examples of its reproduction: R.R., "The Surinam Toad," n.d., Classified Papers on Zoology, 1660–1724, CLP/15i/36, Royal Society of London; and Carolus Linnaeus, *A General and Universal System of Natural History, Comprising the Three Kingdoms of Animals, Vegetables, and Minerals, Arranged under Their Respective Classes, Orders, Genera, and Species* (London: W. Lewis, [18—?]), 12:137–138. Linnaeus's volume corrected Merian's erroneous conclusion:

    > Madame Merian, to whom we owe the first observations on this wonderful subject, mistakenly supposed that the young were conceived beneath the skin on the back of the mother. The fact is, that, after the eggs are excluded from

the female and fecundated by the male, in the same manner with those of all other toads, instead of dispersing them in the water, the male collects them under his belly with his feet, and spreads them over the back of the female, where they stick close by means of the viscid liquor which surrounds them: by some unknown process, perhaps irritated by some property of the male seminal liquor, the skin, or the back of the female tumifies, and forms little cells over all the eggs.

47. Richard Price and Sally Price, introduction to *Stedman's Surinam: Life in an Eighteenth-Century Slave Society; An Abridged, Modernized Edition of "Narrative of a Five Years Expedition against the Revolted Negroes of Surinam" by John Gabriel Stedman* (Baltimore: Johns Hopkins University Press, 1992), xii.
48. Etheridge, "Maria Sibylla Merian."
49. Carolyn Merchant, *The Death of Nature: Women, Ecology, and the Scientific Revolution* (San Francisco: Harper and Row, 1980), xvi.
50. Laura Dassow Walls, *The Passage to Cosmos: Alexander von Humboldt and the Shaping of America* (Chicago: University of Chicago Press, 2009); Dana Phillips, *The Truth of Ecology: Nature, Culture, and Literature in America* (Oxford: Oxford University Press, 2003).
51. Merian likely did not stipulate that habitats were subject to random, intrinsic changes, as contemporary ecologists have theorized. Ecologists call this theory "patchiness, random variation, patter, or grain." Phillips, *Truth of Ecology*, 79.
52. Merian, *Dissertation*, plate 1 textual description.
53. Merian, *Dissertation*, plate 1 textual description.
54. Merian, *Dissertation*, plate 1 textual description.
55. Etheridge, "Biology of *Metamorphosis*," 36.
56. Merian, *Dissertation*, plate 23 text.
57. Etheridge, "Biology of *Metamorphosis*," 35. The Goliath bird-eater injects its prey with a paralytic enzyme, something Merian could not have known from mere observation, though she notes that "they ooze a fluid into the wound," per translation in Lennon, "Translation Original Texts," 180. Bates first named this spider in his 1863 work, *The Naturalist on the River Amazons*.
58. Merian, *Dissertation*, plate 18 text.
59. Merian, *Dissertation*, plate 18 text.
60. Merian, *Dissertation*, plate 18 text.
61. Merian, *Dissertation*, plate 18 text.
62. Etheridge, "Maria Sibylla Merian," 10, 42.

2

THRESHOLDS OF LIVABILITY

Climate and Population Relocation in Anna Maria Falconbridge's *Two Voyages to Sierra Leone*

SHELBY JOHNSON

NEAR THE CLOSE OF HER epistolary travel narrative *Two Voyages to Sierra Leone* (1794), Anna Maria Falconbridge considers the causes for the settlement's embattled existence. She represents the colony's Black settlers who fled to Nova Scotia after the American Revolution and then relocated to Sierra Leone, besieged by the tropical rainy season.[1] In an odd turn, she defends the climate from responsibility for their struggles:

> Methinks I hear you invectively exclaim against the country, and charging those ravages to its unhealthiness; but suspend your judgement for a moment, and give me time to paint the true state of things, when I am of opinion you will think otherwise, or at least allow the climate has not a fair tryal. This is the depth of the rainy season, our inhabitants were not covered in before it commenced, and the huts they have been able to make, are neither wind or water tight; few of them have bedsteads, but are obliged to lie on the wet ground, without medical assistance, wanting almost every comfort of life, and exposed to nauceous putrid stenches, produced by stinking provisions, scattered about town. Would you . . . expect to keep your health, or even live a month in the healthiest part of the world? I fancy not; then pray do not attribute our mortality altogether, to baseness of climate.[2]

Falconbridge focuses on the quotidian concerns of shelter—roofs, floors, bedsteads—which all remain porous to the driving rain and the "nauceous putrid stenches" that permeate the settlement. However, she unexpectedly reads the origins of these "stenches" not in the region's weather patterns, but in the colony's improperly stored food supplies, the "stinking provisions, scattered about town," implying that British goods rather than the area's physical environment have contributed to the settlement's chronic high mortality. Falconbridge's contention that even something so mundane as the food supplies afforded by the British could contribute just as much as climate to the colony's rates of infection during the rainy season constitutes one of her sharpest critiques of colonial rule in the narrative. In *Two Voyages*, Falconbridge offers a diagnosis of colonial administration in ruin, where the toxic smells of the rotting provisions function as a peculiarly odorous metonym for the corrosive miasma of bureaucratic mismanagement in Sierra Leone.

Sierra Leone was colonized through two major relocations of (majority) Black populations: in May 1787, the British government resettled over four hundred of London's "Black Poor" to Granville Town, while in March 1792, the Sierra Leone Company sponsored the emigration of nearly two thousand freed people of color from Nova Scotia to Freetown. Conceived as a shelter for formerly enslaved peoples and Black soldiers and sailors who settled in London and Nova Scotia after the American Revolution, the Sierra Leone projects emerged in the 1780s as a philanthropic venture spearheaded by a diverse coalition of British evangelicals and businessmen, including driving forces of the nascent abolitionist movement.[3] They imagined that the relocation project would promote equitable land distribution and freedom for recently enslaved peoples and military personnel loyal to Britain during the American war.[4] Falconbridge traveled to Sierra Leone twice, from January to September 1791 and from December 1791 to June 1793. Two editions of *Two Voyages* appeared in 1794, and another in 1802, suggesting its popularity in contemporary debates on these experiments in Black resettlement. Falconbridge published *Two Voyages* only a few months after a report accused her husband, the slave ship surgeon-turned-abolitionist administrator, Alexander Falconbridge, of administrative mismanagement in 1794.[5] Defending her (by then late) husband from the charges, Falconbridge contends that London directors' philanthropic ideals failed to take into account the economic and social forces circumscribing the settlement: "It was surely a premature, hair-brained, and ill digested scheme, to think of sending such a number of people all at once, to a rude, barbarous and unhealthy country, before they were certain of possessing an acre of land; and I very much fear will terminate in disappointment."[6] While Falconbridge admits that the climate is "unhealthy," she nevertheless makes a case that the early, troubled years of the Sierra Leone settlement directly resulted from colonial negligence.

In this essay, I explore how the *Two Voyages* intercedes in debates on population relocation in two interconnected ways. First, I argue that Falconbridge's narrative portrays the visual meanings, what she calls the "distress conveyed by the eye," through which populations are *seen* and thus rendered sympathetically *legible* as communities in need of philanthropically driven resettlement.[7] Second, I consider the ways *Two Voyages* offers an early model for imagining how climate could function as an instrument of state violence, where environments are used to discipline or control unwanted populations. I ask: Which populations count to be seen and grieved throughout the Atlantic world? What environments make practical and political sense for resettling these distressed populations? Resettlement was often framed as a realization in reparative justice, where British officials reward loyalty during the American war with land. Falconbridge frequently condemns the resettlement projects as "schemes," however, because the ideal image of the new settlement is far removed from reality.[8] In this way, Falconbridge seems to read resettlement schemes as extensions of colonial management of Black populations. *Two Voyages*, furthermore, juxtaposes mass population relocations to Falconbridge's experiences of marital strife, suggesting that both her perspective as a woman writer and the genre of the travel narrative are uniquely positioned to make connections between toxic paternal values and endemic colonial incompetence.[9] *Two Voyages* thus represents population removal as a way to reflect how closely sympathy, philanthropy, and antislavery—the hallmarks of both benevolent colonialism and domesticity—remained entangled in forms of patriarchy.

Falconbridge's decision to render her account an epistolary travel narrative situates quotidian concerns of reparative justice within a literary global network—what we might call a generic ecology—that linked readers and writers throughout the Atlantic world.[10] Although Falconbridge's female correspondent is never named (and is probably a fiction), that she framed her reflections on Sierra Leone through personal letters between women suggests the extent to which her critique of removal is gendered: white men remain largely culpable for the difficulties experienced by the colony. Falconbridge often understands her position as a white woman as one most able to sympathize with the plight of the Black settlers and textually mediate it to the British reading public.[11] In a few instances, Black settlers seem to have seen her as an important ally. Isaac Anderson, a vocal leader of the Freetown inhabitants, considered *Two Voyages* a "favorite book" and took to "reading aloud relevant passages" to both Black settlers and colonial officials during moments of strife.[12] Falconbridge, however, affirmed the necessity of slavery in *Two Voyages*, diverging from the interests and deeply held political convictions of the Black immigrants.[13] Proslavery and anticolonial positions remain coconstitutive tensions in the text, forming an assembly of political ideologies at odds with the grievances expressed by Black settlers in their own letters and petitions.[14] Falconbridge's attempts to channel the concerns of the colony through her gendered perspective risks co-opting the historical significance of Black readers and writers within the generic conventions of travel writing more generally and the fictional demands of her unnamed correspondent more specifically. The resources of fiction, as contributors to this volume argue in other essays, offer space for female agency and vision across the terrains of the Atlantic world, but in this particular case also elide Black voices.

Indeed, as Deirdre Coleman suggests, Falconbridge "works the epistolary mode for a number of advantages, not least of which is the identification of privacy with authenticity and truthfulness," yet it is worth remaining alert to moments when Falconbridge's inconsistency also punctures that illusion.[15] While other critics have done much needed work considering the concatenation of Falconbridge's proslavery and anticolonial postures, I attend to contradictions in her reflections on colonial population movement because they illustrate how free Black communities unsettle these categories and reveal how these contradictions are woven into her epistolary practices. To that end, near the close of this essay, I read Falconbridge alongside the sole letter we possess written by a Black woman immigrating to Sierra Leone, Susana Smith. Like *Two Voyages*, Smith's letter is concerned with everyday matters of survival. Unlike *Two Voyages*, however, Smith's letter remains in the quotidian, marking how it feels to *dwell* in a threshold of livability Falconbridge primarily *observes*. Individual letters in the archives of women's travel writing, in other words, remain in complex relationships with each other, especially in the experiential differences that distinguished "travelers" from "immigrants." By situating *Two Voyages* within an archive of women's epistolary writing that includes women of color, we are better able to see the illegibility of elements of Black survival within the world depicted in Falconbridge's letters. While Falconbridge's indictment of the routine waste of Sierra Leone's colonial administration offers, then, critical frameworks for tracing the origins and implementation of policies of population management in Britain and West Africa in the 1780s and 1790s, *Two Voyages* also reminds us to be attuned to the ways that modes of population relocation served the interests of benevolent colonialism.

SLOW VIOLENCE IN SIERRA LEONE

By shifting impoverished communities to harsher climates away from imperial centers, British resettlement policies participated in large-scale practices where people of color, as Monique Allewaert reminds us, "were coded as bodies whose destruction by climatic and economic structures were legally justified by metropolitan and colonial law."[16] The Sierra Leone settlement and its chronic high mortality in its early years provoked Falconbridge to ask questions deeply concerned with British motives for embattled settlement schemes: Were Black settlers' interests served by these relocation proposals, or did they betray an (often) unspoken impulse to ensure at least some form of racial homogeneity in Britain and North American colonies? Were harsh climates mobilized as an eighteenth-century version of population management, or were they merely a convenient excuse for explaining why settlements struggled or even failed? Or, if this seems much too unscrupulous for the white evangelical abolitionists spearheading the Sierra Leone settlement, to what extent was British colonial and philanthropic mismanagement accountable for Black settler mortality? Put simply, has climate been given, as Falconbridge claimed, "a fair tryal" or not for the devastating early years of the Sierra Leone settlement? I suggest that by relocating the Black poor in London and Black settlers in Nova Scotia to Sierra Leone, white philanthropists in London used tropical climates as an arrangement of what Rob Nixon calls "slow violence," a violence "that occurs gradually and out of sight, a violence of delayed destruction that is dispersed across time and space, an attritional violence that is typically not viewed as violence at all."[17] Nixon emphasizes that the temporal duration of slow violence frequently occludes its visibility, and thus its legibility in contemporary politico-climatic debates. Rather than instances of ecological contamination and destruction and their attendant impact on impoverished communities, Falconbridge portrays slow violence occurring another way: climates become a vehicle for population control, of removing unwanted populations.

Moreover, by cultivating a sense of immediacy and authenticity, Falconbridge's letters offer a generic resolution to the long temporal durations that render slow violence invisible and illegible because incidents of suffering, especially environmentally provoked devastation, frequently emphasize the descriptive, the experiential, even the somatic. Through its negotiation of local and emblematic experiences of population relocation, the letters of *Two Voyages* advance equivocal strategies for negotiating appeals to reparative justice in the transatlantic world, as well as for describing practical matters of colonial survival. Falconbridge channels her contemplations of the colony's viability and its supposed realization of reparative justice through her reformulations of two conventional tropes of the travel narrative. On a large scale, she evaluates comparative models of population removal and control, particularly the connection, deeply entrenched in public debate, between the Sierra Leone and Botany Bay settlements and their corresponding rationales. On a small scale, she mediates other voices in the text, specifically by including letters and petitions composed by Black settlers near the end of *Two Voyages*.[18] In this way, Falconbridge's letters can encompass something as large as the transatlantic ethics of resettlement "schemes" or something as local as the odor of rotting provisions.

Falconbridge offers perhaps her most revealing instance of inconsistent measures for evaluating colonial practices of population control in the second letter of

Two Voyages. As the first ships were preparing to sail to Sierra Leone in 1787, their arrangements coincided with the sailing of the First Fleet to Botany Bay. Falconbridge commented at length on the contiguous fleets at anchor but managed to sidestep questions of colonial culpability for the slow, climatic violences in the Sierra Leone settlement by transposing it onto the First Fleet:

> The only thing that attracted my notice in the harbour, is the fleet with convicts for Botany Bay, which are wind bound, as well as ourselves. The destiny of such numbers of my fellow creatures has made what I expect to encounter, set lighter on my mind than it ever did before; nay, nothing could have operated a reconciliation so effectually: for as the human heart is more susceptible of distress conveyed by the eye, than when represented by language however ingeniously pictured with misery, so the sight of those unfortunate beings, and the thoughts of what they are to endure, have worked more forcibly on my feelings, than all the accounts I ever read or heard of wretchedness before.[19]

This letter participates in a familiar meditation in the eighteenth century: a moment of sympathetic exchange. Impelled by perceptual proximity, the "misery" of those "unfortunate beings . . . worked forcibly" on her feelings and initiates Falconbridge into an affective circuit that at first opens her to the sufferings of the convicts condemned to transportation. Instead of prompting her to reflect on the rationales that supported large-scale population removals like convict transportation, the spectacle allows her to reconsider the dangers of her own passage to Sierra Leone, where her fate "set lighter on [her] mind." In doing so, Falconbridge makes a case that perceived suffering is legible in a way that described (or written) suffering is not. As with her attention to "nauceous putrid stenches" in the passage I opened the essay with, in this instance Falconbridge prioritizes the sensory, but in such a way that may implicitly undercut what Coleman called the "authenticity and truthfulness" of her letters: suffering has to be *seen* in order to be *felt*.[20] Written narratives, especially those situated in the geographically far-flung spaces of transatlantic territories, offer more attenuated impressions than experience. While Falconbridge's collage of somatic immediacy is not in any way unusual in the eighteenth century, that she invokes its power in a narrative so focused on the optics of population removal suggests that this is a peculiarly tempting colonial fantasy, one that ultimately denies the legibility of convict distress and, potentially, of Black suffering.

In order to contextualize Falconbridge's depictions of Black and convict distress, it may help us to see where *Two Voyages* fits within late eighteenth-century debates on colonial resettlement policies. The American war prompted extraordinary migrations of newly freed populations of people of color, primarily to the comparatively more frigid climates in Nova Scotia and London. Unsettled by the poverty experienced by African-descended peoples in London, who were unable to find work during mass demobilization, one newspaper correspondent observed: "They . . . have served Britain . . . [and] are now left to perish by famine and cold in the sight of that people for whom they have hazarded their lives," reading the northern British climate as contributing to Black settlers' hardships.[21] The Sierra Leone settlement, on the other hand, was also sometimes framed as repayment *to* Britain for the public and philanthropic aid devoted to the impoverished Black residents of London. As the naval officer and botanist Henry Smeathman argued, the settlement would "[remove] such a burthen from the Public for ever; and . . . [put] them in a condition of *repaying* this Country the expense thereof, by opening a new and beneficial channel of trade and commerce."[22]

Yet if the 1780s and 1790s were marked by anything, it was disagreement on the practical ethics of resettlement schemes when climatic viability was disputed. In 1782, for instance, 350 British convicts were transported to Gambia to support slave traders in the region, where most of the prisoners died within the year.[23] Four years later, Parliament's Committee on Convict Transportation, examining various schemes to address England's chronically overcrowded prisons, considered sending shiploads of convicts to Sierra Leone. Edmund Burke, who closely followed the deliberations of the committee, observed in the House of Commons that transportation to West Africa, "the capital seat of plague, pestilence, and famine," constituted nothing less than a "singularly horrid" death sentence "after a mock display of clemency." He considered West Africa the location of "the gates of Hell," which were "open day and night to receive the victims of the law."[24] Smeathman, who had resided in West Africa in the 1770s, decried the region's harsh climate and claimed that "not One in a 100" of the convicts would survive the first six months without adequate medical care, shelter, and supplies.[25] Following Smeathman's testimony, the committee instead recommended Botany Bay as a healthier alternative.

In 1786, however, just as the parliamentary committee was concluding its deliberations, Smeathman underwent a dramatic about-face, recommending Sierra Leone as the ideal location for a Black colony in his *Plan of a Settlement to be Made near Sierra Leone* (1786), a text, according to Coleman, "long on optimism and short on actual details as to how his colony might function and survive."[26] Smeathman suggested that farming and husbandry could proceed "with a rapidity unknown in these colder climates" and was sanguine about the ease with which the settlement could become self-sustaining.[27] By this point, another committee—a philanthropic rather than a parliamentary one—had stepped in to debate the issue of Black poverty: the Committee for the Relief of the Black Poor. Organized to distribute food, clothing, and medical care to impoverished African-descended peoples in London, members of the committee for the Black Poor came to believe that philanthropic assistance constituted only a short-term solution to Black poverty. They cast about for a more permanent solution—namely, resettlement to a more hospitable climate. They considered several alternatives, debating the merits of Nova Scotia, the Bahamas, and Sierra Leone.[28] Smeathman's enthusiastic support for Sierra Leone sealed their deliberations. As Cassandra Pybus dryly notes, the committee "had not thought to ask Smeathman why, if he was so confident of a settlement on the west coast of Africa, he had given such damning evidence to the House of Commons on the deadly prospects for a penal settlement there."[29] Smeathman may have been motivated by the conviction that African-descended peoples were well suited to the climate, better able to adapt to and survive tropical ecologies.[30] And while in later years Black settler survival exceeded that of white colonists, this was not always the case.[31] High rates of mortality marred the early years of the Sierra Leone settlement: of the original 411 colonists who sailed for Sierra Leone from London in April 1787, over 100 were dead after the first wet season, and only around 60 remained by 1791.[32]

By the 1790s, the settlement functioned as an equivocal British colonial fantasy, as both an abolitionist-backed policy of imagined reparative justice and a seemingly crass project for removing the Black poor from sight. Observers criticized the resettlement of Black populations in Sierra Leone by claiming that the British used the comparatively hostile climate of the territory as an effort to visibly erase them from England—where resettlement functioned as a peculiarly subtle tool of racial purification. The Black writer and activist Olaudah Equiano, summarized early settlers' distrust of the British: "[The settlers] fear the design of some in sending them away, is only to get rid of them at all events."[33] Like Equiano, Falconbridge is suspicious of the motives and aims of the Sierra Leone Company's purported fidelity to an equitable freedom for the Black settlers: "I am surprised our boasted Philanthropists, the Directors of the Company, should have subjected themselves to such censure as they must meet, for sporting with the lives of such numbers of their fellow creatures, I mean by sending so many here at once, before houses, materials for building, or other conveniences were prepared to receive them, and for not hurrying a supply after they had been guilty of this oversight."[34] Falconbridge's summation of the practices of the Sierra Leone Company as "sporting with the lives of their fellow creatures" asserts that the colonial administrators failed to meet standards of equity and humanity, and she questions the rationale for the transportation of this population to a far-flung settlement in the British Empire. Falconbridge frames her understanding of colonial mismanagement by white men (both the directors in London and administrative officials in

Freetown) as a competing, largely wasteful ecology, one whose entropic ruin undermines the viability of the settlement.

VISUALIZING VIOLENCE IN TRANSATLANTIC LETTERS

Deliberations on where to transport convicts repeatedly coincided with disputes on where to found Black settlements, and the discursive textures of these debates resonate in the local matters of colonial oversight that Falconbridge remained preoccupied with in her letters. The failed Gambia experiment, the parliamentary deliberations on the viability of Sierra Leone's and Botany Bay's climates, and Smeathman's public about-face on the suitableness of Sierra Leone's climate for a colony constituted only one nexus of policy disagreement on matters of population control. At the level of administrative oversight, the Botany Bay and Sierra Leone settlement often also shared personnel. William Dawes, the governor of Sierra Leone from August 1792 to March 1794, for instance, had accompanied the First Fleet to Botany Bay as an engineer and surveyor. Thoroughly disliked by the Black settlers, Dawes's cold, formal manner contrasted with the previous governor's, John Clarkson's.[35] In *Two Voyages*, Falconbridge questioned the rationale for appointing Dawes to colonial posts with such divergent political goals:

> It may not be *mal-a-propos* to mention here, that Mr. Dawes is a subaltern of Marines; that the prejudices of a rigid military education has been heightened by his having served some time at Botany Bay, where, no doubt, it is necessary for gentlemen to observe an awful severity in their looks and actions; but such behaviour, however suitable for a Colony formed wholly of Convicts, and governed by the iron rod of despotism, should be scrupulously guarded against in one like this, whose *basis is Liberty and Equality*, and whose Police is dependent, in great measure, if not altogether, on the whimsical disposition of an ignorant populace, which can only be advantageously tempered by placidness and moderation.[36]

Falconbridge here juxtaposes the supposed high-minded values of the Sierra Leone settlement—its "*basis*" in "*Liberty and Equality*"—with an acknowledgment of local difficulties of governance, what she (condescendingly) portrays as dual, competing ideals of administrative oversight: the "rigid military" governorship of Dawes and the policing responsibilities of Black magistrates, who display what she calls the "whimsical disposition of an ignorant populace."

Indeed, the letter indulges in a contradictory reading of the meaning of Black freedom: while the settlement ostensibly locates its political origins in the "*Liberty and Equality*" of Black settlers, as an embattled population, their vernacular performances of self-government strike Falconbridge as fancifully incoherent and even unruly. They are, in Michel Foucault's idiom, living not as a "population" subject to governmental regulation but as a "people," or "those who conduct themselves in relation to the management of the population, at the level of the population, as if they were not part of [that] population . . . and consequently the people are those who, refusing to be the population, disrupt the system."[37] Falconbridge contends that culpability for the colony's struggles remains with white administrators like Dawes, who, experienced in the forms of authoritarian oversight deemed necessary in Botany Bay, are ill equipped to oversee Sierra Leone. The letter retains dual consciousness of both anticolonialist and colonialist modes of population management without attempting to reconcile them, suggesting the extent to which her transatlantic letters face certain limits when representing resistant political expression to readers in Britain. If visually removed from England and resettled in West Africa, can Black suffering or Black political self-determination be meaningfully represented in the pages of Falconbridge's *Two Voyages*? Even if seen and observed by Falconbridge in Sierra Leone, how can Black political yearnings be readable if deemed too "ignorant" and "whimsical"? Against these obstacles, how might the political ideals motivating and the ecological and bureaucratic setbacks endangering Freetown ultimately be legible?

These questions become that much more pressing near the close of *Two Voyages* when, frustrated by the Sierra Leone Company's refusal to compensate her for her late husband's expenses in the colony, Falconbridge joins her critiques of colonial negligence to those of the Black settlers. Indeed, she intersperses the letters and petitions of the settlers within her own accounts of the company's negligence. Debbie Lee and Louis Kirk McAuley have argued that in their letters and petitions, the Black settlers "recycled" idioms of political autonomy and affiliation, transforming the "waste" of colonial negligence into a "new product" that affirms their self-determination.[38] We might read Falconbridge's editorial decision to include their letters and petitions as another form of transatlantic literary recycling, one that frames the Black settlers' demands for more just arrangements of political consent and population governance as a shared ideal in the narrative. Given Falconbridge's condescending representation of Black self-governance, however, her incorporation of their transatlantic letters in *Two Voyages* risks transforming literary recycling into appropriation, one that generically parallels the belated and unequitable division of land in the settlement by company administrators. The Black settlers, in particular, understand the fair surveying and partitioning of land as both the fulfillment of promises made by the company *and* a pragmatic policy that takes into account the colony's local terrain and climate. To that end, the petitions dwell on the incompetence and negligence of company administrators, detailed complaints Falconbridge includes in *Two Voyages*.

Falconbridge focuses on the letters and petitions carried in 1793 to the London directors of the Sierra Leone Company by Isaac Anderson and Cato Perkins, a cohort elected to present the Black settlers' grievances directly to the company. In letter 12, for instance, Falconbridge includes much of a petition that affirms "that they should have been satisfied had they got one fifth part of their proportion (*in good land*) time enough to have prepared a crop for the ensuing year, but the rains are now commenced, and the Surveyor has not finished laying out the small allotments, which he might have done, had he not relinquished the work as soon as John Clarkson sailed; and the greater part of those he has surveyed, are so mountainous, barren, and rocky, that it will be impossible ever to obtain a living from them."[39] The petitioners are here preoccupied with settlement sustainability and colonial negligence. The settlers stress the significance of land possession, which for them is always a question that moves from immediate, personal survival to the promised endurance of the community through future generations, what Falconbridge paraphrases as the settlers "dwelling greatly on the happiness and prosperity of their children."[40] In this sense, for the Black community, population always encompasses generational continuity, or kinship arrangements that extend into an inhabitable future. A later petition included in *Two Voyages* goes even further: "You have desired us to commit to writing what we wish to tell you. . . . We beg to have Grants for the land we at present occupy, and a promise in writing for the remainder, or the value, to be given at a future time named in that instrument of writing[, . . .] and we should have the pleasure of knowing we were providing comfort for our children after us."[41] This petition offers a complex vision of settler continuity mediated in domestic practices, genealogical survival, and the written word.[42]

Falconbridge encloses the Black settlers' gestures toward an imagined future, however, within a theory of sympathetic vision that nevertheless questions its legibility, suggesting that *Two Voyages* measures the distance between the possibilities and limits of accounting for reparative justice in this example of an eighteenth-century travel narrative. In order to be legible, forms of racial and climate violence, as we have seen, depend on modes of visuality that in some ways demand intertextual relationships. Falconbridge extends and deepens her critique of the Sierra Leone Company by including letters and petitions by Black settlers, yet her editorial hand also risks subordinating the petitioners' appeals to the political imperatives of white womanhood, especially the sentimental position of the sympathetic spectator of human suffering. What texts, in other words, are left out of the literary ecosystem represented by *Two Voyages*? If *Two Voyages* is situated in a larger literary archive, then Falconbridge's attempts to generically expand who may participate in this transatlantic literary ecosystem end by portraying her as an ephemeral member of it, as only a visitor to this territory.

THRESHOLDS OF LIVABILITY

By reflecting on what Falconbridge's *Two Voyages* integrates, paraphrases, or modifies of the letters and petitions of the Black settlers, I close with a reading of a letter, *not* included in her narrative, because of what it suggests about reading transatlantically—or developing a hermeneutic attuned to varied epistolary practices whereby women, especially women of color, become legible in these archives. A letter by Susana Smith, one of the Nova Scotian emigrants, marks what I call a threshold of livability, a form of survival necessary to meet subsistence in the impoverished, far-flung free Black settlements of the British Empire. Writing to John Clarkson, who oversaw the Nova Scotian migration to Sierra Leone, Smith implores: "Sir I your hum bel Servent begs the faver of your Excelence to See if you will Pleas to Let me hav Som Sope for I am in great want of Som I have not had aney Since I have bin to this plais I hav bin Sick and I want to git Som Sope very much to wash my family Clos for we ar not fit to be Sean for dirt your hum bel Servent Susana Smith."[43] While Lee and McAuley read the emphasis on soap in Smith's letter as an emerging "fetishistic imperial consumer item," I attend to the way the letter and the consumer item it requests indicates a threshold of livability, or an assemblage of peoples, objects, and ecologies needed to support life.[44] By invoking "assemblage," I am drawing from Anna Lowenhaupt Tsing, who in *The Mushroom at the End of the World* refines an earlier definition of an assemblage as a "site for watching how political economy works" to a site that enables "performances of livability," where "performance" suggests the local and intimate routines of habitation.[45] As a Black woman about to undertake the long transatlantic voyage from Nova Scotia to Sierra Leone, Smith's request for soap impresses the everyday routines of survival undertaken against the local specters of disease and poverty during the harsh winter before the settlers sailed to Freetown. Indeed, to reinscribe the substance of her plea reveals the reality of transatlantic travel at its most ordinary and even banal: she wishes to wash her family's "Clos." She wishes to wash their bodies.

For Smith, more importantly, soap matters as both a routine of livability and a routine of *visibility*—with the aid of soap, she and her family will be "fit to be Sean." She will, for one, conform to British standards of cleanliness and maternal care, but her family might also become legible across the barely grievable, transatlantic spaces of suffering, flight, and relocation experienced by people of color. In this sense, Smith's epistolary account of need archives what David Kazanjian, in his examination of a set of letters from the U.S. American–directed resettlement of African Americans in Liberia, has called "heterodox performances of the very meaning of freedom," where freedom marks a mode of survival.[46] Smith's letter, humble though it may be, offers a tremulous flare of somatic detail, of what it might mean to be a body "fit to be Sean," counter to the attenuated sympathy afforded by Falconbridge's "distress conveyed by the eye" and mediated to the reader through the page. But "fit to be Sean" by whom? And to what end?

For Smith, to be a woman traveler, especially a woman of color, is to write oneself into visibility, where a threshold of livability is nearly always already a function of literacy, of appeal to colonial authority. The letter, in other words, signals how closely Smith and her family's domestic health and happiness depends on the legibility of their needs to beneficent colonial philanthropists, like John Clarkson. Perhaps what is necessary for reading transatlantically, then, is to form our own improvised assemblages of texts—to go beyond the intertextual citation already practiced in travel narratives like Falconbridge's—in order to mark alternative thresholds of livability voiced by women living in close proximity, but under different orders of visibility. To read Falconbridge means going beyond even the complex imbedded letters of her text and developing a hermeneutic attentive to the tensions between climatic violences and colonial incompetence, transatlantic resettlement policies and domestic arrangements for women writers throughout the Atlantic world.

NOTES

1. Scholars have debated what to call this particular community. Frequently denoted attributions such as "Black Loyalists" or "Black Nova Scotians" prioritize a political commitment that may have been strategic or a temporary geographical location. I use "Black settlers" for the inhabitants of Freetown, not to align them with the expansionist agendas of white settler colonialism, but to foreground their political agency and aspirations to create a free Black community. Other terms like "immigrants" or "migrants" do not seem to carry quite the same weight.
2. Anna Maria Falconbridge, *Two Voyages to Sierra Leone*, in *Maiden Voyages and Infant Colonies: Two Women's Travel Narratives of the 1790s*, ed. Deirdre Coleman (London: Leicester University Press, 1999), 103.
3. For further historical work on the Sierra Leone settlements of the 1780s and 1790s, see Christopher Fyfe, *A History of Sierra Leone* (London: Oxford University Press, 1962); Christopher Fyfe, *Sierra Leone Inheritance* (London: Oxford University Press, 1964); James W. St. G. Walker, *The Black Loyalists* (Toronto: University of Toronto Press, 1976); Stephen J. Braidwood, *Black Poor and White Philanthropists* (Liverpool: Liverpool University Press, 1994); Gretchen Gerzina, *Black London* (New Brunswick, NJ: Rutgers University Press, 1995); Mary Louise Clifford, *From Slavery to Freetown: Black Loyalists after the American Revolution*

(Jefferson, NC: McFarland, 1999); Simon Schama, *Rough Crossings* (New York: HarperCollins, 2005); Cassandra Pybus, *Epic Journeys of Freedom: Runaway Slaves of the American Revolution and Their Global Quest for Freedom* (Boston: Beacon Press, 2006); Alexander X. Byrd, *Captives and Voyagers* (Baton Rouge: Louisiana State University Press, 2008); Maya Jasanoff, *Liberty's Exiles* (New York: Vintage Books, 2011); and Alan Gilbert, *Black Patriots and Loyalists: Fighting for Emancipation in the War for Independence* (Chicago: University of Chicago Press, 2012).

4. As Simon Schama explains in *Rough Crossings*, compensation practices failed to favor Black claimants. Many Black petitioners who pleaded for lost property or wages, or compensations for injuries sustained during the American war, were met with nothing: "Had the petitioners been slaves until they joined the army? Well, then, it followed that they could not possibly have had any property for which to be compensated! Indeed, it should be enough for them that they had received their liberty!" (180).
5. Deirdre Coleman, introduction to *Maiden Voyages and Infant Colonies: Two Women's Travel Narratives of the 1790s*, ed. Deirdre Coleman (London: Leicester University Press, 1999), 4–5.
6. Falconbridge, *Two Voyages*, 93.
7. Falconbridge, *Two Voyages*, 50. For critical scholarship on *Two Voyages*, as well as the Black settlers' letters and petitions, see Christopher Fyfe, introduction to *"Our Children Free and Happy": Letters from Black Settlers in Africa in the 1790s*, ed. Christopher Frye (Edinburgh: Edinburgh University Press, 1991), 1–19; Srinivas Aravamudan, *Tropicopolitans: Colonialism and Agency, 1688–1804* (Durham, NC: Duke University Press, 1999), 253–269; Helen Thomas, *Romanticism and Slave Narratives: Transatlantic Testimonies* (Cambridge: Cambridge University Press, 2000), 1–5, 228–229, 252–253; Deirdre Coleman, *Romantic Colonization and British Anti-Slavery* (Cambridge: Cambridge University Press, 2005), 28–61, 106–132; Mary Louise Pratt, *Imperial Eyes: Travel Writing and Transculturation* (London: Routledge, 1992), 102–107; and Debbie Lee and Louis Kirk McAuley, "Romantic Recycling: The Global Economy and Secondhand Language in Equiano's *Interesting Narrative* and the Letters of the Sierra Leone Settlers," in *Global Romanticism: Origins, Orientations, and Engagements, 1760–1820*, ed. Evan Gottlieb (Lewisburg, PA: Bucknell University Press, 2015), 169–197.
8. While attentive to rhetoric that framed the settlement as a manifestation of colonial altruism, Falconbridge remains attuned to a much more utilitarian matter: the large-scale organization of populations and their territorial relocations. Michel Foucault argues that in the eighteenth century a diffuse, "regulatory apparatus" emerged to organize populations in the West. Michel Foucault, *Security, Territory, Population: Lectures at the Collège de France, 1977–1978*, ed. Michel Senellart and trans. Graham Burchell (New York: Picador, 2004), 69. The regulatory apparatus Foucault focuses on—such as the police—are those committed to internally regulating the population. This essay seeks to explore the rationales for moving populations from the homeland to geographically far-flung areas of colonial rule.
9. Previous studies of *Two Voyages* have focused on its anticolonial feminism and its participation in Romantic cultures of sentimentality, especially when read through Falconbridge's candid descriptions of her troubled marriage to Alexander. See especially Coleman, *Romantic Colonization and British Anti-Slavery*; and Pratt, *Imperial Eyes*.
10. For considering the interplay between global and local concerns mediated in transatlantic epistolary networks, I draw particularly from the work of Eve Tavor Bannet and Susan Manning, "Introduction: British and American Genres," in *Transatlantic Literary Studies, 1660–1830*, ed. Eve Tavor Bannet and Susan Manning (Cambridge: Cambridge University Press, 2012), 1–9; and David Kazanjian, *The Brink of Freedom: Improvising Life in the Nineteenth-Century Atlantic World* (Durham, NC: Duke University Press, 2016), 7–13.

11. As Deirdre Coleman notes in her introduction to *Maiden Voyages and Infant Colonies*, Falconbridge understood her narrative as a vindication of the grievances of the Black settlers: as a "citizen-critic," she framed herself as "a member of the republic of letters determined to achieve three public ends. The first is self-vindication. . . . The second is vindication of the Nova Scotian blacks, whose sense of betrayal she shared. . . . The third end is public exposure; Falconbridge is determined to publicize the bungling, hypocrisy and greed of a Government-sponsored colonial venture, run entirely by white, male philanthropists" (7).
12. Coleman, introduction to *Maiden Voyages and Infant Colonies*, 21.
13. It is worth noting that Falconbridge bases her proslavery argument by appealing to its value for managing African populations:

    > For a length of time I viewed the Slave Trade with abhorrence . . . but I am not ashamed to confess, those sentiments were the effect of ignorance, and the prejudice of opinion, imbibed by associating with a circle of acquaintances, *bigoted for the abolition*, before I had acquired information enough to form any independent thoughts upon the subject, and so widely opposite are my ideas of the trade from what they were, that I now think it in no shape objectionable either to morality or religion, but on the contrary consistent with both, while neither are to be to found in unhappy Africa; and while three-fourths of that populous country come into the world . . . subject, at any moment, to be rob'd of their lives by the other fourth, I say, while this is the case, I cannot think the Slave Trade consistent with any moral or religious law. (*Two Voyages*, 135)

    For critical assessments of Falconbridge's anticolonial and proslavery sentiments, see Aravamudan, *Tropicopolitans*, 260–264; and Coleman, introduction to *Maiden Voyages and Infant Colonies*, 22–28.
14. See especially Fyfe's edited collection of these letters and petitions, *"Our Children Free and Happy."*
15. Coleman, introduction to *Maiden Voyages and Infant Colonies*, 5. I am also influenced by David Kazanjian's argument in *Brink of Freedom* that "although letters might seem intimate and private, they usually combine artifice with a strong sense of public audience, more like a staged enactment than a transcription of the head or the heart" (13). I want to remain attuned to moments where the letters' evasions, contradictions, misdirections, and sense of artifice are evident.
16. Monique Allewaert, *Ariel's Ecology: Plantations, Personhood, and Colonialism in the American Tropics* (Minneapolis: University of Minnesota Press, 2013), 3.
17. Rob Nixon, *Slow Violence and the Environmentalism of the Poor* (Cambridge, MA: Harvard University Press, 2011), 2.
18. In attending to the multiple texts imbedded within the narrative of *Two Voyages*, I take my cue from Nicole N. Aljoe, *Creole Testimonies: Slave Narratives from the British West Indies, 1709–1838* (New York: Palgrave Macmillan, 2012). Aljoe argues that the Caribbean slave narrative is always a mediated text, or "a collaborative text, drawing on more than one voice" (14). I would like to apply this insight to colonial travel narratives like Falconbridge's.
19. Falconbridge, *Two Voyages*, 50.
20. Coleman, introduction to *Maiden Voyages and Infant Colonies*, 5.
21. Quoted in Schama, *Rough Crossings*, 184.
22. Quoted in Gerzina, *Black London*, 142; emphasis added.
23. For historical considerations of the failed Gambia convict colony, see Aravamudan, *Tropicopolitans*, 255–257; Thomas, *Romanticism and Slave Narratives*, 1–5; Schama, *Rough Crossings*, 187; and Pybus, *Epic Journeys of Freedom*, 96–98.

24. Quoted in Pybus, *Epic Journeys of Freedom*, 97.
25. Quoted in Coleman, *Romantic Colonization and British Anti-Slavery*, 57.
26. Coleman, *Romantic Colonization and British Anti-Slavery*, 57. As Debbie Lee and Louis Kirk McAuley also note: "Smeathman argued that London's black poor would be much happier resettled back in their own country, or—since most were born in America—the country of their ancestors, than they were in frigid England." Lee and McAuley, "Romantic Recycling," 187.
27. Henry Smeathman, *Plan of a Settlement to be Made near Sierra Leona, on the Grain Coast of Africa* (London, 1786), 7–9, quoted in Gerzina, *Black London*, 147.
28. Schama, *Rough Crossings*, 185–187.
29. Pybus, *Epic Journeys of Freedom*, 109.
30. Allewaert, *Ariel's Ecology*, 43.
31. As Schama notes, after the first six months of the Nova Scotian immigration attempt in 1791, mortality ebbed. In the end-of-year census undertaken by Governor John Clarkson, he discovered that "14 percent of the immigrants from Nova Scotia had perished. With the whites it was closer to 70 percent." Schama, *Rough Crossings*, 350.
32. Coleman, introduction to *Maiden Voyages and Infant Colonies*, 3.
33. Olaudah Equiano, *Public Advertiser*, April 6, 1787, 3.
34. Falconbridge, *Two Voyages*, 103.
35. Falconbridge relates one such performance of settler unruliness:

> Mr. Dawes endeavoured to persuade them by argument, that what he wanted to do, was for their protection; but they were deaf to every thing he said, and gave him such language in return which he could not stomach: He told them, if he had imagined they would have treated him with so much indignity, he should not have come among them; and if they continued to behave in the same way, he would certainly leave them as early as he could. To this, with one voice, they exclaimed, "Go! go! go! we do not want you here, we cannot get a worse after you." He was so disgusted at this, that he turned his back, and walked off. It was directly before my door, therefore I witnessed the whole, and could not help feeling for the *Governor*. (*Two Voyages*, 123)

36. Falconbridge, *Two Voyages*, 113.
37. Foucault, *Security, Territory, Population*, 43–44.
38. Lee and McAuley, "Romantic Recycling," 170.
39. Falconbridge, *Two Voyages*, 127.
40. Falconbridge, *Two Voyages*, 127.
41. Falconbridge, *Two Voyages*, 144.
42. Aravamudan notes, "Despite their best intentions, the tropicopolitan settlers in Sierra Leone cannot write themselves into the center of the British nation, nor can they successfully secede from it." Aravamudan, *Tropicopolitans*, 238.
43. Quoted in Fyfe, *"Our Children Free and Happy,"* 24.
44. Lee and McAuley, "Romantic Recycling," 193.
45. Anna Lowenhaupt Tsing, *The Mushroom at the End of the World* (Princeton, NJ: Princeton University Press, 2017), 157–158.
46. Kazanjian, *Brink of Freedom*, 13.

3

TRANSATLANTIC FEMALE SOLIDARITY

Two Women Social Explorers and Their Views on Nineteenth-Century Latin American Women

GRACE A. GOMASHIE

FLORA TRISTAN AND FRANCES "FANNY" Erskine Inglis Calderón de la Barca were travelers who visited Peru and Mexico, respectively, in the nineteenth century and wrote about their perceptions of women and the cultures they observed in their host countries. In Tristan's two-volume French travelogue *Pérégrinations d'une paria*, published in France in 1838, she documents the circumstances surrounding her travel as well as her journey from France to Peru from 1833 to 1834.[1] Calderón also authored a two-volume travel book, *Life in Mexico*, written in English and published in the United States of America in 1843, in which she recounts her two-year stay in Mexico and her travels around the country from 1839 to 1842 as the spouse of the Spanish ambassador to Mexico.[2] These books were highly critical of the patriarchal society in the authors' Latin American host countries, which experienced wars of independence, the forming of new nations, and a move toward modernity.[3] Ultimately, Tristan's and Calderón's writings demonstrate the ways that travel produced and shaped European-born women's beliefs in transatlantic kinship and solidarity among women, including women deemed culturally inferior to them.

The nineteenth century saw an influx of European travelers to Latin America, many of whom had come to take advantage of the continent's vast material resources and others who traveled for adventure and to admire the scenery. June E. Hahner remarks that foreign travel accounts about Latin America were a predominantly male activity before the nineteenth century.[4] Adriana Méndez Rodenas also affirms that, in contrast to most male travelers, female travelers in the nineteenth century sought to engage socially with the Americas while reinforcing their sense of identity.[5] These female social explorers had an interest in being involved in the activities of the new communities they inhabited. Some documented their travel accounts and experiences in diaries, memoirs, or letters, in which they vividly described the happenings of society and provided their personal opinions on social and political issues.

Hahner proposes that many women may have felt compelled by societal pressure and the publishing houses to adopt a discourse of femininity by writing on subjects in the traditional female domain such as social customs and traditions. There is some evidence of the discourse of femininity in the travel accounts of Tristan and Calderón, as they describe the dressing styles, religious beliefs and practices, domestic affairs, local customs, and environs of their host countries. Women authors were in the habit of claiming that their accounts were not meant for the public eye. They often gave apologies for venturing into the male domain or for their coverage of traditionally masculine topics. For example, Calderón apologizes for commenting on politics, but says, "It appears to me, that when bullets are whizzing about our ears, and shells falling within a few yards of us, it ought to be considered extremely natural, and quite feminine, to inquire into the cause of such phenomena."[6]

Reading Tristan's *Peregrinations of a Pariah* and Calderón's *Life in Mexico* gives readers an individualized view of, and valuable insights into, representations of women and societies in the Americas through their eyewitness accounts.[7] Such accounts can also be used as primary sources of information for historians. Since the twentieth century, travel writings, formerly relegated to the background, began to be incorporated into mainstream literature and were also seen as historical texts. As Hahner reminds us, analyses of women's travel writings have come from different perspectives: feminist (biographical or autobiographical methods), postcolonial (analysis of relations of power), postmodern (focus on text only), and historical (context only).[8] Nonetheless, critical reading of travel writing is required because its authors were influenced by their interests, beliefs, and backgrounds. Additionally, authors might present a narrow or stereotyped view of the society as well as make broad generalizations or universalist assertions of people's culture and customs without sufficient knowledge or contact. European and American travelers may portray their host country in a condescending tone, based on their social conditioning and notions of superiority.

The socio-economic status and ideologies of women travelers can influence their choice of social encounters and their descriptions. Therefore, Sara Mills situates women's travel writings in the colonial discourse rather than presenting them as a search for identity or as going against the status quo.[9] Studying travel writing from the mid-nineteenth to the late twentieth century, she remarks that female discursive strategies would have been similar to those of their male counterparts, were it not for the "discursive frameworks that exert[ed] pressure on female writers."[10] She cautions against reading these travel accounts as autobiographical, or "straightforward transcriptions of the lives of women travelers . . . [or] faithful representation of the writer."[11] She also considers how different interpretations of the text by readers and the pluri-significance and connotations of words can obscure the representation of an author's self. Additionally, Mills suggests that the label "autobiographical" is not helpful, as it casts doubts on the authenticity of the events narrated and implies that female authors are incapable of creating cultural and historical artifacts. Another limiting factor that casts doubts on travel accounts is the possibility that certain episodes can be changed, omitted, or embellished at the time of publishing. For example, the preface to Calderón's *Life in Mexico* states that certain elements were omitted (but which are not specified). What is certain is that Calderón coded the names of her characters and omitted some controversial issues based on her delicate position as the wife of the Spanish ambassador to Mexico.

Being mindful of the historical context and the strengths and limitations of women's travel accounts, this essay reveals the views and attitudes of Flora Tristan and Fanny Calderón on Peruvian and Mexican women, respectively. Comparing the views of these two transatlantic social explorers is informative because they both provided detailed commentaries about the status of women during the same historical period in Latin America, and their progressive views on women's rights reinforce each other. Their forthright opinions on gender relations and women's social conditions in nineteenth-century Latin America break the mold of conventional female attitudes of this era and provide an inadvertent glimpse into the authors' conceptions of their home countries.

Before exploring themes in each traveler's writings, we must consider the circumstances surrounding their travels and shaping their outlooks. In order to help readers understand the perspectives of French-born Tristan's travelogue, she narrates in her introduction, preface, and prologue the events and circumstances that led to her travel to Peru. She informs her readers that she was the illegitimate daughter of Don Mariano Tristan de Moriscos, a Peruvian creole of noble birth who served in the Spanish army, and Thérèse Laisnay, a Frenchwoman. The untimely death of Don Mariano left Flora and her mother in dire financial straits. Under pressure from her mother, Flora married her employer, André Chazal, a lithographer. This abusive and disastrous union bore three children, of whom two survived. To escape her abusive husband, thirty-year-old Flora undertook a voyage to Peru on April 7, 1833, to seek the protection of her father's family, headed by Don Pio de Tristan. Before then, she had supported her children for eight years after separation from her husband. Upon the counsel of one of her paternal relatives, she embarked on this peregrination to Peru disguised as an unmarried woman. Her untenable situation as a married woman, enforced by France's laws against divorce, and the need for financial security motivated her travel. Her pilgrimage to Peru is a story of claiming her paternal legitimacy and inheritance. Contrary to her expectations, she was denied her paternal right by her greedy uncle Pio but was given a meager monthly allowance instead. However, Tristan focused her energy on improving the condition of women, a course that she continued after her return to France in late 1834 or early 1835. In *Peregrinations*, she identifies with women who are oppressed under patriarchy and celebrates female superiority, leadership, and excellence.[12] She also criticizes heavily patriarchal and religious institutions and the seeming lack of leadership and progress in post-independence Peru.

Tristan's book was out of the ordinary, as it described her marital woes in detail. Initially, she published a few episodes of her travels, but she decided to publish the whole memoir after her husband published a book about her, labeling her as unfaithful and unfit to be a mother.[13] She saw the condition of women as similar to enslavement, with both women and enslaved people needing emancipation. Jennifer Law-Sullivan identifies the influence of the *Gazette des femmes* and the feminist literary circles of the Saint-Simonians on Tristan's activism.[14] She is often criticized for being too dramatic, hyperbolic, duplicitous, and self-important, and for universalizing her personal trials with serious issues such as injustice, enslavement, and oppression.[15] Nonetheless, Tristan's work exemplifies the activism and literary protest of the women's movement in France at that time. She dedicated her book to the Peruvians and signed "your compatriot and friend."[16] One of her recommendations to the Peruvians was the importance of formal education: "Educate the people, that is the pathway to prosperity."[17] She frames her personal experiences as part of a shared collective experience of female victimization: "I do not wish to draw attention to myself, but to all the women who find themselves in the same position, the number increases daily. They experience the same tribulations and sufferings I face."[18] In her book, Tristan portrays herself as a concerned Peruvian citizen who seeks the welfare of her fellow compatriots. She also establishes herself as an insider with the right to comment on social issues in Peru. She further positions herself as an advocate or a voice for women, having personally experienced tribulations and sufferings. She personalizes her narratives.

In the translator's introduction to *Peregrinations of a Pariah*, Jean Hawkes states that this is not just a travel account, but "a personal odyssey, a record of temptations she [Tristan] had to face in the course of her transformation from a self-centered young woman into a single-minded champion of the oppressed."[19] After its publication *Peregrinations* was negatively received in Lima because of its critical comments about the ruling class. Some Peruvians, especially those loyal to her uncle, burned an effigy of Tristan to show their displeasure. However, in France, her travel account was so popular that a second edition was printed soon after the first one.[20] Following a prolonged period of obscurity that began after her death in 1844, there was a revival of the persona of Tristan in the mid-twentieth century, and she is now hailed as a pioneer in the fight for women's rights. Feminists such as Bolivian Carolina Freyre de Jaime and Peruvian Magda Portal reclaimed Tristan.[21] As a fitting memorial, Peru created the women's rights organization Centro de la Mujer Peruana Flora Tristán in 1979, with the mission "to fight the structural causes that restrict the citizenship of women and/or affect their participation."[22] In sum, Tristan presented herself as a vocal and legitimate voice for women's liberation. Her reclamation and acceptance by feminists and women's rights organizations are a testament to and recognition of her efforts to advance the rights of women.

Unlike Tristan, Calderón's travel to Mexico was not motivated by desperate circumstances. Her memoir focuses on her experiences during her stay as the wife of the first Spanish ambassador to Mexico. She belonged to a wealthy and noble Scottish family that lost its sizable fortune due to the economic depression of the late 1820s; the family then moved to France for its cheaper cost of living. After the death of William Inglis, Fanny's father, some of Fanny's family members moved to the United States and in Boston started an elite school for girls. Fanny, already a published writer, joined the local literary circle, where she met some notable writers such as William H. Prescott. Prescott would later be instrumental in Fanny meeting her husband, Angel Calderón de la Barca y Belgrano (the then Spanish ambassador to the United States), and in assisting her in the publication of her travel account. During her two-year residence in Mexico, she recorded her experiences, including witnessing two revolts. She portrayed the inept leadership of post-independence Mexico and the selfishness of its political activists.

Her account has been labeled imperialist because it seems to call for intervention by a superior country. Miguel A. Cabañas believes that Calderón's account contributed to the knowledge needed by the United States to intervene militarily in Mexico in 1846.[23] Calderón portrayed Mexico as being an incompetent state and suggested that it could not govern itself as one catastrophe followed another. Cabañas describes the personal friendship between Prescott and Calderón, as well as Prescott's use of empirical information from Calderón's letters and his endorsement of her account. Interestingly, Prescott's classic *History of the Conquest of Mexico* benefited immensely from Calderón's descriptions of Mexico, since Prescott had never visited the country.[24] Calderón and Prescott were invited to meet with American political leaders for a discussion about military intervention. Taking into consideration her position as the spouse of the ambassador, she coded people's names in her book by using the first and last letters of their surnames. In fact,

Hahner is certain that Calderón revised her source material, omitting many contentious passages before publication.[25]

Calderón's book was very controversial in Mexico: there were two main sources of opposition, the Mexican press that dismissed it as "a collection of despicable trivia" and Spaniards residing in Mexico who perceived it as "a poisonous satire against Mexicans."[26] The latter viewed it as an act undeserving of a representative of the Spanish government. The press, unamused by Calderón's witty and satirical portrayal of Mexico, maintained that the author "betrayed the generous hospitality which she and her husband had been shown by Mexicans."[27] As the privileged wife of the first Spanish ambassador, she had access to many sites, which were otherwise closed to strangers. Nevertheless, Calderón's book has received many accolades. Charles A. Hale considers it "the best Latin American travel account."[28] Prescott asserted that "for spirited portraiture of society—a society unlike anything existing in the Old World, or the New—for picturesque delineation of scenery, for richness of illustration and anecdote, and for the fascinating graces of style, no [other travelogue] is to be compared with *Life in Mexico*."[29] Cabañas highly recommends Calderón's book for her "critique of patriarchy and the creation of an enlightened female self."[30] While Calderón's criticism of patriarchy may not have been as passionate as Tristan's, there is no doubt that she favored women's rights.

Analyzing Tristan's and Calderón's accounts side by side provides two different perspectives regarding the issue of women's rights in mid-nineteenth-century Latin America: that of an insider (Tristan) and of an outsider (Calderón). Tristan was much more militant about women's rights in her book than the more satirical Calderón was in her account. From her privileged position as an ambassador's wife, Calderón portrayed her female acquaintances from a distance, while Tristan, a self-proclaimed pariah who was also Peruvian, identified personally with the women she encountered. Their economic, social, and national status played a role in how they portrayed their female acquaintances. Tristan's militancy was motivated by her grievance toward society, with its absurd laws and prejudices concerning women. She blamed French society for her status as a pariah for having "banished [her] from its midst" and its laws against the dissolubility of marriage.[31] She even compared her abusive marriage to enslavement. Nonetheless, she was always proud of her strong will and courage to resist in the face of opposition: "I am a victim of the very laws and prejudices which make your lives so bitter, but you lack the courage to resist."[32] Irrespective of Tristan's and Calderón's different lived experiences and backgrounds, they were both passionate about denouncing patriarchy, as demonstrated by several examples in the argument that follows.

The two authors are similar in that each can be categorized as being an *exploratrice sociale* (social explorer), a term used by Mary Louise Pratt to describe women travelers engaged in "the political work of social reformers and charity workers."[33] Both Tristan and Calderón visited convents, madhouses, hospitals, and orphanages in their host countries. Pratt views their biting critique of these social institutions as a sort of "political practice" or form of imperialism anchored in their sense of superiority or high-class values.[34] Tristan and Calderón reveal their presumed superiority in some of their descriptions, especially their many comments about the education of women. Nonetheless, from this overview of the lives and writings of these two female authors, we can appreciate that they differed from their female peers as they discussed women's issues, politics, and the national policies of their host countries. These two writers were not afraid to speak their minds about what they perceived as flaws and shortcomings in Mexico or Peru. Both Calderón and Tristan criticize the despotic regimes, constantly fraught by divisions, which abused power to the detriment of the public good. Similarly, they are critical of the treatment of women in Mexican and Peruvian societies. In the following paragraphs I examine the views and attitudes of Tristan and Calderón on Peruvian and Mexican women, respectively, in terms of three themes: the oppression of women through religion and marriage, women's agency and power, and advocacy for women's education.

Tristan was highly critical of the Roman Catholic Church and what she saw as its collusion with the ruling class to "keep the oppressed people in a state of submission" by means of superstition and prejudice.[35] She was unimpressed by the manipulative strategies of the Church, which "exploits popular taste to increase its hold over people" (111). She notes, "The clergy may have supported the revolution, but they had no intention of giving up their power, and they will keep it for many years to come" (110). Her critique also extends to convents for their oppressive atmosphere. Tristan's interest in convents and nuns was piqued when she heard about her cousin Dominga's escape from the convent of Santa Rosa. Dominga entered the convent after her heart was broken by a man who left her for a richer woman: she escaped from the convent after eleven years. Tristan visited the Santa Rosa convent and realized how imprisoning and dismal the conditions were. In her book, she constantly highlights the theme of death as it related to this convent. For example, she mentions that the sleeping cells of the nuns, called tombs, actually bore this name with reason. She describes that the greeting among the sisters was "Sister, we must die," and the reply was "Sister, death is our deliverance" (191). Tristan indicates that Dominga chose to live rather than consign herself to these conditions. However, Tristan was not against all convents, because she praised the convent of Santa Catalina, a less strict religious order, for its numerous works of charity. Nonetheless, she states that a convent is not a place for "women [who] are too beautiful and too lovable" (204). After her escape, Dominga lived in isolation, shunned by society and her own mother. Dominga revealed to Tristan the futility of having escaped from the convent. She was extremely frustrated by the reactions of the local people, who refused to allow her to re-integrate into society. As societal pressures and prejudices did not let Dominga forget that she was the bride of Christ, neither did they permit Tristan to forget her marital status. Despite the efforts of these two women to follow their dreams, they could not escape the judgment and criticism of society. Momentarily resigned to their fate, Dominga and Tristan acknowledge respectively, "I shall always be a nun!" and "I shall always be married!" (241).

Calderón was even more critical of the Catholic Church in Mexico for oppressing women. She contrasted the living conditions of the nuns with the monks: whereas the cloistered nuns lived a life of penitence and self-denial, the monks lived comfortably. Calderón attributed this difference to the patriarchy of the Church. She noted that in cities like Puebla, taking the veil was as common as getting married. She was granted permission by Archbishop Manuel Posada to visit the convent of La Encarnación, "the most splendid and richest convent," where the family of novices paid five thousand dollars each into the common fund.[36] When the novices are presented to her and her two female companions, she refers to them as "poor little entrapped things! who really believe they will be let out at the end of a year if they should grow tired, as if they would ever be permitted to grow tired!" (1:220–221). Calderón felt that taking the veil was a very depressing event: "I have now seen three nuns take the veil; and, next to a death, consider it the saddest event that can occur in this nether sphere" (1:291). She explains the motives for the common occurrence of these "human sacrifices." Taking the veil was very attractive to "a young girl, who knows nothing of the world, who, as it too frequently happens, has at home neither amusement nor instruction, and no society abroad, who from childhood is under the dominion of her confessor, and who firmly believes that by entering a convent she becomes sure of heaven" (1:291). The glamorous ceremony initiating a novice into a convent was appealing to most aspiring nuns.

Others took the veil because they did not have a dowry or very fine looks. One lady without a dowry was accepted into the convent, or "sacrificed" in Calderón's view, because of her fine singing voice. Calderón points out the painful separation between a mother and her daughter, neither of whom had a say in the decision made by the father and the church confessor. In one of the convent ceremonies, she remarks, "The most terrible thing to witness was the last, straining, anxious look which the mother gave her daughter through the grating." A countess opined that taking the veil was "worse than a marriage!" Calderón does not hide her sentiments as she openly shares to all present her "horror at the sacrifice of a girl so young that she could not possibly have known her own mind" (1:308). She believed that the novice was being consigned to a living tomb. She was not against convents per se; what saddened her was their initiation of young lively girls: "That a convent may be a blessed shelter from the calamities of life, a haven for the unprotected, a resting place for the weary, a safe and holy asylum, where a new family and kind friends await those whose natural ties are broken and whose early friends are gone, I am willing to admit; but it is not in the flower of youth, that the warm heart should be consigned to the cold cloister" (1:307–308). Both Tristan and Calderón criticized the complicit nature of the society, mostly men, and the Church in sacrificing and condemning young girls to such a restrictive life as nuns. Becoming a nun was not about a woman's personal calling, but about the dictates of one's father and confessor.

They also criticized what they saw as marital oppression of women. Tristan uses the story of her cousin Doña Carmen Pierola de Florez to demonstrate the enslavement of marriage. Carmen, a self-educated, intelligent woman, having had to choose between marriage and the cloister, opted for the former. Her husband turned out to be a womanizer and a gambler, who squandered her rich dowry: "The proud Doña Carmen had to suffer every torture imaginable during her ten years that her marriage lasted."[37] When she complained about his excesses, she was told to be grateful: "People found in the ugliness of the wife and the beauty of the husband sufficient justification for the plundering of her fortune and the constant indignities to which she was subjected. Such is the morality which proceeds from the indissolubility of marriage!" (101). Tristan criticizes the absurdity of marriage rooted in patriarchy. When her husband returned, financially broke and diagnosed with a strange (venereal) disease, Carmen took care of him "with the secret pleasure people like her obtain from displaying their superiority in the exercise of a noble vengeance" (101–102). Tristan highlights the moral superiority and resilience of Carmen over her husband.

From Carmen, we have a sense of the plight of women in Peruvian society:

> Ah Florita, it is plain to see that you have not been oppressed by a tyrannical husband, dominated by an arrogant family or exposed to the wickedness of men. You are not married, you have no family, you have been free in all your actions, absolute mistress of yourself; you have no obligations towards society, so you have never been affected by its calumnies. Florita, there are very few women in your fortunate position: most marry very young and their faculties can never develop because they are oppressed to some extent by their masters. . . . [T]his is what happens in

> our backward society. . . . Marriage is the only hell I acknowledge. (105–106)

In this tirade, Carmen expresses a wish for women to be free from the bondage or control of their husband, their family, and society. Being single was a million times better than getting married. Tristan informed Carmen that European women also experienced similar oppression: "There is suffering wherever there is oppression and there is oppression wherever there is the power to oppress. In Europe women are men's slaves just as they are here, and have to suffer even more from men's tyranny. But in Europe God has given women more moral strength to free themselves from the yoke" (106). Tristan informs Carmen that "freedom is a matter of *will*. Those to whom God has given a will strong enough to overcome every obstacle are free, whereas those whose will is weak and yields to opposition are slaves and will be slaves even if some freak of fortune placed them upon a throne" (105; Tristan's emphasis). Tristan implies that her cousin, and by extension Peruvian women, had reluctantly accepted the status quo. Tristan pushes back on what she felt were excuses from Carmen for remaining in a country she considered "loathsome [and] condemned to live in" (104). Through her visit to Peru, Tristan realized that her own situation was not unique: "Married women here are just as unhappy and oppressed as they are in France, and the intelligence God has given them is doomed to sterility and inertia" (106). Thus, Tristan felt a close sense of solidarity with Peruvian women. It is ironic that while Tristan self-identified with the marital plight of Peruvian women, her statement to Carmen about European women having a God-given freer will born of having more moral strength reveals her sense of superiority over her Peruvian counterparts. Tristan took immense pride in her steps to overcome her marital woes, including coming to Peru despite being poorer than her cousin, while Carmen would not leave Peru due to financial and social constraints. Carmen blames "the harshest of all laws, necessity! If you have no money you are a dependent, a slave, you have to live where your master puts you" (104). Carmen also pushes back on the notion that a strong will is required to break the yoke of marriage, pointing to Tristan's lack of experience in married life. Tristan, who hid her marital status from her Peruvian family, vehemently and indirectly defended herself and underlined her sense of superiority by identifying with European women, who, she claimed, had experienced more tyranny from men but still had more moral strength.

Calderón was not as critical of marriage as Tristan was, perhaps because her marriage was not an abusive one. She, instead, mentions how instrumental women are to their husbands' success. She claims that the distinguished men of Mexico married "women who are either their equals or superiors, if not in education,—in goodness, elevation of sentiment and natural talent."[38] Calderón praises Mexican women for their modesty, tact, hospitality, decorum, impeccable reputation, loyalty, and warm manners. Nonetheless, she shows the abusive side of marriage with her depiction of female prisoners in the Acordada (public jail). Most of them were convicted for "murdering their husbands; which is the chief crime of the female prisoners" (2:280). In the Acordada many prisoners, including noblewomen, had murdered abusive husbands or lovers. Observing the demeanor of the prisoners, Calderón notes that "few looked sad; most appeared careless and happy, and none seemed ashamed" (2:280–281). In other words, none of them were repentant of their actions. Calderón seemed to understand the actions of the women in saying, "It is some comfort to hear that their husbands were generally such brutes, they deserved little better" (2:281). Tristan and Calderón reveal the abusive relationships that women of all social classes endure in the name of marriage. Women were treated as second-class citizens in these societies and had to bear the indignities from their husbands in silence. If Peruvian society could not accept Dominga, the ex-nun, after she escaped from a convent, it stands to reason that it would not condone a woman leaving her husband. Abused married women seemed to have no recourse.

Both Tristan and Calderón showcase women's intelligence and superiority. Calderón witnessed two revolutions in Mexico that she considered baseless, but she praised female agency, bravery, and wit during times of peril. She lauded the acts of women who braved the dangers of cannons and bullets to find safety for their loved ones. She ridiculed the incompetence of the soldiers: "The cannon directed against the palace kill people in their beds, in streets entirely out of that direction, while this ball, intended for the citadel, takes its flight to San Cosme! Both parties seem to be fighting the city instead of each other."[39] Contrary to the official news that portrayed women as victims of war, she shows women as survivors: "Ladies and children escaped, in many instances, by the azoteas, going along the street from one roof to another, not being able to pass where the cannon was planted. The Señora, with her six beautiful boys, escaped in that way to her brother's house, in the evening, and in the very thick of the firing" (1:204). Calderón was also extremely critical of the second revolution: "[It has] neither principle, nor pretext, nor plan, nor the shadow of reason or legality. Disloyalty, hypocrisy, and the most sordid calculation, are all the motives that can be discovered" (2:228). In her view, feckless men started unnecessary wars that endangered the lives of women and children. With courage and bravery, women confronted the consequences of men's actions.

In terms of women's agency, Tristan documents more examples than Calderón does. Three case studies worth noting in *Peregrinations* feature the *rabonas*, Indigenous women fighters; Doña Pencha Gamarra, a former first lady of Peru;

and the *limeñas,* women of Lima. *Rabonas* were Indigenous women who served soldiers in the Peruvian army by setting up and tending their camps. According to Tristan, their Indigenous male counterparts would rather die than become soldiers, but these women embraced this way of life. Tristan had great admiration for the *rabonas* and idealized them as strong, powerful, self-sufficient, and autonomous women, thus making them a symbol of women's power:

> The *rabonas* . . . form a considerable troop, preceding the army by several hours so that they have time to set up camp, obtain food and cook it. The *rabonas* are armed. . . . When the army is on the march it is nearly always on the courage and daring of these women four or five hours ahead of them that it depends for its subsistence, and when one considers that in leading this life of toil and danger they still have the duties of motherhood to fulfill, one is amazed that any of them can endure it. . . . It is worth observing that whereas the Indian would rather kill himself than be a soldier, the Indian women embrace this life *voluntarily*, bearing its fatigues and confronting its dangers with the courage of which the men of their race are incapable. I do not believe it possible to adduce a more striking proof of the superiority of woman in primitive societies; would not the same be true of peoples at a more advanced stage of civilization if both sexes received a similar education? We must hope that some day the experiment will be tried.[40]

Tristan was impressed with the *rabonas*' fighting spirit and their "fierce courage [that] over[came] all resistance" in their endeavors (180). They were "exposed to the same dangers [as the soldiers] and endure[d] far greater hardships than the men" (180). For Tristan, these superwomen were proof of female superiority over men in a primitive society. Using the *rabonas* as an example, Tristan makes a case for female superiority in what she refers to as a more civilized society. In her opinion women would surpass men if provided with similar educational opportunities. Her characterization of the *rabonas* as primitive, however, once again reflects her Eurocentrism.

In addition to the *rabonas*, a woman named Doña Pencha Gamarra captured Tristan's imagination. For Tristan, this ex–first lady of Peru represents female power and leadership: "The fate of the republic is in her hands. . . . [She] dictated policy and commanded the troops" (174). Her life inspired Tristan so much that she contemplated entering politics as an "open revolt against a social order which sanctioned the enslavement of the weaker sex [and] the spoliation of the orphan" (174). As she contemplated her disastrous marriage, illegitimacy, and inability to take her rightful position (as heiress) in Peruvian society and her rich uncle's inheritance of her father's fortune, Tristan was extremely bitter about her situation.

Tristan's dream to enter politics, following the example of Doña Pencha, was motivated by her desire to correct social injustices and serve the public. Tristan engaged actively in politics when she returned to France.

Tristan portrayed Doña Pencha as the one who performed most of the presidential duties when her husband, Augustin Gamarra, was president of Peru from 1829 to 1833. Due to her political scheming, she became widely disliked and was exiled to Chile in 1834. Even after being exiled, Doña Pencha was still defiant. She referred to herself as the "terror of all Peru!" and demanded that Tristan should give her a place in her journal. She wanted to write her name into history from outside of Peru. Tristan was impressed with her demeanor of superiority and remarks that "though a prisoner, Doña Pencha was still the president's wife" (293). Doña Pencha described some of the ploys and tactics she used to maintain her position. She told Tristan, "To compensate for the weakness of our sex I have had to retain its attractions and exploit them as need arose in order to enlist the support of men" (296). She was well aware of her status as a woman in a man's world and the disadvantages it implied. That realization shattered Tristan's idealistic image of her. Seeing Tristan's judgmental look, Doña Pencha retorts, "You think you are stronger than I am. . . . You know nothing of the never-ending struggle I have had for the past years, the humiliations I have had to endure! I have begged, flattered, lied: I have tried everything and stopped at nothing . . . and yet it was not enough" (296). Included in her humiliations were slanders spread about her epileptic seizures and her sexual life. She died seven weeks after her exile, and in tribute to Doña Pencha, Tristan praises her leadership and governance, which she believed was even superior to that of Simón Bolívar. She writes: "Yet this woman, raised in a convent, without education, but gifted with a strong moral sense and an uncommonly powerful will, governed a people even Bolívar had found ungovernable with such success that in less than a year order was restored, rival factions were tamed, trade flourished, the army regained confidence in its leaders; and even if parts of Peru were still unsettled, most of the country enjoyed peace" (303). Tristan's comments still resonate today with the widely held sentiment that women in politics are held to higher standards and more scrutiny than men.

Another group of women that fascinated Tristan were the women of Lima. She envied their freedom: "There is no place on earth where women are so free and exercise so much power as in Lima" (269). She attributes the "great freedom" and "powerful influence" the *limeñas* enjoy to their special outfit, noting, "I must tell the reader about the costume peculiar to the women of Lima, the advantage it gives them and the influence it has on their morals, customs and character" (270–271). This special outfit was the *saya*, "a skirt, worn with a sort of sack," or *manto*, a type of material that "envelops the shoulders, arms and head . . . leaving only one eye uncovered" (270–271). This special way of dressing afforded the *limeñas* anonymity and the perfect disguise, to pursue their interests, even to indulge in intrigues, when they went out. In Lima, "every woman may go out alone" (273). Not only did this dress style emphasize or draw attention to their "fine supple figures"; it also entranced foreign men so much that they tended to commit follies and extravagances for *limeñas*. Tristan provides a very interesting reading of their costume. Comparing the *limeñas* with European women, who were "the slaves of laws, morals, customs, prejudices, fashions and everything else," she notes that "in every situation the woman of Lima is always herself; never does she submit to any constraint. . . . Freedom of action characterizes everything she does" (275). The *limeñas* smoked cigars, rode in breeches, gambled, and did other activities usually considered to be masculine. Actively interested in politics, they were instrumental in lobbying and securing posts for their male relatives and for men they fancied. Tristan claims that the *limeñas* were "far above them [their men] in intelligence and will-power" (273). While appreciative of the charms and freedom of the *limeñas*, Tristan was highly critical of their lack of education.

Another common theme in both writers' books is the importance of education. Tristan and Calderón found women's education in Latin America sorely lacking. They pointed out that for women to reach their potential, education was key. Tristan's and Calderón's preoccupation with the weaknesses of the educational system in their host countries indicates that their home countries enjoyed a relatively high level of education among women. Both writers considered that improvement in education would be a positive agent of change that would empower women in Latin American countries. Tristan's concern about women's education is evidenced in her examples of female agency and power. Citing female superiority in the *rabonas*, Tristan believed that when men and women are given similar opportunities to be educated, women will indeed surpass men. With regard to Doña Pencha, Tristan comments on her achievements irrespective of her lack of education. Just as she was critical of the former first lady of Peru for using her feminine wiles on men, Tristan was very disapproving of the *limeñas*. Her depiction of the *limeñas* suggests that Tristan thought the society women of Lima used their sexuality more than their intelligence to gain the upper hand. She sermonized about God's given power and endowment to woman of "a heart more loving and devoted than that of man" and "an incontestable superiority over man," which must be harnessed by practicing self-control and developing intellectually.[41] Tristan directly calls out the *limeña* for her behavior: "She fails to recognize her mission when, instead of being the inspiration of man and improving his character, she seeks only to seduce him. . . . [H]er authority disappears together with the desire she has aroused."[42] Thus, Tristan expresses conflicting feelings about the *limeñas* in both admiring their freedom and disparaging their use of sexuality to gain the upper hand over men. Tristan advocated that education, not sexuality, was the way for women to make social progress.

Similar to Tristan's view of Peruvian women, Calderón identifies a deficiency in the education of Mexican women, whom she had praised for their modesty, loyalty, decorum, and many excellent qualities:

> Generally speaking, then, the Mexican Señoras and Señoritas write, read and play a little, sew, and take care of their houses and children. . . . If we compare their education with that of girls in England, or in the United States, it is not a comparison but a contrast. . . . In the first place, the climate inclines everyone to indolence, both physically and morally. . . . Then as to schools, there are none that can deserve the name, and no governesses. Young girls can have no emulation, for they never meet. . . . It frequently happens that the least well-informed girls are the children of the cleverest men, who, keeping to the customs of their forefathers, are content if they confess regularly, attend church constantly, and can embroider and sing a little.[43]

Calderón laments the lack of formal education for girls and the deficient school system. She bemoans the failure of men, even the most educated ones, to formally educate their female children, thus leading them to hold on to antiquated traditions. Both Calderón and Tristan saw education as a pathway to enlightenment for women. Opportunities for the education of girls and women in Peru and Mexico in comparison to those in the United States and Europe were very limited.

Peregrinations and *Life in Mexico* are accounts of transatlantic female solidarity that express deep concerns for women's rights, in spite of reservations concerning the presumption of superiority by Tristan and Calderón. Tristan and Calderón were intelligent, inquisitive, observant, and forthright social explorers. Both women were early proponents of women's rights in Latin America. They were concerned with women's issues in relation to marriage, family, education, and social status, and their forthright opinions on these matters transcends female attitudes of that time. Their views on Latin American women indirectly give us some insights into the condition of women in European societies. Calderón, with greater social privilege as the wife of an ambassador, portrayed women from a distance, while Tristan, a feminist socialist and social pariah, identified with the personal struggles of the women she encountered. Calderón portrayed a male-dominated world detrimental to the advancement of women's issues. Most women that Tristan described went against the status quo and were superior to men. Tristan documented the trials of strong and resilient women who were battling a male-dominated society in Peru. By her description, it appears that only the women of

Lima were left unscathed by Peruvian society, and they had the freedom to be themselves by accentuating their anonymity and sexuality. However, it is doubtful that this approach would be a sustainable way of achieving freedom and influence. Instead, Tristan recommended education as key to women's liberation.

Tristan and Calderón sometimes showed their sense of superiority in their descriptions. Even Tristan, who largely identified with the women of Peru, often showed her European pride. She referred to the *rabonas* as "a primitive society," implying that France was a more civilized country. She also believed that married European women suffered more than their Latin American counterparts and that God gave European women stronger willpower. Tristan thought herself to be morally superior to the ambitious and power-grabbing Doña Pencha, who sometimes used underhanded tactics to achieve her political ambitions. Additionally, even though Tristan envied the women of Lima for their freedom, she was still critical of their sexual immorality and low educational level.

Irrespective of these reservations, *Peregrinations* and *Life in Mexico* are beacons of transatlantic female solidarity and a call to rectify women's rights. The books of Tristan and Calderón show commonalities between Peruvian and Mexican women and their shared destinies as either wife or nun. Additionally, both authors demonstrate that Latin American women had to contend with oppression and abuse rooted in their patriarchal societies. Tristan and Calderón also used their platforms to showcase strong, resilient women and to advocate for better women's education. Their books are now well accepted as being groundbreaking travel narratives and will remain objects of enduring public interest and academic study.

NOTES

1. Flora Tristan, *Pérégrinations d'une paria (1833–1834)*, 2 tomes (Paris: Arthus Bertrand, 1838).
2. Frances Erskine Inglis Calderón de la Barca, *Life in Mexico during a Residence of Two Years in That Country*, 2 vols. (Boston: Charles C. Little and James Brown, 1843).
3. Adriana Méndez Rodenas, *Transatlantic Travels in Nineteenth-Century Latin America: European Women Pilgrims* (Lewisburg, PA: Bucknell University Press, 2014), 2.
4. June E. Hahner, *Women through Women's Eyes: Latin American Women in Nineteenth-Century Travel Accounts* (Wilmington, DE: Scholarly Resources, 1998), xii.
5. Méndez Rodenas, *Transatlantic Travels*, 2.
6. Calderón de la Barca, *Life in Mexico*, 1:200.
7. Eve Tavor Bannet and Susan Manning, "Introduction: British and American Genres," in *Transatlantic Literary Studies, 1660–1830*, ed. Eve Tavor Bannet and Susan Manning (Cambridge: Cambridge University Press, 2012), 1–9.
8. Hahner, *Women through Women's Eyes*, xx–xxvi.
9. Sara Mills, *Discourses of Difference: An Analysis of Women's Travel Writing and Colonialism* (London: Routledge, 1993).
10. Mills, *Discourses of Difference*, 6.

11. Mills, *Discourses of Difference*, 36.
12. For the purpose of this essay, patriarchy is broadly defined as "the manifestation and institutionalization of male dominance over women and children in the family and the extension of male dominance over women in society in general." Gerda Lerner, *The Creation of Patriarchy* (New York: Oxford University Press, 1986), 239.
13. André Chazal, *Mémoire à consulter pour M. Chazal contre Madame Chazal* (Montmartre: Imprimerie de Cosson, 1838).
14. Jennifer Law-Sullivan, "Liberté, Egalité, Sororité: Flora Tristan and the Contact Zone between Race and Gender," *Nineteenth-Century French Studies* 39, no. 1–2 (2010–2011): 62–76.
15. Law-Sullivan, "Liberté, Egalité, Sororité," 65.
16. Tristan, *Pérégrinations d'une paria*, 1:xi; my translation
17. Tristan, *Pérégrinations d'une paria*, 1:xi; my translation.
18. Tristan, *Pérégrinations d'une paria*, 1:xxviii–xxix; my translation.
19. Jean Hawkes, translator's introduction to *Peregrinations of a Pariah*, by Flora Tristan, trans. and ed. Jean Hawkes (London: Virago Press, 1986), x–xi.
20. Marjorie Agosín and Julie H. Levison, eds., *Magical Sites: Women Travelers in 19th Century Latin America* (Buffalo, NY: White Pine Press, 1999), 65.
21. Mary Louise Pratt, *Imperial Eyes: Travel Writing and Transculturation* (London: Routledge, 1992).
22. Centro de la Mujer Peruana Flora Tristán, "Misión y vision," accessed March 5, 2020, http://www.flora.org.pe/web2/index.php?option=com_content&view=article&id=198&Itemid=27; my translation.
23. Miguel A. Cabañas, "North of Eden: Romance and Conquest in Fanny Calderón de La Barca's *Life in Mexico*," *Studies in Travel Writing* 9 (2005): 1–19.
24. William H. Prescott, *History of the Conquest of Mexico* (New York: Harper and Brothers, 1843).
25. Hahner, *Women through Women's Eyes*, 44.
26. Méndez Rodenas, *Transatlantic Travels*, 113.
27. Méndez Rodenas, *Transatlantic Travels*, 113.
28. Charles A. Hale, review of *Life in Mexico. The Letters of Fanny Calderón de la Barca*, ed. Howard T. Fisher and Marion Hall Fisher, *Hispanic American Historical Review* 47, no. 4 (1967): 581.
29. William H. Prescott, review of *Life in Mexico during a Residence of Two Years in That Country*, by Madame Calderón de la Barca, *North American Review* 56, no. 118 (1843): 137–170.
30. Cabañas, "North of Eden," 2.
31. Flora Tristan, *Peregrinations of a Pariah*, trans. and ed. Jean Hawkes (London: Virago Press, 1986), 1.
32. Tristan, *Peregrinations of a Pariah*, 2.
33. Pratt, *Imperial Eyes*, 160.
34. Pratt, *Imperial Eyes*, 161.
35. Tristan, *Peregrinations of a Pariah*, 111.
36. Calderón de la Barca, *Life in Mexico*, 1:218.
37. Tristan, *Peregrinations of a Pariah*, 101.
38. Calderón de la Barca, *Life in Mexico*, 2:128.
39. Calderón de la Barca, *Life in Mexico*, 1:187.
40. Tristan, *Peregrinations of a Pariah*, 179–180; Tristan's emphasis.
41. Tristan, *Peregrinations of a Pariah*, 272.
42. Tristan, *Peregrinations of a Pariah*, 272.
43. Calderón de la Barca, *Life in Mexico*, 1:340–343.

4

"THE FAIR DAUGHTERS OF TERRA NOVA"

Women in the Settler Cultures of Early Nineteenth-Century Newfoundland

Pam Perkins

In October 1825, Sir Thomas Cochrane decided to mark his arrival as the first civil governor of the colony of Newfoundland by holding a formal drawing room for the wives and daughters of the local elite. The plan was, according to Cochrane, greeted with considerable pleasure. "I hear that the ladies are all in great glee," he wrote in his journal a few days ahead of the event, adding that "every Milliner" in the capital St. John's "is in requisition."[1] As it turned out, the ladies had a few more days of pleased anticipation than Cochrane had intended: the drawing room had to be postponed twice because storms made it impossible for them to travel the short distance to Government House without destroying their finery. Cochrane's friends in Britain would probably have been unsurprised by news that the weather was a problem, given that in the limited space that Newfoundland occupied at the time in the British cultural imagination it tended to be aligned more closely with the North American subarctic than with the settler colonies of the eastern seaboard and Caribbean.[2] Given those ideas, Cochrane's presentation of Newfoundland's unwelcoming landscape and weather as the backdrop of a gently feminized world of drawing rooms and delicate millinery would have been both surprising and striking then, and perhaps remains as much so now. Women tend to be all but invisible in many of the accounts of eighteenth- and early nineteenth-century Newfoundland, but paying attention to the glimpses of them in documents from that time is important. As Cochrane and a few other writers from this period bring women into their published and unpublished representations of the island, they are implicitly countering the more usual representations of Newfoundland as an unfamiliar, even uninhabitable outpost of empire and incorporating it into an imaginative version of the wider British world.

There are of course several good reasons that Anglo-Newfoundland women have not left much of a mark on the transatlantic literature of the long eighteenth century. For one thing, there was no Newfoundland counterpart of Frances Brooke or Charlotte Lennox—that is, writers who drew upon direct experience in their representations of transatlantic landscapes and societies. These writers were doing significant cultural work: by merging historical "facts" and fiction, they brought narratives of settler colonial life to those reading more for pleasure than information and did so in a way that incorporated unfamiliar transatlantic locales into an extension of British life and culture. In contrast, the handful of late eighteenth- and early nineteenth-century novels by women that have episodes set on or near Newfoundland—most notably Laetitia Matilda Hawkins's *Memoirs of a Scots Heiress* (1791) and Emily Clark's *The Esquimaux* (1819)—not only make no attempt to offer a realistic depiction of the British settlements there but also give no reason to think that the authors knew anything of the island other than its name. The first published literary work by a woman who had unquestionably lived in Newfoundland did not appear until 1839; it was a collection of verse called *Poems Written in Newfoundland* by Henrietta Prescott, the daughter of Cochrane's successor in the governorship. Even that offers little scope for anybody attempting to reconstruct a female perspective on nineteenth-century Newfoundland colonial life, as it includes only a few poems that are about the island, focusing instead on European historical romance. Nor did that handful of poems inspire any wider discussion about or understanding of Newfoundland in British literary circles, as the book attracted little attention beyond a few notices announcing its appearance and paying polite compliments to the "talents" of the "fair authoress."[3]

The absence of literary contributions by Anglo-Newfoundland women from the turn of the nineteenth century is not of course all that surprising. Most of the permanent British settlers of the island were fishermen and their families, and even if they were literate, women of that class would have had little time to spare for writing about their experiences and less opportunity to share or circulate their work, even in the form of an occasional letter to family in Britain or elsewhere along the North Atlantic seaboard. As Sarah M. S. Pearsall has noted, "Atlantic distance" made sustaining family ties by sharing news of their new lives "a luxury" for many transatlantic emigrants.[4] That said, there were a few leisure-class women in the capital, St. John's, who had that "luxury"; they were mainly the wives and daughters of military men and other colonial administrators, and at least some of what these women wrote about their time on the island survives. Mary Elizabeth Brenton (1791–1884), for example, the daughter of the lawyer and judge Edward Brabazon Brenton, was a correspondent of the botanist Sir William Jackson Hooker and has a claim to being among Newfoundland's first women writers, as she provided Hooker with much of his information on the plants of Newfoundland.[5] More tangentially, the archives of Sir Thomas Cochrane contain a few letters by and about the women with whom he mingled in St. John's society.

Yet even if the relatively few surviving records of Anglo-Newfoundland women in the eighteenth and early nineteenth centuries do not in themselves offer anything approaching a full account of women's experience of life on the island, the few traces that remain are worth exploring. If one reads the material left by the women themselves in the context of public and private narratives by some of their male compatriots, it is possible to build a more complex and nuanced picture of the ways in which not just the elite but also some of the otherwise silent women working in the fisheries were central to the imaginative construction of a recognizably British identity for Newfoundland colonists. Doing so is all the more important because in the relatively few published narratives of eighteenth- and early nineteenth-century Newfoundland society, there is a marked tendency to depict colonial settlers as having their identities as Britons, and perhaps even their humanity, eroded by the harshness of their new home. A Mr. Lacy, a chaplain stationed on the island in the 1720s offered a particularly lurid account of the "frightful Tribe" of Anglo- and Irish Newfoundlanders, who survive their "willing Banishment" from Britain by sinking into a drunken existence on the bare edge of survival, content to

> lodge upon the Skin of some wild-beast,
> On whose rank Flesh they first had made a feast.[6]

Matters had not much improved by the end of the century, at least according to the Missionary Society, which introduced its account of Newfoundland by lamenting that its British settlers were living in a situation "as deplorable as that of the heathen world" and then praised a missionary who arrived on the island in 1799 for persevering in his endeavors despite both the "severity of the climate" and the "uncivilized manners" of the people he had to live among.[7] Two young naval officers who visited St. John's during the Napoleonic Wars were similarly shocked by their experiences with the locals. Edward Chappell, who was there in the summer of 1813, was dismayed by what he saw as the "vulgar arrogance" and "debauchery" of "all ranks" of society, while Robert Steele, who had been there four years earlier, painted a vivid picture of a city that he found "barely habitable," reeking as it was of fish offal and seal oil and swarming with rats and stray dogs.[8]

There were, of course, more positive images of Newfoundlanders available. By 1813, the year of Chappell's visit, the Scottish-born physician and politician William Carson was mocking the reflexive tendency to depict Anglo-Newfoundlanders as "a race of savages untameable by civilization" and insisting that, on the contrary, they were a "hardy race, fearless of danger and capable of undergoing the greatest corporeal exertion."[9] (Marina Seifert has traced the much later stereotype of the "hardy, happy Newfoundland fisherman" back to Carson.[10]) Yet perhaps the most immediately striking aspect of Carson's more positive vision of this settler colonial culture is his insistence that the admirably masculine virtues of the Newfoundland fishermen are dependent upon the barely acknowledged women in the background. While Lacy uses what he sees as the utter degradation of Newfoundland women—they are, he claims, indistinguishable from the men in their taste for rum and squalor—to further emphasize the colonists' supposed fall from British values, Carson implores the "inhabitants" of Newfoundland whom he is addressing to consider their duties as husbands and fathers, grounding their implicitly "British" virtues in feminine domesticity.[11] The aim of Carson's pamphlet was to encourage more settled communities (something that he sees as essential to ensuring continued British control of Newfoundland, and, in turn, continued British influence in North America), and that settlement, he argues, is dependent upon creating firm ties to home and family. "The fisherman," he writes, risks losing "his attachment to that spot of his nativity possessed by the tiller of the ground and the feeder of the flocks, which is in these the source of patriotism."[12] Carson argues that it is only by exploiting the "personal interest" that binds the fisherman to his wife and children and by convincing him that taking up farming will allow him to better support his family that the government can help establish a settled Anglo-Newfoundland society.[13]

This idea, that the domestic ties created by women were essential to the successful establishment of a transatlantic fishing colony, was not limited to paternalistic addresses to the lower classes. A decade and a half later, Sir Thomas Cochrane was complaining bitterly to the Colonial Office about the lack of "a respectable" and non-transient local "gentry."[14] In order to flourish, he argues, the colony requires a stable upper-middle and ruling class, something that he implies will never happen unless administrators' families—and thus, obviously, women—are willing to make the island their home. Notably, even though Cochrane is perhaps best remembered in Newfoundland history for his interest in building roads and for his difficulties with the newly established House of Assembly, his private journals and letters demonstrate his interest in introducing a form of feminized public sociability that would make the island more appealing to the wives and daughters of his staff and colleagues.[15] The first years of his residence in St. John's appear to have been a whirl of social engagements, ranging from picnics at his cottage outside the city to regular evening parties at Government House. In marked contrast to the views of St. John's provided by Chappell and Steele, a French visitor to the city in 1828 was impressed not just by the amusements offered there, including balls and plays, but also by the "miniature court" that Cochrane had established, filled, as the visitor noted, with "fresh and pretty" ladies.[16]

Cochrane's papers in fact provide a valuable starting point for examining the ways that, in the early decades of the nineteenth century, both elite and non-elite women helped shape attempts to imagine Newfoundland as part of a transatlantic British world, as opposed to being simply a way station for fishermen or a "nursery for seamen."[17] While the roles played in the cultural imagination by outport women were inevitably very different from those of the St. John's elite, looking at them together reinforces the significance of women in general, not just women of a particular class, in creating and maintaining a sense of British identity in this part of the North American seaboard.

THE FAIR DAUGHTERS OF TERRA NOVA

Ruling-class men of 1820s St. John's appear to have taken as a matter of course the idea that their women compatriots were elegant exemplars of British culture, however much Lacy or Chappell might have disagreed. Newspapers of the day regularly feature accounts of events such as cricket matches, boat races, and political dinners that might not have been geared toward women but which nonetheless routinely finished with toasts to the "fair daughters of Terra Nova" and speeches that absorbed the elite women of the city into a very conventional discourse about the civilizing role of "the gentler kind of our creation."[18] The implication, clearly enough, is that a "daughter of Terra Nova" is also, and uncomplicatedly, a daughter of Britain.

Yet there are several reasons to examine that assumption a little more closely. Most basically, there is a sense in the literature of the day that, on the one hand, a "new" transatlantic identity can be achieved only by the loss of the original self and that, on the other, one can preserve one's Britishness only by rejecting any sense that the new land can be "home." One of the standard tropes in the letters and journals of British-born women who made the transatlantic journey—to Newfoundland or elsewhere—in the decades on either side of the year 1800 is that the inevitable discomforts of shipboard life are a literal and metaphorical sea change that cuts them off from the comforts, pleasures, and intellectual pursuits of their familiar British world. As Pearsall explains, "the ability of transatlantic distance to fracture families" left individuals feeling "adrift."[19] Cochrane's first wife, Matilda, who accompanied him to his Caribbean station in 1813 (she died before his posting to Newfoundland), exemplifies this anxiety. In the journal that she kept to record her "sensations on commencing an undertaking which in health w[d] have appeared formidable," she reports her misery upon reflecting that she has "small hope of seeing again that Country and those friends from whom [she] was separated."[20] A decade and a half later, Frances Simpson, wife of the governor of the Hudson's Bay Company, was similarly distressed, as she contemplated her voyage to Montreal with "a mind agitated by the various emotions of Grief, Fear, and Hope"—adding hope into the mix only because she clung to the belief that it might be possible "at some future period (however distant)" to see once again "the home of [her] infancy."[21] Prescott did not leave any such direct account of her journey or of any anxieties that she might have felt on leaving England, but in a gloomy poem called "The Departure," she imagines the thoughts of the passengers on a British ship heading for the "Western world":

> A shadow was on ev'ry brow, and tears in silence fell,
> They knew not, till that parting hour, they loved their land so well!
> . . . .
> They look'd on lawn and meadow, on deep wood and breezy hill,
> And almost seem'd to hear the voice of some far-gleaming rill;
> They thought upon their trackless voyage,—on ocean's raging foam,
> And, turning to that peaceful scene, they felt it was their *Home.*[22]

As with Simpson, the only way that that Prescott's imagined travelers retain a sense of identity is by clinging to the hope of "glad returning to their home, when years had roll'd away."[23]

Admittedly, these presentations of transatlantic travel as little more than miserable exile might be undercut later in the works in question; Matilda Cochrane decided, after braving seasickness, storms, and encounters with enemy American ships, that she was "charmed with a naval Life," while Prescott followed "The Departure" with a cheerful poem of celebration with "A Spring Morning in Newfoundland."[24] Yet the point remains that in these journals and poems, the only way to avoid the trauma of fractured social and familial identities is to cling to an idea of "home" as being unequivocally England. Prescott might be able to offer a Wordsworthian celebration of spring, even when it arrives in Newfoundland instead of England, but she constructs the Newfoundland spring as a sequence of absences of such typically English signs of the season as "yellow cowslip[s] glowing" or "primrose[s] hidden in the hawthorn shade."[25] Likewise, Brenton presents her joy in the genteel Englishwoman's pursuit of botanizing as being compromised by the harsh climate and landscape of the island. Late, icy springs prevent plants from blooming; short seasons kill them before they have a chance to flourish, and unwelcoming terrain makes many of the more interesting specimens simply inaccessible. It can be difficult, she notes ruefully, to find people willing "to penetrate into a bog up to their knees" merely to procure a flower for her.[26]

Yet what complicates this familiar idea of an absolute divide between "home" and "away" is the fact that by the later 1820s, few of the more prominent women in Newfoundland government and military circles were straightforwardly miserable exiles ripped from a grieving family on the far side of the ocean. The women who formed Cochrane's innermost circle during his first year on the island were in fact remarkably cosmopolitan, with ties all around the Atlantic world. Mary Bruere Tucker (ca. 1790–1851), the wife of Cochrane's first chief justice, met and married her husband in England, but they were both from a wealthy Bermuda family—their shared grandfather had been governor of the island—and she eventually died in London, Ontario.[27] Elizabeth Dunscombe (1779–1859), the wife of a Bermuda-born merchant who was also Cochrane's aide-de-camp, was originally from Connecticut and later moved with her husband to Montreal and then England. Anne Theresa Haly (ca. 1807–1874), the daughter of an Irish military officer, moved between Newfoundland, England, and Gibraltar, where her husband eventually became chief justice. Anne Aplin (ca. 1800–1879), with whom Cochrane fell in love during her stay at Government House in the first half of 1826, was the Jersey-born wife of a ship's captain who traveled with her husband around what are now the Atlantic provinces of Canada before returning to England. (In another indication of the transatlantic reach of these families, Aplin was also Prescott's maternal aunt.) Perhaps most strikingly, Brenton, despite her regrets about Newfoundland's climate and growing season, was born in Atlantic Canada, to an established Halifax family, and it was not until her father retired to England in the late 1830s that she settled in that country. The fact that none of these women was rooted in Newfoundland might give weight to Cochrane's complaint to Bathurst about the transience of the local gentry, but what is more important here is the point that these "fair daughters of Terra Nova," who defined and transmitted ideologies of Britishness on the island, were women whose own cultural identities had been shaped by movement around a wider transatlantic world. As Janet Sorenson has noted, "travel across the Atlantic" can in fact be "a counterintuitive means of producing Englishness."[28]

In Newfoundland, as elsewhere in the transatlantic world, that "Englishness" (or, more generally, Britishness) was produced and maintained in part through the reproduction of a British material culture, a point that becomes clear if one looks beyond the rather sensationalist Newfoundland travelogues of the early nineteenth century. As mentioned earlier, the tendency in English-language literary accounts of St. John's is to focus on dirt and discomfort; such narratives imply strongly that the city has nothing to offer—and, indeed, is no fit place for—a proper British lady. Yet in both their advertisements and their contents, Newfoundland papers from the 1810s to the 1820s suggest that observers such as Chappell and Steele were a little overstrained in their dismissal of the city as a pit of dissolute squalor. By 1814, merchants were advertising "Ladies' Kid Shoes and Gloves" alongside more sturdy and practical wares; thirteen years later, the papers indicate the availability of a far wider range of luxury goods, ranging from "2 Piano Fortes of very good tune" to "40 Dozen Eau de Cologne" and "an assortment of LACE."[29] Newspaper advertisements also promoted the amateur theater and the local lending library, which in March 1829 announced the arrival of a selection of new periodicals, poetry, plays, and a novel by Walter Scott.[30] Nor was it just the library that offered material directed toward a leisured female readership; the newspapers themselves regularly reprinted from the British press items that would, at the time, have been seen as catering to women's tastes. Women who picked up the St. John's *Public Ledger* in the summers of 1827 and 1828 would, for example, have found light reading ranging from poetry by Felicia Hemans to information from *La belle assemblée* on the latest English summer fashion to a gothic tale about a ghostly ice ship.[31] Granted, this haphazard variety of texts might suggest that Anglo-Newfoundlanders in the 1820s were still struggling with what Richard B. Sher has identified as the central problems of the eighteenth-century American print trade with Britain: that the material available tended to be "expensive, uncertain, and a bit out of date."[32] Yet the simple fact that the newspapers chose to establish a feminized version of print culture in early Newfoundland colonial society makes clear the presence of an audience of literate, leisured, Anglicized women.

Such material accoutrements of femininity as lace, library books, and musical instruments were not the only means by which elite Anglo-Irish Newfoundland women maintained their cultural identities in a transatlantic setting. Stinking streets notwithstanding, St. John's claimed to offer more well-to-do female inhabitants the opportunity to cultivate the usual accomplishments of genteelly educated British women. By 1822, the city had a "professor of music," and there was a drawing master there no later than 1829.[33] By 1834, there was even a boarding school at which "YOUNG LADIES" were promised "the advantages of French conversation and constant attention to their intellectual advancement."[34] Granted, such "intellectual advancements" probably did not involve anything more than, at best, the smattering of accomplishments promised by British boarding schools catering to the daughters of newly prosperous but non-gentry families, schools that were much mocked at the time in the more elite British media. Even so, the glimpses of his female compatriots that Cochrane provides in his journals suggest an attempt to absorb women of the Newfoundland elite into a sociable world that was more or less interchangeable with that of the provincial gentry in Britain. Haly, for example, appears to have spent the spring and summer of 1826, when she was around nineteen, in the sort of gentle pleasures that would have been familiar to Jane Austen's heroines, including shopping, dancing, amateur concerts, rounds of visiting, and even occasional visits to the theater. Haly was a frequent luncheon guest at Government House, and she regularly accompanied Aplin on walks or drives to Virginia Cottage, Cochrane's "rural" retreat on the outskirts of St. John's, where they sewed, gardened, fished on the lake, or "rambled about in the woods for birds nests."[35] Aplin's social life is even more fully delineated: Cochrane's journal entries for May 1826 are peppered with accounts of the informal dances that she attended at Government House. On Saturday the sixth, for example, he reports that he "danced with Mrs A——," while the following Monday he "danced 3 quadrilles" and then another two a few days later.[36] On the evenings when she did not dance, Aplin read aloud (or listened to Cochrane reading aloud while she worked or drew), played guitar, or sang; she also helped to turn Virginia Cottage into a comfortably English version of a rural cottage orné by making curtains and drawings to hang on the walls as well as by assisting with the plans for flower gardens and decorative walks.

What makes these glimpses of a world of sunny Austenian pleasures all the more striking is that even as Cochrane presents his women friends enjoying the pleasures of English country life, reminders that they are in a very different part of the world continually slip through. In March 1826, Aplin was thrown from a sleigh and left with a badly swollen eye, which Cochrane treated by taking her into a nearby "Tilt" (a local term for a fisherman's temporary lean-to) and rubbing the eye with snow.[37] On May 5 it was so cold that Aplin and Haly had to spend their afternoon at Virginia Cottage huddling over a fire, while five days later, Haly and her mother were stranded at Government House for the night when a sudden snowfall made it impossible for them to get home after dinner. Yet Aplin appears to have been unperturbed by the challenges of the climate: according to Cochrane, they enjoyed the May blizzard by taking "a short turn in the sleigh in spite of it then snowing that [they] might say [they] had done so on the 11th May," and she refused to let fog or rain deter her from outings to Virginia Cottage.[38] While neither Haly nor Aplin left any direct account of their time in Newfoundland, the picture of them that emerges from Cochrane's journal is that of women who are determined to maintain an unequivocally genteel British woman's tastes, habits, and accomplishments even without being firmly rooted in Britain themselves and even in a part of the North Atlantic world that is emphatically un-British in its landscape and climate.

This sense of British gentility skewed slightly to fit the constraints of transatlantic life is even clearer in a March 1827 exchange of letters between Cochrane and Elizabeth Dunscombe about a planned outing to Virginia Cottage. Cochrane had invited Dunscombe and one of her daughters to come to Government House before heading out to meet the other guests on the way; Dunscombe was infuriated both by what she saw as a degree of informality that bordered on impropriety and by an apparent disregard to her comfort. "I knew I was the only lady invited to go without a gentleman," she writes. "My embarrassment . . . could not escape your observation, not being accustomed to disguise my feelings."[39] Her hope, as she goes on to explain, was that the bad weather would have led to the outing being canceled, sparing her embarrassment and discomfort, but when she met Cochrane on her way and "understood [she] was expected . . . to wait in the snow until [he] had ascertained if the other ladies would choose to go, the aukwardness [*sic*] of [her] situation so forcibly struck on [her] mind that [she] certainly thought [he] must have invited [her] to offend [her]."[40] Dunscombe's rhetoric—complete with underscored references to her "excessive feelings" and (in a second letter) to the "fatal party"—makes clear that she was well versed in the language of fashionable literary sentimentalism; neither her initial hurt and anger nor her subsequent protestations of respect and friendship would be out of place in any of the contemporary novels about long-suffering women of feeling.[41] Yet Dunscombe's implicit appeal to a clear and unambiguous code of British propriety—gentlemen call on ladies; ladies' comfort is paramount—is undercut by the specifics of place, as Cochrane insists upon the unpredictability of the weather and the relative inaccessibility of the Dunscombes' property as justification for relative social informality. There were, in other words, checks on the ability of women such as Dunscombe, Aplin, and Haly to recreate genteel British society in Newfoundland. Yet the simple fact that Dunscombe was prepared to quarrel with the governor himself about the finer points of etiquette indicates the importance, to these women, of maintaining a properly "British" way of doing things, even if—like Dunscombe—they were in fact born and raised in a transatlantic society. In effect, their adherence to the values and customs of genteel femininity becomes a measure not just of their own but also, and more generally, of their society's "Britishness."

LABORIOUS UNFEMININE TOIL

Anne Theresa Haly, Anne Aplin, Elizabeth Dunscombe, and Mary Elizabeth Brenton may not have left very many records of their transatlantic life, but their contemporaries among the Anglo-Newfoundland women who lived outside St. John's are even more difficult to track, as few of them left traces other than a name. A Mrs. Selby—her given name is unknown—who accompanied the trapper and fur trader George Cartwright to Newfoundland and then to Labrador in the 1770s is one of the very few European woman whose life in rural Newfoundland prior to the nineteenth century has been documented in any detail. Her experiences, as recorded by Cartwright in his journal, suggest the challenges faced by women outside St. John's: he provides vignettes of her sheltering from the rain with him under a canvas sail while he shot a bear, whose "rank" flesh was necessary "to satisfy a craving appetite"; breaking her leg when trying to reach a neighboring house on Fogo Island; and, once in Labrador, traveling by dogsled over the ice to stay in a tilt while on a caribou hunting expedition.[42] Even recognizing that this was some fifty years before the women of Cochrane's St. John's were enjoying their lives of visits and dances, the gap between rural and "urban" Newfoundland life is striking. Indeed, the extent to which Mrs. Selby's experiences run counter to the expectations of "proper" British femininity might explain why she has been one of the very few Anglo-Newfoundland women from the eighteenth or early nineteenth century to enter the twentieth- and twenty-first-century popular imagination.[43]

Yet if Mrs. Selby was atypical in having her transatlantic life documented, at least to some degree, other scraps of information about outport Anglo-Newfoundland women of this era suggest that she was also atypical in her apparent freedom from the constraints of British femininity. Reports by missionaries and educators note approvingly when girls and women from the outports meet their expectations of a virtuous peasantry; the clergyman Lewis Amadeus Anspach, for example, was pleased to see that the fishermen's wives were both "remarkable for their ingenuity and industry" and "characterized by a steady attention to domestic duties."[44] Other observers were scornful of women from the more remote settlements who failed to meet those standards. Chappell mocked the young women he encountered in St. George's Bay, on the west coast of the island, for what he presents as their bad attempt to imitate gentry manners. According to Chappell, they invited the officers to a local "hut" for "a sort of rustic ball," after which the men amused themselves with "comic description[s]" of their dance partners' "most burlesque finery."[45] At least one of Chappell's reviewers found this mockery distasteful, but his grounds for complaint—that Chappell had not modified his criticism with a "conciliating compliment . . . as, for instance, that among the fishermen's daughters some were handsome"—reinforce Chappell's implication that women of the lower classes are interesting or appealing only insofar as they meet his aestheticized standard of English femininity.[46]

This point is even more strongly emphasized in the few accounts that Cochrane provides of Anglo-Newfoundland women outside the capital. In a tour of the Burin Peninsula in July 1827, he encountered a woman whom he identifies only by the surname Pike, but who clearly fascinated him. She is one of the few people in his journal described physically: she is "above the middle height" and though not "handsome" has "a pleasing expression of countenance."[47] Yet what seems to be most striking about her, according to Cochrane, is the absence of any physical trace of what he calls "the laborious unfeminine toil" of the salt cod industry (158). Significantly, according to Cochrane, she also self-identifies as English despite having been born on the Burin Peninsula, laying "great Emphasis" on her father's "being an Englishman born" and lamenting "that Newfoundland was thought nothing of at home," that is, in England (157). In effect, Mrs. Pike embodies a version of non-elite femininity in which Englishness remains so powerful that traces of Newfoundland are almost completely erased. Yet at the same time, as Cochrane emphasizes the ways in which Mrs. Pike seems at odds with or out of place in her surroundings, he implies a less comfortable idea that English femininity is fundamentally incompatible with the demands of rural Newfoundland life.

This idea is reinforced a little later on the same expedition when Cochrane visits an island in White Bear Bay on the southwest coast of Newfoundland inhabited only by two brothers who had settled there with their wives and children. In this case, Cochrane initially stresses the families' distance from British culture, noting that they are barely literate. One of the women was able to read print, he observes, but not to write or read handwriting, and she had taught the others as best she could. Their only books were a Bible and prayer book, but "never having even seen a Minister" they remained "ignorant how the Church Service should properly be performed" (160). While impressed and moved by their determination to follow a regular system of family worship, Cochrane uses these women less as an example of enduring Britishness than as a reminder to himself of the power of virtuous feeling to endure in the absence of "education—example—or precepts" (160). In effect, Cochrane depicts these women and their families as living in something akin to a state of nature, and while he derives an unexceptionably moral lesson about piety and resignation from observing them, he does not appear to see them as being, like Mrs. Pike, displaced compatriots. Cut off by a generation or two from Britain, the women of White Bear Bay are an unsettling reminder of the potential fragility of Englishness in a remote and impoverished transatlantic setting.

That said, it is significant that the main vestige of British culture left to these people—the ability to read a prayer—is transmitted by a woman. There is a very great distance between Anne Aplin's ability to smooth Cochrane's way into St. John's life through her dancing, drawing, and singing and the struggles of a barely literate woman on a remote coastal island to share prayers with her husband and in-laws. In both cases, however, it is a woman who is able to maintain an element of "English" identity in a colony that was depicted, at the time, as being more or less unpleasantly foreign. Mrs. Pike and the woman from White Bear Bay function as counterpoints to the worries of missionaries that the British settlers of Newfoundland were degenerating into "heathens," while Aplin's guitar and quadrilles make clear that, Steele and Chappell notwithstanding, St. John's offered its visitors and inhabitants more than forbidding terrain, dreadful weather, and streets full of rotting fish guts. Even without having written a word about their transatlantic experiences, these and other women of this era thus offer a fuller and more rounded vision of Newfoundland's settler colonial society than would be available if their presence and experiences remained overlooked.

NOTES

1. Thomas Cochrane, "Selections from Thomas Cochrane's Newfoundland Journal," comp. and ed. Pam Perkins, in "Thomas Cochrane and Newfoundland in the 1820s," by Pam Perkins, *Journal of Newfoundland and Labrador Studies* 29, no. 1 (Spring 2014): 127.
2. Pam Perkins, "A 'Remote and Cheerless Possession': Early Nineteenth-Century Newfoundland in the British Cultural Imagination,'" in *Romantic Norths: Cultural Exchanges 1750–1850*, ed. Cian Duffy (London: Palgrave, 2017), 234–237.
3. Anon., "Weekly Record," *Boston Weekly Magazine* 2, no. 46 (August 1, 1840): 367.
4. Sarah M. S. Pearsall, *Atlantic Families: Lives and Letters in the Later Eighteenth Century* (Oxford: Oxford University Press, 2008), 43.
5. I am very grateful to Ann B. Shteir for introducing me to the botanical work of Mary Elizabeth Brenton.
6. [B. Lacy], *Miscellaneous Poems Compos'd at Newfoundland, on Board His Majesty's Ship the* Kinsale (London: printed for the author, 1729), 14–15.
7. London Missionary Society, *Transactions of the Missionary Society in the Years 1803, 1804, 1805, and 1806* (London, 1806), 2:106–107.
8. Edward Chappell, *Voyage of His Majesty's Ship* Rosamond *to Newfoundland and the Southern Coast of Labrador* (London: J. Mawman, 1818), 52; Robert Steele, *A Tour through Part of the Atlantic; or, Recollections from Madeira, the Azores (or Western Isles) and Newfoundland* (London: J. J. Stockdale, 1810), 100–101.
9. William Carson, *Reasons for Colonizing the Island of Newfoundland, in a Letter Addressed to the Inhabitants* (Greenock, Scotland: William Scott, 1813), 5, 9.
10. Marina Seifert, *Rewriting Newfoundland Mythology: The Works of Tom Dawe* (Berlin: Galda and Wilch, 2002), 33–34.
11. Carson, *Reasons*, 1.
12. Carson, *Reasons*, 9.
13. Carson, *Reasons*, 9.
14. Thomas Cochrane, unpublished letter to Lord Bathurst, May 1, 1827, MS 2370, fol. 43, National Library of Scotland, Edinburgh.
15. D. W. Prowse, *A History of Newfoundland* (Portugal Cove, NL: Boulder Publications, 2002), 424–426, 436.
16. Eugene Ney, "The English Shore," in *French Visitors to Newfoundland: An Anthology of Nineteenth-Century Travel Writings*, trans. and ed. Scott Jamieson and Anne Thareau (St. John's, NL: ISER Books, 2013), 66.
17. Carson, *Reasons*, 6.
18. *Public Ledger* (St. John's, NL), August 7, 1827.

19. Pearsall, *Atlantic Families*, 47.
20. Lady Matilda Cochrane, Commonplace Book 1813, MS 2485, fol. 1, National Library of Scotland, Edinburgh.
21. Lady Frances Simpson, (Journal of a Voyage from Montreal thro' the Interior of Canada to York Factory), 1830, 1, D.6/4, Hudson's Bay Company Archives, Winnipeg, MB.
22. Henrietta Prescott, *Poems, Written in Newfoundland* (London: Saunders and Otley, 1839), 119–123, lines 15–16, 21–24.
23. Prescott, *Poems*, 123, line 48.
24. M. Cochrane, Commonplace Book 1813, fol. 10; Prescott, *Poems*, 124–127.
25. Prescott, *Poems*, 125.
26. Mary Elizabeth Brenton, unpublished letter to Sir William Jackson Hooker, October 20, 1832, Directors' Correspondence 61/54, fol. 2, Library and Archives at Royal Botanic Gardens, Kew, London, accessed September 1, 2017, http://plants.jstor.org/stable/10.5555/al.ap.visual.kusdc152.
27. *Weekly Herald and Conception Bay General Advertiser* (Harbour Grace, NL), May 14, 1851.
28. Janet Sorensen, "Literature of the Ocean," in *Transatlantic Literary Studies, 1660–1830*, ed. Eve Tavor Bannet and Susan Manning (Cambridge: Cambridge University Press, 2012), 126.
29. *Royal Gazette and Newfoundland Advertiser* (St. John's), June 30, 1814; *Public Ledger*, December 18, 1827.
30. *Public Ledger*, March 3, 1829.
31. *Public Ledger*, August 1, 1828; August 17, 1827; July 6, 1827.
32. Richard B. Sher, "Transatlantic Books and Literary Culture," in *Transatlantic Literary Studies, 1660–1830*, ed. Eve Tavor Bannet and Susan Manning (Cambridge: Cambridge University Press, 2012), 11.
33. Gerhard P. Bassler, *Vikings to U-Boats: The German Experience in Newfoundland and Labrador* (Montreal: McGill-Queen's University Press, 2006), 70; Alexandra E. Carter, "William H. Eagar: Drawing Master of Argyle Street, Halifax," *Journal of Canadian Art History* 7, no. 2 (1984): 139.
34. *Public Ledger*, January 3, 1834.
35. T. Cochrane, "Selections," 141.
36. T. Cochrane, "Selections," 136–137.
37. Thomas Cochrane, unpublished journal, November 12, 1824–September 20, 1826, MS 2590, p. 101, National Library of Scotland, Edinburgh.
38. T. Cochrane, "Selections," 136.
39. Elizabeth Dunscombe, unpublished letters to Sir Thomas Cochrane, March 13 and 15, 1827, MS 2350, fols. 15v–16, National Library of Scotland, Edinburgh.
40. Dunscombe to T. Cochrane, fol. 16v.
41. Dunscombe to T. Cochrane, fols. 17, 22.
42. George Cartwright, *A Journal of Transactions and Events, during a Residence of Nearly Sixteen Years on the Coast of Labrador*, 3 vols. (Newark, England: Allen and Ridge, 1792), 1:15, 18, 220.
43. See Valerie E. Legge, "With 'High Hearts': Women Travelers to Newfoundland and Labrador," in *Pathways of Creativity in Contemporary Newfoundland and Labrador*, ed. Maria Jesús Hernáez Lerena (Newcastle upon Tyne: Cambridge Scholars Publishing, 2015), 56–57.
44. Lewis Amadeus Anspach, *A History of the Island of Newfoundland* (London: printed for the author, 1819), 468–469.
45. Chappell, *Voyage*, 72.
46. "Chappell's Voyages to Hudson's Bay and Newfoundland," *Monthly Review*, n.s., 87 (September 1818): 72.
47. T. Cochrane, "Selections," 157.

5

BUSTY BUCCANEERS AND SAPPHIC SWASHBUCKLERS ON THE HIGH SEAS

Ula Lukszo Klein

ANNE BONNY AND MARY READ are two of the most well-known female pirates not only of the eighteenth century, but perhaps of all time. Appearing in Captain Charles Johnson's *A General History of the Robberies and Murders of the Most Notorious Pyrates* (1724), their legacy continues in various forms throughout the centuries after their deaths.[1] Even for twenty-first-century audiences unfamiliar with the eighteenth-century text, they continue to fascinate, as Bonny, Read, and Bonny's pirate captain lover Jack Rackam all feature in the video game *Assassin's Creed IV: Black Flag* (2013), and Bonny and Rackam are main characters on the Starz network show *Black Sails* (2014–2017).[2] Clearly, Bonny and Read hold a fascination for both eighteenth-century readers and modern consumers of popular culture related to a larger cultural fascination with pirates. More importantly, though, their existence as *female* pirates, specifically, captures our interest precisely because of how they survived in the quasi-mythical, male-dominated world of the golden age of piracy.

Bonny's and Read's stories draw on and combine various tropes of the independent, plebeian woman in the eighteenth century, including the tropes of the cross-dressing warrior woman, the female criminal, and the whore's story.[3] The female cross-dresser of eighteenth-century narrative is often, though not always, a transnational figure, one whose roots lie beyond the borders of England or whose travels *en cavalier* take her far beyond the reaches of the British Isles, or both. The larger cultural phenomenon surrounding the fascination with the stories of women who dressed in men's clothing and, at times, "passed" as men is often also concerned with additional ways that these women assert their Otherness.[4] The stories of Bonny and Read are part of a larger conversation about the role of women in the home and outside of it in the late seventeenth and early eighteenth centuries.[5] As laboring-class women whose stories emphasize their desire to leave behind the constraints of England and English domesticity, Read and Bonny are shown attaining economic independence as well as independence of movement that was, at the time, often only available to men. Further, as members of a transatlantic seafaring world, their stories tap into a world defined by its nationlessness, its romance, and its endless possibilities, as much as by its dangers and hazards.

In this essay, I examine the narratives of Bonny and Read in the eighteenth-century transatlantic context and consider how their stories of outlaw mobility reveal a dual move in which gender and even sexual deviances are, if not fully accepted, consumed by readers for pleasure and entertainment, while at the same time they obscure naturalized racial differences. I argue that, like many tales of cross-dressing women, the stories of Bonny and Read use the body to construct and deconstruct gender while also illustrating the possibility of female same-sex desires—but between two white, European women, albeit of lower-class origins. In the transatlantic context, the female pirate comes to exemplify a specific trope of female masculinity and laboring-class independence predicated on the white, European status of the two women. Further, the elements of romance that differentiate Read's and Bonny's stories from the other male pirates' life stories in the *General History* gesture toward how pirate stories will develop in the following centuries: as part of a predominantly white adventure world of the Atlantic. Thus, the stories of female pirates emphasize the freedoms available to white women of the transatlantic world who appropriate the behaviors and clothing of men, while also illustrating how categories of race and class are imbricated in the representations of gender and desire.

FEMALE PIRATES AS TRANSATLANTIC SUBJECTS

For many scholars of the transatlantic and, specifically, the transatlantic eighteenth century, the transatlantic space is at once one of mobility and possibility for the lower-class subjects of empire as well as a dangerous space of ravishment and enslavement. Eve Tavor Bannet argues that works by Daniel Defoe and Penelope Aubin, for example, as well as slave biographies "gesture towards the outlines of a transnational subaltern subculture in and between those rival Atlantic empires that were 'Poor Man's Country' for people who experienced and portrayed empire from below."[6] Similarly, Laura Doyle argues that in the transatlantic milieu, "everyone is a *contingent* member of this race-empire of freedom. Everyone is free to rise, and free to fall, to rule or be ruined, financially or bodily."[7] Pirates in particular, as Margaret Cohen explains, inhabit a transatlantic world of spectacular liberty where "might made right, and the only freedom was the 'freedom of the seas,' an amoral

Figure 5.1 "Ann Bonny and Mary Read convicted of Piracy Nov. 28th 1720 at a Court of Vice Admiralty held at St. Jago de la Vega in the Island of Jamaica" (*A General History of the Robberies and Murders of the Most Notorious Pyrates*, 1724). © British Library Board. C.121.b.24, opposite page 117.

freedom of movement without regard for the purpose of such travel."[8] While there is ample risk to be ruined "financially or bodily" in these stories, even Bonny's and Read's eventual captures, as noted in figure 5.1, are defined textually through their fierce independence and resourcefulness, eschewing the tragic in favor of the titillating. Charles Johnson's *General History of the . . . Pyrates* overwhelmingly represents Bonny and Read as women who take advantage of the freedom of the sea in spectacular and seductive ways.

When writing about Bonny and Read, it is important to note that very little of their lives remains in the public record. Their fame in England was made through their inclusion in Johnson's *General History of the . . . Pyrates*, which, though first published in 1724, went through a number of issues and reprints throughout the eighteenth century and, in increasingly fictionalized and edited versions, in the nineteenth century as well.[9] Johnson's narrative is based on the women's official trial report, which Johnson had access to; the report circulated both through newspaper printings contemporary to the trials and in pamphlet form afterward.[10] However, Johnson's narrative embroiders the original facts extensively, even imagining origin stories for Bonny and Read in which they cross-dressed as young girls. Margaret Cohen and Hans Turley have noted the qualities of traditional romance that characterize the narratives of Bonny and Read within the *General History of the . . . Pyrates*, drawing attention to how Johnson sets their stories apart from those of the male pirates: "Johnson goes to a lot of trouble to 'prove' that Bonny and Read are women . . . once they actually turn pirate. The 'facts' are lost to history by the romantic mythologizing that preserves the heterocentric status quo."[11] In order to avoid speculating about the lives of the "real-life" Bonny and Read, this essay focuses on their representation in Johnson's *General History of the . . . Pyrates* in its various iterations. At a time when the female adventurer in novels by Defoe and Aubin will soon be displaced by the heroines of Samuel Richardson and Frances Burney, their representation of female autonomy stands out for its emphasis on ambiguous virtue and celebrated independence. Unlike indentured servants, enslaved people, or even middle- and upper-class European women who inhabited the transatlantic world, Bonny and Read are represented as active agents in these narratives and as women who navigated their lives, as well as the high seas, with their own interests at heart. In this way, they resemble other female adventurers such as the female soldier Hannah Snell; in stark difference to Snell's virtuous representations in print culture, however, Bonny and Read are cast as outlaws and vicious fighters. As Sally O'Driscoll notes, "The romance of the female outlaw draws the audience in, and is too powerful an image to be utterly reduced to a moral tale."[12] The adventure and romance of Bonny's and Read's narratives avoid easy categorization or narratorial moralizing, as the text prioritizes these women's adventurous qualities.

In part, this freedom of movement and freedom from social mores is directly related to being a pirate. As Marcus Rediker explains in *Between the Devil and the Deep Blue Sea*, "[Pirates'] experience as free wage laborers and as members of an uncontrolled, freewheeling subculture gave pirates the perspective and occasion to fight back against brutal and unjust authority."[13] Both women disguise themselves as men and use their disguises to remain on board privateer and pirate ships for the purposes of pillaging and plundering. Both also use their disguises in order to carry on affairs with men on board the ships, demonstrating how piracy and cross-dressing together facilitate financial as well as sexual independence.[14] In both cases, their cross-dressing purportedly begins at a young age.[15] In the story of Read, her cross-dressing begins when her mother passes her off as a boy for financial gain, and, as an adolescent, Read remains in men's clothes. At thirteen, she works as a footman until, "growing bold and strong, and having a roving Mind, she enter'd herself on board a Man of War, where she served some Time, then quitted it," as she was unable to "get a Commission, they being generally bought and sold."[16] Thus, Read, as a lower-class woman, suffers from the same class-based limitations as her fellow men: "Discounting her gender—Read's case is similar to that of many soldiers and sailors in eighteenth-century England who could not afford to buy their commissions."[17] Read eventually tries to leave behind her life in men's clothing and life aboard ship, but her Flemish lover-turned-husband soon dies, and she returns to the sea as a privateer and, later, pirate.

Johnson's narrative is contradictory about Read's motivations once she becomes a pirate. The narrative explains that "it is true, she often declared, that the Life of a Pyrate was what she always abhor'd, and went into it only upon a Compulsion, both this Time, and before[,] . . . yet some of the Evidence against her, upon her Tryal, who were forced Men, and had sail'd with her, deposted upon Oath, that in Times of Action, no Person amongst them was more resolute or ready to board or undertake any Thing that was hazardous, than she and Anne Bonny. . . . This was Part of the Evidence against her, which she denied."[18] Frederick Burwick and Manushag Powell have argued that the text appears forgiving of Read's piracy, casting her as the "virtuous" female pirate and Bonny as the "vicious" one.[19] Indeed, the narrator continues here by saying that although he is uncertain about Read's motivations, "thus much is certain, that she did not want Bravery, nor indeed was she less remarkable for her Modesty, according to the Notions of Virtue."[20] The narrative represents Read as brave and bold, while also underscoring her choice to hide her identity; these elements of Read's character allow her to pursue adventure and survive adversity on the high seas, even garnering the admiration—or fear—of fellow pirates. Read's narrative channels the trope of the woman warrior from broadside ballads, in which lower-class women maintain their virtue despite engaging in a martial or seafaring lifestyle, provided they do not have sex out of wedlock. The narrative constructs the seafaring female pirate as a type of exemplary transatlantic subject: one who obeys the dictates of domestic femininity even as she channels explicitly masculine qualities of valor, bravery, and courage.

Although Bonny's narrative swings more toward the whore end of the "'whore'/ 'faithful mate' dichotomy" that Turley proposes for understanding their stories, it does, like Read's, represent piracy as a mode through which to achieve independence in a transatlantic setting, casting Bonny as another exemplary transatlantic subject.[21] Bonny is Irish and illegitimate, purportedly brought into her father's home in breeches so as to deceive his wife about the extramarital affair that brought Bonny into the world. As a young woman, Bonny keeps house for her father in Carolina until she marries without her father's consent a man "not worth a Groat" and is summarily "turn'd . . . out of doors."[22] Soon after, she meets the pirate captain Jack Rackam and "consented to elope from [her husband], and go to Sea with Rackam in Men's Cloaths."[23] Significantly, a revised version of this exchange takes place in the appendix to the first volume, in which the narrator alludes to the possibility that Bonny orchestrated her own wife sale: "Rackam lived in all Manner of Luxury, spending his Money liberally upon Anne Bonny, who was so taken with his Generosity, that she had the Assurance to propose to her Husband to quit him, in order to cohabit with John Rackam; and that Rackam should give him a Sum of Money, in Consideration he should resign her to the said Rackam by a Writing in Form."[24] In reality, wife sale was a dangerous practice through which a man might pimp out his wife to other men for financial gain.[25] In the *General History of the . . . Pyrates*, however, it functions as yet another element of Bonny's representation as a canny and resourceful transatlantic subject, willing to exploit her status as a commodity to end up where she wants. At the very least, we might surmise that the *General History of the . . . Pyrates* works to preserve the notion of female pirates as displaying positive plebeian characteristics of being intrepid, resourceful, and cunning, but also, in keeping with notions of piracy, the pirate characteristics of spontaneity and volatility.[26] Bonny has a "fierce and courageous Temper" whose reputation literally outgrows the truth: even the narrator of the *General History of the . . . Pyrates* acknowledges that some rumors of her vicious behavior were "upon further Enquiry . . . found . . . to be groundless."[27] The notion that Read is cast as more virtuous than Bonny is a tenuous one at best, as the narrative acknowledges a good amount of ambiguity with regard to their motivations for piracy, ultimately underscoring both women's shrewd survival instincts, their courage, and their willingness to take action.

Notably, although Bonny's story is much shorter than Read's and, according to Burwick and Powell's evaluation, much more negative about her legacy and character, hers is the one that ends ambiguously. Read is reported to have died of a fever in prison, while Bonny, we learn, is ultimately reprieved and "what is become of her since, we cannot tell; only this we know, that she was not executed."[28] While Read may nominally function as a tragic female victim of piracy or the transatlantic world writ large, Bonny's character resists easy dismissal or categorization, and she successfully avoids execution. Considered together, however, Read's and Bonny's stories show us that being a female pirate had its peculiar advantages. When Read is set to be executed for piracy, she is able to plead her belly, and thus "her Execution was respited, and it is possible she would have found Favour, but she was seiz'd with a violent Fever, soon after her Tryal, of which she died in Prison."[29] It is not piracy that finally kills Read, but disease. For Bonny, the mobility and independence offered her through piracy does not end, we learn, with imprisonment; instead, her future, at least according to Johnson's text, is left vague and full of exciting possibilities. The rendering of Read as "the virtuous one" and Bonny as "the vicious one" is, in this reading, problematic and perhaps not fully convincing. As O'Driscoll notes, the women's stories are linked: "The women are always presented as a pair. . . . Iconographically, they are presented together . . . joined more firmly by their relationship than they are with the men they supposedly love."[30] As inseparable representatives of female piracy, Bonny and Read manage to avoid classification as fully virtuous or fully vicious; to a certain extent, their low social origins free them from typical definitions of feminine behavior. Additionally, their relationship as female pirates becomes linked not only through gender and class, but also through sexuality and race.[31]

As transatlantic female subjects whose stories draw on laboring-class values, women warrior archetypes, as well as concepts of pirate freedoms, Bonny and Read appear to have a variety of options for mobility and independence. As members of a "seaborne citizenry," Bonny and Read, oddly enough, emblematize one of the most positive and exciting of the various "disparate expressions of the . . . profound impulse to escape imperious, manly British rule."[32] From this perspective, female pirates become emblems of an "up by the bootstraps" type of shrewdness, practicality, and resolve, not unlike that asserted by stereotypical eighteenth-century women warriors. These women are often as good as, if not better than, their male counterparts at drinking, swearing, fighting, working, and even, on occasion, wooing other women.[33] At the same time, as pirates, these women can never be lauded and praised in the same way as a virtuous female soldier like Hannah Snell, in whose narrative she is praised, no less, as "the real *Pamella*" for her extraordinary virtue aboard ship.[34] As pirates, Bonny and Read are members of a specific class of persons whose lifestyle was not only outside the law, but also outside the nation. Textually, the pirate is an antihero: we read about him/her with disgust and fascination; we are disgusted by his/her violence but attracted by the image of the pirate as "a kind of libertine of the seven seas. He thumbs his nose at any conventions, economic or cultural, that might link him to the status quo."[35] The female pirate is, then, doubly of interest both as a pirate and as a public woman who, as O'Driscoll puts it, "is available for public scrutiny."[36] The role of Read and Bonny within this transatlantic context of danger and freedom becomes increasingly complex when we consider how the gender presentation and sexuality of these women functions in the text in contrast to their racial identity as white European women.

FEMALE PIRATES: RACE AND DESIRE IN THE TRANSATLANTIC WORLD

The narratives of Bonny and Read in Johnson's *General History of the . . . Pyrates* present both women as accessing sexual independence through their plebeian initiative, combined with their cross-dressing and piracy. Their sexual independence, however, is not limited to heterosexual desires. Moments of sapphic possibility arise in their narratives as, in Bonny's, we learn that the two women met aboard ship and Bonny attempts to seduce Read, a narrative move that gestures to the possibility of a transatlantic sexuality defined in part by non-normative sexual desires. O'Driscoll makes a case for the sapphic overtones of their stories that would have been legible to eighteenth-century readers, arguing that "the possibility of a same-sex affair remains available to the reader, couched in the conventions of cross-dressing theatricality—thus presented as playful misrepresentation. The original edition neatly labels this playful possibility as impossible, yet later editions indicate that readers and publishers found it appealing."[37] Although Bonny purportedly believes Read to be a man, and Read immediately rebuffs Bonny's sexual overture and instead reveals her true identity to Bonny, the ambiguousness of the exchange and its existence in the narrative at all alludes to the titillating quality of same-sex female desires that were available to contemporary readers.[38]

Importantly, though, the text defines appropriate sexual bodies through racial difference: specifically, through the white breasts of Read. In the transatlantic context of slavery and the "race-empire of freedom" that Doyle delineates in *Freedom's Empire*, the whiteness of Read's breasts takes on added importance. Doyle argues that the eighteenth-century Atlantic world saw the creation of freedom as a race-defined category: "Herein lie the deepest ideological (as opposed to economic) roots of what we now call whiteness, whose purported superiority rests on its racially inherited, mastering capacity for freedom. To be white is to be fit for freedom."[39] In the case of Read, to be white or, specifically, to have white breasts is to be female and white and fit to be desired. Read, therefore, is a suitable sexual partner for a fellow sailor not just because she is a woman, but because she is specifically a white woman.

The racial coding of Read's breasts, along with the assumptions of whiteness via British and Irish nationality, suggests that unlike gender identity or sexuality, racial identity is much less flexible. This aspect of the text, however, has been overlooked by critics who have discussed at length the importance of gender and sexuality in Bonny's and Read's narratives. For Rediker, for example, their lives "represented a subversive commentary on the gender relations of their own time," while Lizabeth Paravisini-Gebert sees the women's breasts as well as their pregnant bellies functioning textually as "evidence of their purportedly true female nature . . . juxtaposed to, and serv[ing] to counter, their reported statements of a wanton cruelty and disregard for life of which only males should be capable."[40] For Turley, the women serve as a counterpoint to the lack of male sexuality aboard pirate ships. Indeed, the "women *have* to be women in order for sexuality to be disclosed on board a pirate ship," meaning that gender and sexuality are defined through absence in pirate histories until the introduction of Read and Bonny.[41] The piratical subject is linked to the sodomitical subject in the eighteenth century, and the appearance of Read and Bonny in the *General History of the . . . Pyrates* is in part poised to alleviate readers' concerns about sodomy and the homosocial world aboard a pirate ship. For Turley, therefore, Bonny and Read are represented as breaking with gender and sexual conventions, yet their stories "preserv[e] the heterocentric status quo," showing that the transatlantic world is yet another space in which heterosexual norms and patriarchal dictates must be upheld, even as they are constantly at risk of being exposed as unstable.[42]

The narratives of Bonny and Read, like women warrior ballads, propose an alternative to the all-male world aboard ship; however, they do not preclude the possibility of female same-sex desires either. Building on Turley's arguments, O'Driscoll argues that the narratives of Read and Bonny are important signifiers in the history of sexuality in the eighteenth century, as they represent normative female bodies as implicitly those of heterosexual women and, further, that these categories are normalized and reified in the text, not unlike in Paravisini-Gebert's analysis.[43] Yet, it is the femaleness of the breast that allows the text to gesture to female same-sex desires that were standard elements of eighteenth-century cross-dressing narratives. Importantly, the attempted seduction of Read by Bonny figures as only one of at least three such seduction scenes that render the transatlantic voyage as one of amorous possibilities, as long as both partners are white. Transatlantic sexuality is only flexible with regard to gender, while racial differences, which highlight the difference between free and enslaved persons in the transatlantic setting, are much more strictly defined.

It is in Read's narrative in the *General History of the . . . Pyrates* that readers learn the titillating details of how Bonny tried to seduce Read. This attempted, quasi-lesbian seduction happens only after we have read about one of Read's own seductions, which are illustrated through what Paravisini-Gebert calls the "breast-revelation motif."[44] Early on, Read falls in love with a Flemish soldier; rather than reveal outright to him who she is (that is, a woman), the narrator writes that "as they lay together in the same Tent, and were constantly together, she found a Way of letting him discover her Sex, without appearing that it was done with Design."[45] Her method for revealing her sex is unclear until she reveals it again, to a young man taken captive aboard ship, immediately after we learn of her meeting with Bonny. Read uses all her skills to seduce the young man, first gaining his confidence in her masculine disguise by disparaging the pirate lifestyle and, subsequently, by revealing her female sex. "When she found he had a Friendship for her, as a Man," the narrator writes, "she suffered the Discovery to be made, by carelessly shewing her Breasts, which were very White."[46] It is not the size and shape of the breasts that bear the marker of gender here, but their color. As readers, we may infer that Read's "accidental" revelation of her gender to the Flanders cadet was through a similar means.

In Read's story, breasts *are* gender. Presumably, the whiteness of Read's breast indicates her femininity because a woman's breasts are never exposed to the sun in the way a laboring-class man's might be; however, two problematic points arise here. First, an aristocratic or middle-class male might also have a very white chest, for example. Second, and more to the point, is the indication of racial preference in a female breast.[47] The sailors and soldiers who see Read's breast, we might surmise, would identify her as female due to the size or shape of her breasts; the text, however, reveals that it is the whiteness of her breasts that makes her recognizable as both female and an appropriate partner for a romantic relationship. If, indeed, the female breast was becoming increasingly "colonized" and recoded as an important part of the imperial project, as Ruth Perry has argued, then the whiteness of Read's breast is not merely coincidental.[48] This moment in the text reveals not just Read's breast, but the growing concerns about who has access to the freedoms of the transatlantic world, and who does not.

Keeping these earlier seductions in mind, we turn to Read's seduction by Bonny. We are told that Read was exceptionally brave and that no one suspected she was a woman; no one knows her secret until she meets Bonny. The narrator explains: "Anne Bonny took her [Read] for a handsome young Fellow, and for some Reasons best known to herself, first discovered her Sex to Mary Read; Mary Read knowing what she would be at, and being very sensible of her own Incapacity in that Way, was forced to come to a right Understanding with her, and so to the great Disappointment of Anne Bonny, she let her know she was a Woman also."[49] This short section contains several suggestive possibilities. First of all, the narrator is remarkably coy about Bonny's motivations. Where he does not mince words when recounting Read's love for the Flemish soldier, or Bonny's desire to leave her husband for Rackam, he writes that Bonny reveals her sex to Read "for some Reasons best known to herself." If we, the readers, believe that Bonny desires Read because she is a "handsome young Fellow," then the obvious reason for revealing her sex (as we see in Read's narrative) is to entice this fellow into bed with her, as the narrator explains that Read "kn[ows] what she would be at." By describing Bonny's motivations as "reasons best known to herself," the narrator gestures to the *amor impossibilis* of lesbian desire—the desire that dare not speak its name. Read's decision to reveal her true identity to Bonny is also unclear, as it seems that she took great care, up until that point, to keep her identity hidden. Read's decision—or desire—to reveal herself as a woman to Bonny is at the very least suggestive of same-sex female desire, even more so when we speculate on how Read and Bonny reveal *their* sex to each other. Given the only specific "revelation" of sex in these two narratives, the reader may imagine that they also showed their breasts to each other as a means of seduction and confession.

The text gleefully allows and encourages its readers to imagine both women baring their breasts to each other, for Bonny, as a sign of a desire, and for Read, as a signifier of her lack, or, as the narrator pens it, "her own Incapacity in that Way" (122). Even this phrase, however, implies that Read is unable to fulfill Bonny's desires (physically) rather than return them. Significantly, their mutual revelations become fodder for Rackam's jealousy: "This Intimacy so disturb'd Captain Rackam, who was the Lover and Gallant of Anne Bonny, that he grew furiously jealous, so that he told Anne Bonny, he would cut her new Lover's Throat[;] therefore, to quiet him, she let him into the Secret also" (123). Rackam's jealousy, like Bonny's initial attraction to Read, signifies that Read passes unquestionably as a man to others. Yet, the narrator's allusive remark that Bonny's attraction to Read was unaccountable calls on the reader to consider the possibility that Bonny was attracted to Read precisely for her female qualities or appearance. As pirate women who transgress norms of femininity and domesticity in addition to transgressing the rule of law, Bonny and Read are perhaps, not surprisingly, coded as sapphic. Bonny's and Read's performance of masculinity and the narrative allusions of secret liaisons and illicit desires link back to the notion of the transatlantic world as one of unbounded possibilities for female independence and unconventional morality. The flexibility of these categories, however, exists in contrast to the inflexibility of their racial identities—identities which would have had significant resonances in the eighteenth-century transatlantic world that was, by that point, defined by the slave trade.

Both Bonny and Read are represented as accessing male freedoms and even outperforming their male counterparts in the tough transatlantic pirate world of the eighteenth century. Read is stronger and more courageous than her lovers, saving one from death many times on the field of action and, in another case, defending her lover in a duel while dressed in men's clothes. Bonny, though perhaps not as selfless as Read, is reported to be brutally tough, much tougher than her male lover. When Rackam is scheduled to be executed and is allowed to see Bonny one more time, her reputed words to him, as they are recorded in the *General History of the . . . Pyrates*, are "that she was sorry to see him there, but if he had fought like a Man, he need not have been hang'd like a Dog" (133). Pirate and plebeian archetypes merge in these stories, as Bonny and Read take up the mantle of exaggerated masculinity, even as they are able to use their femininity to get what they want. Part of their iconic appeal is their ability to be simultaneously male and female, masculine and feminine, and capable of appealing to the desires of both men and women. This dual power, however, stems in part from their whiteness, which functions as a blank slate or canvas on which to project European notions of valor, working women's resourcefulness, imperial sea power, and the white female domesticity that, over the course of the century, would rise as the ideal structuring notion of country and empire. In this way, their stories typify the representation of the golden age of piracy: as a romance of whiteness on the high seas.

CONCLUSION: FEMALE PIRATES AND THE ROMANCE OF WHITENESS

The Atlantic world has been characterized by various scholars as an ideal setting for the traditional romance genre. According to Gretchen J. Woertendyke, "The sea's material and psychic vastness saturates virtually every sphere; and romance is the genre singularly capable of maintaining a poetics of relation *both* on its surface and within its deeper structures of language and history."[50] The stories of Bonny and Read, as already intimated, take up this strand of romance in the *General History of the . . . Pyrates*, as discussed by Burwick and Powell, Cohen, and Turley. Cohen writes, "Captain Johnson himself noted the likeness of his biographies to 'a Novel' apropos of the female pirates Anne Bonny and Mary Read, who, however, were historical figures, in a fusion of fact and fiction characteristic of craft's romance of practice."[51] If indeed "modern romance after the rise of the novel is signaled by the fictional, no longer magical and unreal, but still unimaginable against the everydayness of common life," then we can easily see how these narratives fit this definition.[52] Bonny's and Read's exploits are notable precisely because they are unusual; further, they are not judged like typical eighteenth-century women. In the logic of the romance text, these women are self-sufficient, exciting, and desirable, and their ability to transcend gender and sexual expectations is at once extraordinary and acceptable. The romance of Bonny and Read is only possible, though, because they are white and European.

Despite the possibilities open to persons of lower-class origins in the transatlantic world of the eighteenth century, their stories are a romance of possibility that obscures the harsh realities that Bannet argues are central to the transatlantic world. Further, whiteness becomes a guarantor of additional freedoms and the possibility of becoming heroines of high seas romance. The legacy of the golden age of piracy, visible through works of literature such as *Treasure Island*, its film adaptations, and other pirate products such as the Pirates of the Caribbean ride at Disney World, its subsequent film adaptations, and pirate-themed television shows like *Black Sails*, points to a predominantly white, adventure-themed legacy of piracy. More specifically, the stories of Bonny and Read similarly function in their retellings as signifiers of the white romance of piracy. According to Burwick and Powell, "post–*General History*, and specifically post–Anne Bonny, they [women] cross-dress in part for mischief and because no one love is enough for their unruly appetites. Their trousers signify less loyalty, than lust."[53] In fact, "it is the latter case, Anne Bonny's, that has ended up being compatible with the sultry she-pirates of more recent years."[54] In *Black Sails*, for example, it is Bonny, not Read, who plays a starring role as *the* female pirate of the show. And although Bonny's character is coded not as "whore" but rather as "faithful mate," she remains imbricated in the structures of gender, race, and nation that characterize her story in the *General History of the . . . Pyrates*.[55]

The stories of Anne Bonny and Mary Read in the *General History of the . . . Pyrates*, as well as their fictional afterlives, suggest that female pirates emblematize a transatlantic subject who offers the fantasy of female empowerment within a white, European context. The sapphic qualities of the female pirate, as exemplified first and foremost through Bonny's character in Read's story, are acknowledged as an alternative, titillating possibility within a dangerous, seafaring world, and which, perhaps, goes hand in hand with stereotypes of the lesbian as embodying one type of female masculinity. The masculine gender performance of both women is, however, disturbed by the likewise titillating body of the female pirate and, specifically, her breasts—which we see underscored in the illustration of Read and Bonny in the Dutch edition of their stories, as shown in figures 5.2 and 5.3. Unlike the joint image from the English edition, where the women pose together, fully dressed, the Dutch edition reimagines these women, explicitly merging masculine and feminine qualities. While the exposed breasts may be titillating and sexualized, these images also literalize the gender fluidity of the women, their power, and the fascinating romance of their masculine/feminine existence. In both images, the masculine garb and stance, as well as the rather phallic seam on the women's trousers, compete visually with the exposed breasts.

Thus, we might surmise that these women are able to negotiate between masculine and feminine expectations as their desires and whims dictate; however, their apparent freedoms are always tied to their status as white women within a transatlantic world marked by excitement and danger, as well as freedom and enslavement. In this way, their stories are not unlike those of other transatlantic white women who take advantage of what the Atlantic world can offer them, often at the expense of enslaved or Indigenous peoples. Aphra Behn's Widow Ranter, for example, reaps the benefits of being a white woman in the British Colonies, and her cross-dressing figures as a whim or eccentricity. By contrast, Semernia, the Indian Queen of Behn's play, is literally caught in the colonial cross fire; *her* cross-dressing

Figure 5.2 Anne Bonny, Dutch edition (*Historia der Engelsche Zee-Roovers*, 1725). © British Library Board. 9555.aaa.1, opposite 221.

Figure 5.3 Mary Read, Dutch edition (*Historia der Engelsche Zee-Roovers*, 1725). © British Library Board. 9555.aaa.1, opposite 222.

eventually leads to her death. Similarly, Daniel Defoe's heroines Moll Flanders and Roxana are able to travel the globe and reap vast rewards for themselves, and their monetary gain is directly linked to global slave trades involving non-European peoples. Gender, sexuality, and desire are at the heart of all these stories and, as the case of Anne Bonny and Mary Read suggests, whiteness functions as a crucial category that enables sexual and gender fluidity, as well as monetary success and social mobility, for European women.

NOTES

1. Charles Johnson, *A General History of the Robberies and Murders of the Most Notorious Pyrates* (London: T. Warner, 1724). References are to this edition unless otherwise noted. Lizabeth Paravisini-Gebert notes that the first publication making mention of Bonny and Read was actually a pamphlet published in Jamaica in 1721. Lizabeth Paravisini-Gebert, "Cross-Dressing on the Margins of Empire: Women Pirates and the Narrative of the Caribbean," in *Women at Sea: Travel Writing and the Margins of Caribbean Discourse*, ed. Lizabeth Paravisini-Gebert and Ivette Romero-Cesareo (New York: Palgrave, 2001), 60.
2. Ubisoft, *Assassin's Creed IV: Black Flag* (Montreal, 2013). *Black Sails*, aired 2014–2017, on Starz.
3. I use the term "plebeian" and "laboring-class" interchangeably in order to signify persons of the lower social classes at this time, but also to describe the virtues that were attributed to this class of persons. Scholars such as Fraser Easton and Catherine Craft-Fairchild have likewise used these terms when writing about cross-dressing women warriors and female husbands of the eighteenth century. For more on the role of class and cross-dressing women, see Catherine Craft-Fairchild, "Cross-Dressing and the Novel: Women Warriors and Domestic Femininity," *Eighteenth-Century Fiction* 10, no. 2 (1998): 171–202; Fraser Easton, "Gender's Two Bodies: Women Warriors, Female Husbands, and Plebeian Life," *Past and Present* 180 (2003): 131–174; and Fraser Easton, "Covering Sexual Disguise: Passing Women and Generic Constraint," *Studies in Eighteenth-Century Culture* 35 (2006): 95–125.
4. The stories of Bonny and Read have clear parallels with the stories of female husbands like the notorious Mary Hamilton and Catherine Vizzani, both of whom cross-dressed in order to seduce other women; the tales of courageous-yet-virtuous female soldiers and sailors like Hannah Snell and Christian Davies; and the widespread tradition of female soldier balladry. For more about the cultural fascination surrounding such women's narratives, see, for example, Theresa Braunschneider, "Acting the Lover: Gender and Desire in Narratives of Passing Women," *Eighteenth Century: Theory and Interpretation* 45, no. 3 (2004): 211–229; Rudolf Dekker and Lotte van de Pol, *The Tradition of Female Transvestism in Early Modern Europe* (New York: St. Martin's Press, 1989); and Julie Wheelwright, *Amazons and Military Maids: Women Who Dressed as Men in the Pursuit of Life, Liberty and Happiness* (London: Pandora, 1989).
5. Dianne Dugaw notes that representations of lower-class cross-dressing women were often in tension with the eighteenth-century "ethos of female delicacy." Authors of such narratives negotiated this tension by describing such women as beautiful, brave, or both. Dianne Dugaw, "Female Sailors Bold: Transvestite Heroines and the Markers of Class and Gender," in *Iron Men, Wooden Women: Gender and Seafaring in the Atlantic World*, ed. Margaret S. Creighton and Lisa Norling (Baltimore: Johns Hopkins University Press, 1996), 35.
6. Eve Tavor Bannet, *Transatlantic Stories and the History of Reading, 1720–1810: Migrant Fictions* (Cambridge: Cambridge University Press, 2011), 4.

7. Laura Doyle, *Freedom's Empire: Race and the Rise of the Novel in Atlantic Modernity, 1640–1940* (Durham, NC: Duke University Press, 2007), 11.
8. Margaret Cohen, *The Novel and the Sea* (Princeton, NJ: Princeton University Press, 2010), 4.
9. The afterlives of Read and Bonny in print culture and onstage are traced in Frederick Burwick and Manushag Powell, *British Pirates in Print and Performance* (New York: Palgrave Macmillan, 2015).
10. A Jamaican printer, Robert Baldwin, published the trial proceedings in a pamphlet that later served as a trial report sent to the Council for Trade in England, as noted in Paravisini-Gebert, "Cross-Dressing," 93n2. Marcus Rediker has traced reports of the women's arrest to the *Boston News-Letter* of December 1720 as well as a pamphlet on the trials published in 1720: *The Tryals of Captain John Rackam and Other Pirates* (Jamaica, 1720). See Marcus Rediker, "Liberty beneath the Jolly Roger: The Lives of Anne Bonny and Mary Read, Pirates," in *Iron Men, Wooden Women: Gender and Seafaring in the Atlantic World*, ed. Margaret S. Creighton and Lisa Norling (Baltimore: Johns Hopkins University Press, 1996), 230n1.
11. Hans Turley, *Rum, Sodomy, and the Lash: Piracy, Sexuality, and Masculine Identity* (New York: New York University Press, 1999), 100. It is also notable that the stories of Bonny and Read are the only ones in the *General History* that also explain how they became pirates and give details about their childhoods.
12. Sally O'Driscoll, "The Pirate's Breasts: Criminal Women and the Meanings of the Body," *The Eighteenth Century* 53, no. 3 (2012): 360.
13. Marcus Rediker, *Between the Devil and the Deep Blue Sea* (Cambridge: Cambridge University Press, 1987), 268.
14. This trope is common in the stories of female soldiers, both in the ballad tradition and in other forms of eighteenth-century print. See Dianne Dugaw, *Warrior Women and Popular Balladry, 1650–1850* (Cambridge: Cambridge University Press, 1989).
15. It was not uncommon for stories of cross-dressing women to attribute their behaviors to earlier cross-dressing tendencies in their childhood, as in actress Charlotte Charke's autobiography. Charlotte Charke, *A Narrative of the Life of Mrs. Charlotte Charke*, ed. Robert Rehder (London: Pickering and Chatto, 1999).
16. Johnson, *General History*, 119.
17. Turley, *Rum, Sodomy, and the Lash*, 98.
18. Johnson, *General History*, 122.
19. Burwick and Powell, *British Pirates*, 132–138.
20. Johnson, *General History*, 122.
21. Turley, *Rum, Sodomy, and the Lash*, 97.
22. Johnson, *General History*, 132.
23. Johnson, *General History*, 133. Rackam's name is spelled variously; the *General History* spells it "Rackam"; in the credits for *Black Sails* it is spelled "Rackham." Thus, I use the spelling for the respective text I am writing about.
24. Charles Johnson, *The History of the Pyrates, Containing the Lives of Captain Misson. Captain Bowen. Captain Kidd. . . . And Their Several Crews* (London: T. Woodward, 1728), 285. This is a reprint of the original *General History* with added materials. The extended title notes: "to the whole is added an appendix, which compleats the lives of the first volume. . . . Collected from journals of pyrates . . . and from those of commanders, who had fallen into their hands."
25. For an overview of the practice of wife sale, see E. P. Thompson, *Customs in Common: Studies in Traditional Popular Culture* (New York: New Press, 1991), 404–466; Samuel Pyeatt Menefee, *Wives for Sale: An Ethnographic Study of British Popular Divorce* (Oxford, UK: Basil Blackwell, 1981); and Lawrence Stone, *The Family, Sex, and Marriage in England, 1500–1800* (New York: Harper, 1977), 40–41.

26. Dugaw has discussed the ways in which lower-class women who cross-dressed for reasons of necessity were often lauded in popular ballads; in many such ballads or stories like that of Snell, the heroines' laboring-class background is emphasized, as well as certain virtues often associated with lower-class life: intrepidity, courage, and resourcefulness. See Dugaw, "Female Sailors Bold," 37–38. Easton also notes that certain virtues associated with warrior women had plebeian connotations, such as "industriousness." Easton, "Gender's Two Bodies," 145.
27. Johnson, *General History*, 132.
28. Johnson, *General History*, 133–134.
29. Johnson, *General History*, 126.
30. O'Driscoll, "The Pirate's Breasts," 365.
31. Although racial categories are still in flux in the early eighteenth century and do not signify in the same way as they do today, I argue that skin color and ethnic or national origins play an important role in defining Read and Bonny within the transatlantic context.
32. See Elizabeth Mancke and Carole Shammas, *The Creation of the British Atlantic World* (Baltimore: Johns Hopkins University Press, 2015), 4; and Bannet, *Transatlantic Stories*, 4, respectively.
33. For more on how lower-class women accessed and performed archetypal male qualities of physical strength and determination, see Dugaw, *Warrior Women and Popular Balladry*. For more on how female cross-dressers appealed to other women and how they used this appeal to their advantage, see Ula Lukszo Klein, "Eighteenth-Century Female Cross-Dressers and Their Beards," *Journal for Early Modern Cultural Studies* 16, no. 4 (Fall 2016): 119–143.
34. *The Female Soldier; or, The Surprising Life and Adventures of Hannah Snell* (1750), Augustan Reprint Society, publication no. 257 (Los Angeles: William Andrews Clark Memorial Library, University of California, 1989), 41.
35. Turley, *Rum, Sodomy, and the Lash*, 40.
36. O'Driscoll, "Pirate's Breasts," 372.
37. O'Driscoll, "Pirate's Breasts," 365.
38. See Susan Lanser, *The Sexuality of History: Modernity and the Sapphic, 1565–1830* (Chicago: University of Chicago Press, 2014); and Klein, "Eighteenth-Century Female Cross-Dressers."
39. Doyle, *Freedom's Empire*, 3.
40. Rediker, "Liberty beneath the Jolly Roger," 15; Paravisini-Gebert, "Cross-Dressing," 66.
41. Turley, *Rum, Sodomy, and the Lash*, 100.
42. Turley, *Rum, Sodomy, and the Lash*, 40.
43. Despite the sapphic resonances she identifies in the text, O'Driscoll ultimately asserts, "The tale of the female pirates displays unease about the possible implications of the misappropriation of gender by bodies sexed as female. It is in this context that the breast takes on a vital role: it becomes the signifier of femaleness that betrays passing women and thus attempts to prove that passing is impossible." O'Driscoll, "Pirate's Breasts," 368.
44. Paravisini-Gebert, "Cross-Dressing," 66.
45. Johnson, *General History*, 120.
46. Johnson, *General History*, 123.
47. Both Londa Schiebinger and Kathleen Wilson have noted how the size and shape of women's breasts took on added importance in the transnational eighteenth century. Schiebinger notes that the eighteenth-century ideal breast was a "virginal" one. The qualities of the virginal breast—small and rounded—were thought to exemplify a civilized society. Schiebinger points out that the colonial enterprise contributed to this classification: "The ideal breast—for all races—was once again young and virginal. Europeans preferred the compact 'hemispherical type,' found, it was said, only among whites and Asians." Londa Schiebinger,

Nature's Body: Gender in the Making of Modern Science (Boston: Beacon Press, 1993), 64. Similarly, Wilson finds evidence for such emphasis on small-breastedness in the eighteenth century. She argues that British historians and writers on the Cook voyages to the Pacific frequently cite the size and shape of native women's breasts to determine the level of civilization in that society. According to Wilson, the ideal eighteenth-century mother had "round and moderately sized breasts with well-formed nipples." Kathleen Wilson, *The Island Race: Englishness, Empire, and Gender in the Eighteenth Century* (New York: Routledge, 2003), 178.

48. See Ruth Perry, "Colonizing the Breast: Sexuality and Maternity in Eighteenth-Century England," in "The State, Society, and the Regulation of Sexuality in Modern Europe," pt. 1, special issue, *Journal of the History of Sexuality* 2, no. 2 (1991): 204–234.
49. Johnson, *General History*, 122.
50. Gretchen J. Woertendyke, "Geography, Genre, and Hemispheric Regionalism," *Atlantic Studies* 10, no. 2 (2013): 214.
51. Cohen, *Novel and the Sea*, 94.
52. Woertendyke, "Geography, Genre," 216.
53. Burwick and Powell, *British Pirates*, 123.
54. Burwick and Powell, *British Pirates*, 132.
55. In *Black Sails*, Bonny and Rackham are central to the plot of the show, and they are lovers, just as in the *General History*. Their relationship becomes complicated, not when Bonny meets Read, but rather when Bonny's relationship with Max, a mixed-race prostitute in the pirate town on New Providence Island, becomes sexual in season 2. As in the *General History*, Bonny must negotiate her relationship with her lovers, especially Rackham, who immediately becomes jealous of her nightly dalliances in Max's bed. The romance of the female pirate persists here: Bonny is strong and willful, while Max is perpetually at risk of being raped, and her rape is a central plot point in the first season. Thus, the female pirate archetype remains defined by whiteness and her alignment with sources of power that are masculine and imperialist, while the prostitute archetype remains defined by weakness, objectification, and her ability to offer comfort while receiving none.

Part Two

FICTIONAL WOMEN'S TRAVELS

6

GENDER PERFORMANCE AND THE SPECTACLE OF FEMALE SUFFERING IN SAMUEL JACKSON PRATT'S *EMMA CORBETT*

Jennifer Golightly

IN THE LAST THIRD OF Samuel Jackson Pratt's epistolary novel *Emma Corbett, or the Miseries of Civil War* (1780), the eponymous heroine has disguised herself as a man and fled from England to the American colonies in an effort to save the man she loves, Henry Hammond, who is fighting in North America with the British army. The merchant ship upon which Emma makes her transatlantic crossing has been attacked, and Emma has been imprisoned in America as an enemy combatant. In his letter to Charles Corbett, Emma's father, Robert Raymond describes how Emma is freed from prison and permitted to search for her lover by General George Washington. In the guise of a Native boy, she seeks out Henry, eventually finds her beloved wounded, and nurses him back to health. Emma's various disguises enable her to survive her voyage to and journey within the war-torn colonies, but it is her display of sensibility—and consequent lapses into insensibility—that enable her to move relatively freely through the country. While Pratt's depiction of an eighteenth-century woman's transatlantic travels read as somewhat familiar—after all, Emma Corbett is not the first female character to don a male disguise in order to cross the Atlantic—*Emma Corbett* offers readers an uncharacteristic image of a transatlantic woman whose performances of gender and sensibility ultimately alter those of the men closest to her and change the way they view patriotism. The role women play in the fictional world of the novel is thus largely representational. It allows Pratt to explore questions about masculinity and femininity raised by the war and to imagine a way in which women—simply by embodying a sensibility that the novel casts as a quality shared by both men and women, Britons and American colonists—could reconcile men on opposite sides of the hostilities between Britain and its colonies in North America.

In *Emma Corbett*, sensibility represents more than the display of female tears and emotion, though both play an important role in the novel. I argue that *Emma Corbett* shows that the display of female sensibility, manifested physically through the body of a suffering woman, has the power to "unman" men in the novel. Moreover, the novel suggests this unmanning is exactly what is needed in a conflict it depicts as civil strife. The spectacle of female suffering—which seems to overcome all disguise—elicits male sensibility. In *Transatlantic Stories and the History of Reading, 1720–1810*, Eve Tavor Bannet points out that Emma in particular takes on different roles open to women at the time, including the position of the woman following men into battle: "Her disguise as a man, the battle on the ship and her capture place her in the subject-position of women like Deborah Sampson who disguised themselves as male soldiers or sailors and fought alongside the men."[1] In order to cross the Atlantic, a liminal space that is neither wholly British nor American, a lawless, international place frequently portrayed as filled with perils of various sorts—marauding pirates, slave ships, French warships, hurricanes, and tempests—Emma adopts the dress of a figure that allows readers to suspend disbelief about the feasibility of a young woman making a transatlantic crossing alone during a time of war with relative ease. During her journey, Emma's sentimental, virtuous femininity is no passport, and her disguise as a young British sailor, a "fair-looking boy," more realistically allows her to travel safely across the ocean.[2] While so disguised, the ship upon which Emma has sailed is attacked, and she is wounded; being a man is in fact no protection in the present circumstances, and she is taken prisoner. Emma is recognized first by Robert Raymond and then by her brother, Edward Corbett, both times revealing her true identity through a display of emotion: she shrieks upon seeing Raymond and sinks to the floor when her brother enters her room. In this scene, Emma's disguise seems to slip away without narrative comment. She is taken prisoner while dressed as a young boy, but in the emotional prison episode with Robert Raymond and her brother, Emma's male disguise goes unremarked by the narrator, and she is, by the end of the scene, clearly identified as a woman: George Washington calls her "the beauteous prisoner" and "she."[3] Once freed from the prison, Emma adopts another disguise to allow her to search for Henry safely in war-torn North America. Using berries to darken her skin, she dresses as an Indigenous person. Her disguise permits her to move through the North American countryside searching for Henry as battles rage around her, but ultimately, as in the case of her previous disguise, Emma's safety consists in revealing her sensibility. Upon discovering Henry's nearly lifeless body in a forest, Emma nurses him and shelters him for days until, when they are both at the point of death, a group of soldiers pass by on their way to provide supplies to a general fighting in the area. Raymond writes to Charles Corbett that it is Emma's "winning address" and the "moving simplicity of her grief" that gain "so entirely upon the soldiers and the people who attended the sledges and wagons, that they administered whatever could promote the wish of Emma, and even furnished her with a sledge, a mule, and a guide, to carry Captain Hammond to John's-Town."[4] There is no clear indication in this episode of whether the soldiers and townspeople see Emma in her male disguise or whether she has set aside her disguise. The focus instead is on Emma's sensibility as a catalyst for the humane treatment she receives.

The novel thus uses sentiment as a code that enables characters to live in a transatlantic world in which hostilities are suspended in recognition of a common moral code. Janet Todd has described sensibility as a "cult," primarily developed through the fiction of the second half of the eighteenth century in Britain. The term "sensibility" conveyed the sensitivity and emotional refinement of the character to whom it was applied. As Todd notes, "sensibility" and "sentiment" were used somewhat interchangeably during the eighteenth century, but "sentiment" carried the added "denotation of moral reflection."[5] Both sensibility and sentiment embody emotion of various sorts, but in the literature of sensibility, the emotion expressed is an indicator of virtue and overall moral worth in a character, particularly when combined with sympathy, or the ability to feel or identify with the emotions expressed by others. In *Emma Corbett,* sensibility elicits sympathy that enables Britons and American colonists to respond to one another not as Britons or Americans but as fellows. Emma's sensibility is part of this sentimental code. For this reason, Emma's displays of sensibility, the excess of which leads to the spectacle of her insensible body, enable her to move freely through war-torn British North America, to enter prison an enemy combatant and leave prison with George Washington's blessing, or to acquire a sledge, a mule, and a guide to save both her own and Henry's life. When strong enough, female suffering recalls men from the vain pursuit of "honor" and glory and refocuses their attention on what is really important in the moral world of the narrative: bonds between fathers and children, brothers and sisters, and lovers. Emma's wordless suffering, her collapse into a near-death state, essentially removes all of the characters involved in the scene from the context of the war and places them outside it. Though the novel's ending raises questions about the long-term prospects for the generation most affected by the war's violence, Emma's suffering, itself in part a product of her transatlantic travel, erases the national identities in which the male characters have so invested themselves and redraws those identities as existing more broadly within the circle of humanity.

PSYCHOSOMATIC SENSIBILITY AND SUFFERING

The sensibility displayed by Pratt's female characters, particularly Emma, is mostly apparent in ways that we would consider psychosomatic. It is the physical manifestation of an excess of emotional pain and produces madness, physical debility, or, frequently in Emma's case, something akin to a "corpse-like" state. G. J. Barker-Benfield has discussed the ways in which novels of sensibility use the manifestation of emotion through the body as a technique for conveying what is otherwise internal and thus fundamentally inexpressible.[6] Physiological symptoms such as tears, trembling, sighing, blushing, and fainting were codes for internal emotion so strong that it overwhelmed the individual experiencing it (but was difficult for the author of a novel to convey without descriptions of its physical manifestation).

Pain, in the lexicon of the British novels of the mid-eighteenth century, could be a physical condition, but it could just as often indicate an intellectual state. Barker-Benfield in particular has explored the ways that such an intellectual state, produced by an excess of feeling, could evoke a physical response in the body. However, as Bill Wandless points out, Enlightenment theorists such as Anthony Ashley Cooper, third Earl of Shaftesbury, Francis Hutcheson, and David Hume associated pain with morality, an association adapted and used frequently in sentimental British novels of the later part of the eighteenth century.[7] According to Wandless, the depiction of pain in the fiction of this period "evokes moral response. . . . Pain becomes a reliable and productive index of character, an essence that confirms appearance in various ways and may be turned to various uses."[8] As Wandless suggests, the portrayal of pain in eighteenth-century novels prompts readers to determine value and make judgments: "The novel of sensibility explored the means by which an audience could make sense of an author's techniques, a character's behavior, and the reader's own affective responses."[9] Indeed, Pratt's use of pain is strongly connected with morality in *Emma Corbett*.

Emma suffers pain because she is both humane and moral and thus cannot withstand the brutality that the men she loves are working to inflict on those who disagree with them. Her suffering is emotional but is expressed physically, and the degree of her suffering is indicative of her morality, which, in the novel, is rooted in her pacifism. Thus, in line with Barker-Benfield's arguments about sensibility and its connection to physiology, I use suffering and pain here to mean the experience of physical debility or sickness produced by an excess of emotion. Instead of being able to express her emotion verbally, as she frequently does with great power, Emma, at various points in the text, faints, drops on the floor, sickens, withdraws, loses her bloom, becomes pale and listless, and eventually dies. By the end of the novel, both Emma and her sister-in-law, Louisa Corbett (née Hammond), are dead. The spectacle of dying or dead women recalls the men around them to humanity (portrayed in the novel as prioritization of family over nation) from the brutality into which the war and their roles in the war—patriot, soldier, citizen—have cast them.

GENDER PERFORMANCE

Recent scholarship on Pratt's novel has focused on the text's insistent questioning of identity in terms of national, personal, and gender boundaries.[10] In "Gender, Neutrality, and the Nursing Father in Pratt's *Emma Corbett*," Trevor McMichael argues that "Pratt explored a variety of gender identities in a process that linked proper masculine hybridity, a hybrid of balanced feminine and masculine sides, to psychological balance, political neutrality, and domestic efficacy."[11] McMichael argues that the novel shows the need for men to restrain their own sensibility so they do not risk becoming "too emotional or effeminate" (280). As McMichael points out, one of the emotions to which men were particularly susceptible, one that *Emma Corbett* shows as most requiring regulation, was patriotism, which was dangerous "precisely because it can lead men either to behave effeminately or too emotionally" (279). McMichael writes that "Pratt argues for stable gender identities in *Emma Corbett*, especially for women in their conventional function as mothers in this period," and he argues that "Emma paradoxically . . . reflects cultural anxieties about women subverting proper feminine conduct" (284). However, McMichael's argument overlooks the fact that all of the mothers are dead by the end of the novel and that rather than pointing to the need for men to restrain their own sensibility, the novel concludes with two older men, one of whom has learned at great cost to express rather than restrain his sensibility, who will provide maternal and paternal nurturing to the two children orphaned by the war. While the novel's conclusion is not wholly optimistic about the fate of the generation of young people fighting in the war, it depicts Robert Raymond and Charles Corbett as embracing traditionally feminine qualities of sympathy, nurturing, and compassion in order to raise the children orphaned as a result of the war.

Rather than insisting on the performance of traditional gender roles, the novel instead provides a series of examples that demonstrate how in the Britain and North America of the revolution everything, including national and gender identity, has been turned upside down. Emma's decision to travel to North America in male disguise marks the true beginning of this dilemma. In his essay "The English Problem of Identity in the American Revolution," Dror Wahrman argues that "subverted gender boundaries" served as a "metonymic representation of the

American war."[12] Wahrman writes that the late 1770s "witnessed a far-reaching shift in cultural attitudes toward gender categories and their possible limitations," a shift that Wahrman suggests is represented in Pratt's novel through Emma's cross-dressing and assumption of masculine roles.[13] Wahrman sees Pratt as depicting Emma's cross-dressing as a "disruption of nature in the shape of a woman forced—against her nature, of course, but also against the narrative logic of the novel—to dress as a man" in order to depict the unnaturalness of the conflict itself.[14] For Wahrman, *Emma Corbett* is one example of a fairly numerous body of works across genres—textual, visual, spectacular—published or staged around the time of the American Revolution that use gender to discuss "the bigger issues of identity categories and their threatening inadequacies as they were raised by this crisis."[15]

It is Emma's love for Henry Hammond and her determination to be with him that prompts her to cross the Atlantic and simultaneously transgress conventional gender roles assigned to women. Bannet suggests that Pratt's novel shows Emma moving through different "subject positions": as "daughter, whose first challenge is to determine where her duty lies" and then as "the woman who chose not to stay behind when men went to war."[16] Bannet argues that though Pratt intended Emma to be "the hero whose actions in wartime are supposed to command the reader's wonder and admiration," Emma's death ultimately suggests "Pratt did not view her as the model of female conduct that was going to be desirable or appropriate once peace was restored."[17] The problem is that there are no women present at all at the end of the narrative, so it is hard to determine which character the novel presents as an appropriate model for female conduct at the novel's end: Louisa and Emma, the two primary female characters in the novel, are both dead. The only other woman who has a voice in the text is on the fringes of the plot. She is Caroline Arnold and primarily serves as a companion and nurse to Louisa and a onetime correspondent to Emma, sending her, in response to Emma's questions about how it is possible to reconcile the infliction of death and injury upon humanity with claims of masculine honor, the fragmentary story of the Carbine family. By the end of the novel, though, Caroline Arnold has been silent for forty-three pages, and because there is relatively little attention paid to her, it seems unlikely that Pratt identified her as an appropriate model of female conduct either.

I suggest Emma is the model Pratt has in mind even though the women in the text are more valuable when they are dead, enshrined in male memory as having suffered to the ultimate extent as a result of the actions of the men they leave behind. The memories of dead women who suffered in consequence of male pursuit of public fame serve as an enduring touchstone to perpetually elicit male sensibility. *Emma Corbett* is not unique in using "the spectacle of suffering womanhood to elicit the melting humanity of male onlookers," as Claudia L. Johnson has argued.[18] Moreover, sentimental novels use spectacle as a means of eliciting sympathy, not just from other characters in the novel, but from the reader as well. The sentimental spectacle of suffering women positioned eighteenth-century readers, British and colonial American, alongside the male characters in the novel who are moved to renounce nationalistic and patriotic ambitions in favor of affective ties of affinity, brotherhood, and sympathetic identification. The novel therefore has an explicitly political if not partisan agenda: it aims to use the sentimental response to question the necessity of a war that many in Britain viewed as akin to a civil war waged against fellow British citizens and to unite these readers by highlighting values shared by both sides.

Readers of Pratt's novel are cued to understand the suffering of women in exactly this way by the inclusion of the Carbine fragment, enclosed in a letter from Caroline Arnold to Emma near the opening of the narrative. The fragment tells the story of two brothers, Nestor and Julius, both of whom have dedicated their lives to serving their country as soldiers. Nestor, the eldest, is a "remnant" of a man: one leg and a foot have been amputated, and his face is so scarred from battle on one side that the narrator of the fragment describes him as having only "the residue of a face."[19] Julius, the younger brother, is likewise missing one leg, lost to a parapet, and an arm, in addition to most of one side of his face and half an ear. The narrator of the fragment describes the brothers as having left their now invisible limbs "scattered in different quarters of the globe."[20] The dedication of the brothers to warfare as a career is made clear by their given names—Roman names—and by their surname, Carbine, a word used to describe a type of weapon since the beginning of the seventeenth century. Their professionalism as soldiers is further emphasized by Nestor's commitment to outfitting and educating his six young sons in preparation for their own careers as soldiers. Nestor has been forced to assume the roles of both mother and father to his six sons and one daughter after the death of their mother, who dies after dutifully nursing Nestor through a fever, which she then contracts. The memory of this dead, dutiful wife is evoked several times in the Carbine fragment and serves to move both Carbine brothers, but particularly Nestor, to tears.

The story of the Carbine family establishes a framework through which readers of Pratt's text can understand the behavior of Emma and the men who love her. In sending it, Caroline claims that the Carbines' story will demonstrate to Emma that "humanity and bravery are nearly allied, and that the tender husband and good soldier often form the same character, though they cannot always exert themselves in the same moment; or, perhaps, were we to scrutinize nicely, we should, in reality, find, that when the soldier is hazarding his life and liberty for that of his wife, his children, his countrymen, and his King, he is *then* the tenderest lover, the worthiest husband, the best parent, the most loyal subject, and the most valuable citizen."[21] Caroline's reading of the fragment and indeed of Emma's circumstance opposes not only Emma's own, but also that advanced by the novel itself. Emma cannot read the actions committed by soldiers in the name of war as anything but brutal and dehumanizing, and she cannot reconcile the soldier's duties with the ones required of men as fathers, brothers, husbands, and sons. The Carbine fragment points to an ongoing tension in the novel between the obligations of humanity, which the novel broadly associates with those of domestic life, and the demands of the life of a soldier. While Emma's father and lover see their civic duties as tied to the needs of their countries, she sees family, not country, as the center of society. The pathos of the Carbine fragment makes clear that the novel supports Emma's evaluation of which of these—family or country—should be primary. Both brothers are mutilated beyond recognition as a result of their time as soldiers, and the reader understands that though the Carbines recognize the depth of their sacrifice—the loss of their health, their physical integrity, and, in the case of Nestor, his wife—they still cannot, due at least in part to their social class, prioritize what should be most important, a fact made clear by the instruction of Nestor's small sons in the arts of war. Though it does not, as Caroline hopes it will, soothe Emma's fears and reconcile her to the need for men to kill other men in the name of country, the Carbine fragment is crucial in preparing the reader of Pratt's novel for the destiny that awaits Emma and Louisa. By the end of the novel, we know, both women will be dead as a result of the actions of the men around them, and their suffering will serve, much as Frances Carbine's does, as a spectacle that will elicit remorse from the men who loved them.

THE POWER OF SENSIBILITY TO REFORM MEN

After Emma leaves England in pursuit of Henry, it is increasingly Robert Raymond who reports, journal-style, to Charles Corbett what Emma says and does. This shift is significant because it coincides with an increase in episodes in which displays of Emma's sensibility move the narrative action forward. These episodes demonstrate more than Emma's conventional femininity; they show her disengagement with masculine, military attitudes evinced by many of the male characters in the novel. Rather than writing letters demonstrating this sensibility, Emma enacts the emotion she feels physically, either through a kind of despondent though determined activity, characterized by physical debilitation, weakness, or illness, or by a lapse into lifelessness, which has the effect of resolving conflicts between the male characters in the novel, even suspending the pursuit of fighting by Edward and Henry.

The first of these incidents, narrated by Robert Raymond in a letter to his silent correspondent, Frederick Berkeley, focuses upon Emma's resistance to notions of martial honor and military glory, indicating her emphasis instead upon humanity, love, and pacifism. The episode takes place before Emma leaves England, when Raymond finds her in the library at Castleberry contemplating a painting. The painting depicts a battle scene. Emma, who is recovering from an illness brought on by her father's insistence that she renounce her love for Henry, describes to Raymond her feelings upon looking at various pieces of the scene and becomes increasingly frenzied: "In that lacerated body there yet seems life. It is panting in the picture!—how the streams of—Ah, my God! the hoof of a horse seems ready to stamp upon his bosom—another sword is pointed at his throat.—Stop, stop barbarian—he is of thy *kind*—he is thy fellow-creature—perhaps he is closely, dearly, TENDERLY connected—restrain thy sacrilegious hand—kill not her whose existence is interwoven with his—kill not his helpless *children*—respect the tender state of unprotected infancy."[22] Emma cannot sustain the emotions that overwhelm her when she considers the women and children left behind by these soldiers, who will suffer as much, if not more, than the soldiers themselves. The broken nature of her speech, demonstrated by Pratt's frequent use of dashes and Emma's incomplete sentences, which begin before she can finish articulating her previous thought, indicates the swell of emotion Emma experiences as she gazes upon the bloody scenes depicted in the painting. Ultimately, Raymond writes to Berkeley, "She fell lifeless on the floor. Her soul was filled with images of the deepest horror. It was a noble frenzy of tenderness and humanity, but it trod too quickly on her late recovery.—She is again carried to her bed" (144). As in similar instances later in the novel, Emma's fall into lifelessness serves to remove a source of conflict between men: as a result of her collapse, Raymond tells Emma's father he will no longer seek Emma's hand in marriage because it is clear she is in love with Henry. From this point forward, Raymond strives to use reason to control his love for Emma, which grows rather than abates, and he becomes her friend, ally, and protector rather than suitor.

A second incident revealing the sympathetic power of Emma's sensibility is the one with which this essay begins. Emma's shock at the sight of her brother, whom she has heretofore believed dead, causes her to fall unconscious on the floor of the prison. The spectacle of Emma's lifeless body is enough to secure her own and Robert Raymond's release from the prison into which they have been thrown after both have been captured by colonial forces during their transatlantic crossing. This spectacle is also enough to prompt General George Washington, under whose command Edward Corbett is fighting, to weep upon hearing of Emma's attempts to reach Henry. In an interview with Raymond, Washington declares that he is "not at war with the *affections*. Ever privileged be *their* emotions"; he continues, "I feel them all. The beauteous prisoner is at liberty, Sir Robert, to go where she pleases. I shall appoint persons to attend her, who may prevent all interruption and insult; but *you*, methinks, Sir Robert, should continue to follow her fortunes as a *friend*,—you are *both* free" (182). Washington consequently allows Edward a temporary relief from his duties so that he may spend time with his sister. Like Henry at the beginning of the novel, Edward is nearly "unmanned" by the sight of his sister and the revelation she makes to him of the birth of his son. Robert Raymond writes that he enters the room after his interview with Washington to find Edward and Emma weeping together: "Your son was pronouncing, or rather attempting to pronounce, the names of wife and parent, of Louisa and his little Edward" (183). Emma's presence and her conversation with Edward, all of which centers upon the same themes of love, family, home, parents, spouses, and children, force Edward to drop "for a while the fierceness of the soldier, and [act] as a man—as the child of nature—as the husband of Louisa, and the brother of Emma" (183). By the end of the scene, Edward has to beg Raymond to remove Emma from his arms because "she is gaining on [his] emotions," and Edward is afraid, if given "leisure to reflect" or "opportunity to consider the consequences," he will renounce his commitment to fighting to defend his country and property. The consequence, as it turns out, is Edward's own death, which occurs only a few pages after Raymond and Emma leave him to continue Emma's pursuit of Henry. Edward cannot "support [their] departure," and so seeks permission from Washington to follow Emma and either "guide her to the arms of Henry, or persuade her to return" (187). On his way to Emma, Edward encounters a party of English soldiers who are burning a village and is killed by them as he attempts to defend the colonists living there.

A third incident revealing the power of Emma's sensibility to reform the men in the novel occurs immediately after Emma learns of Edward's death. After burying her brother, Emma receives reports of Henry, whom she believes to be dead. News of Henry's death and a reminder from Raymond of her father, to whom he is writing, cause Emma to lapse from speech into lifelessness: "I have ventured to whisper it very softly to Emma, that I am about to seal the packet that my trembling hand has written as it could snatch the flying minute—'*To my father*!' said she. Oh God, oh God! Tell—tell him—Here she folded her arms, looked up to heaven, tried to articulate more, and sunk upon the bed" (191). Raymond's whisper at the moment Emma learns of Henry's (false) death recalls her father's intractability on the subject of Emma's love for Henry, and her collapse while she is trying to find words to relay to her father serves as a reproach to him. In letters to Charles Corbett, Raymond describes the spectacle of Emma's inert body, lying speechless and near death: "The silver chord is not quite broken: yet the cold, cold dews descend so fast—No—I have, after the pause of another hour, visited her again. In her pulse there is yet promise. In her eye there is yet hope" (191). Raymond's certainty that Emma is near death leads him to deplore the war that has caused so much misery, not just within the Corbett family, but to families across Britain and North America: "Unfortunate Corbett! This fatal war has reduced all the honours and blessings of your house to the dust! Alas! how many thousand fathers besides has it not wounded beyond the reach of this world's remedies?" (191). The point here is not that Raymond himself has just recognized the cost of the war but that these scenes, described in great detail to the most intractable man in the novel, Charles Corbett, serve to provide an ongoing scourge to a father who was once willing to sacrifice everything, even his daughter, for the love of his country.

The novel's point that women embody the suffering and anguish caused by the war is driven home in a fourth incident that begins when Emma, disguised as a Native boy, locates Henry, who is alive but at the point of death. Emma sets out alone to find Henry's body so that she can "pay to him the mournful offices which she has paid to Edward" (193). She finds Henry "lying as dead, with an arrow sticking in his bosom" (194). Emma removes the arrow, and, because she has "heard of the Indians using shafts whose points were envenomed," she sucks the poison out of Henry's wound, enabling his recovery but ensuring her own eventual death. In the months that follow their marriage, the poison that Emma has ingested begins to manifest itself in her physical decline, a metaphor for the poison spread by the war. When he learns that the venom Emma removed from his wound is the source of her illness, Henry realizes that he is to blame for her inevitable death. The spectacle of Emma's weakening body leads Henry to renounce his participation in any further warfare: "Yes, Sir Robert, I and only I have murdered her. I am the accursed cause. . . . Curse on the war! I will have no more to do with it" (209). Once again, though she is physically weak and knows she is destined to die, Emma works to save Henry's life, asking Raymond to pretend with her that they have found a cure for the poison. Their scheme backfires when Henry proves unable to withstand the drastic movements between happiness and despair and dies. Emma, who has discovered she is pregnant, returns to Britain with Robert Raymond—a return that is remarkably uncomplicated, given the disguises, attacks, and captures that characterized their journey to North America. They arrive at the Corbett house in time to see Louisa's coffin being borne away: Louisa, tormented by a succession of grief, joy, and renewed grief, has gone mad, declined, and died. Emma's death follows shortly after she gives birth to a baby girl, whom she leaves to be raised by Raymond with Louisa and Edward's son. The sight of the distracted Louisa, coupled with Raymond's detailed accounts of Emma's suffering, have caused Charles Corbett to renounce his partisanship and to pray instead only that the conflict might end quickly. The novel ends with Raymond taking on the role of what Bannet and McMichael have termed "the nursing father": Raymond will perform the duties of both mother and father to the children left behind by the dead couples and, what is more, will continue to educate Charles Corbett to undertake the same role.[23] The novel's ending ostensibly provides hope for a new social order outside of the theater of war, one in which national identities have been submerged under the more significant ties of family and love.

However, the novel's end is not unequivocal in the hope it provides for the future of British society. What are we to make of the fact that there are no women left alive by the end of the novel, and that, like the Carbine family, Robert Raymond and Charles Corbett are left in their old age to raise the children orphaned by the young adults in the novel? Emma's challenging of the code of martial masculinity is most effective when she is lifeless, either due to a lapse into insensibility as a result of excessive sensibility or, eventually, from her actual death. The spectacle of Emma's inert body can reform the men around her, but this reformation comes too late for the younger generation of men to be effective. As Kate Davies argues, by the end of the 1770s, images of the "violated or abandoned national body of 1775" had been replaced with images of "monstrous maternity": women "nursing dead children or consuming their own offspring."[24] Emma's suckling of the poison from Henry's chest after he has been shot with a poison-tipped arrow is one example of the monstrous maternity of which Davies writes. The deaths of all of the women in the novel—all of whom are mothers by the end—is another kind of monstrosity. Within this context, a nation of children without mothers or fathers, raised by older men who have assumed an oddly maternal kind of role, it is difficult to see the novel's ending as without some reservation about the hope it offers for a reformed society.

From the outset, it is clear that *Emma Corbett* is engaged in a variety of complex debates about identity, gender, and nationality created by Britain's imperial project but made sharper by the onset of hostilities between Britain and the North American colonists. Bannet writes that in *Emma Corbett*, Pratt "put the transatlantically shared soldierly ideal under such pressure that it cracked apart to reveal conflicts between honor and humanity, duty and sensibility, reason and loyalty, ideology and reality."[25] The novel applies this pressure to the soldierly ideal Bannet describes by simulating and ultimately embracing the deaths of its female characters. In addition to these fissures, the novel investigates questions made sharper by the war: the nature of public and private and masculinity and femininity. Emma in particular is preoccupied with these questions and with the tension between honor and humanity. She, like Robert Raymond, cannot convince herself that honor should be placed above humanity or indeed that there is honor to be gained from participating in the deaths of fellow human beings. Throughout the novel, from the time of Henry's departure, Emma argues for the superiority of demands made by family, love, and home over those of fortune, fame, glory, honor, or property. The conflict between the demands of "public" life upon men and their subsequent neglect of the "private" duties of the home and family is a central problem in *Emma Corbett*, and it is resolved only at the end of the novel when both Charles Corbett and Henry Hammond have disavowed their partisanship and national identity in favor of family bonds. This disavowal comes at a huge cost, however. Though there are moments throughout the text where Edward, Charles, and Henry are all on the brink of recognizing their folly in pursuing the war, it is only when they are confronted with the spectacle of women suffering to the utmost extent—women who are near death, distracted, or dead—that these male characters are recalled from their engagement with problems of property, patriotism, and national identity and are made to realize the importance of the bonds of love, family, and home.

NOTES

1. Eve Tavor Bannet, *Transatlantic Stories and the History of Reading, 1720–1810: Migrant Fictions* (Cambridge: Cambridge University Press, 2011), 220.
2. Samuel Jackson Pratt, *Emma Corbett, or the Miseries of Civil War*, ed. Eve Tavor Bannet (Peterborough, ON: Broadview Press, 2011), 179.
3. Pratt, *Emma Corbett*, 182.
4. Pratt, *Emma Corbett*, 196.
5. See Janet Todd, *Sensibility: An Introduction* (London: Methuen, 1986), 7.
6. See G. J. Barker-Benfield, *The Culture of Sensibility: Sex and Society in Eighteenth-Century Britain* (Chicago: University of Chicago Press, 1992). For good introductions to the culture of sensibility and how it became pervasive in British novels of the later part of the eighteenth century, see Todd, *Sensibility*; and John Mullan, *Sentiment and Sociability: The Language of Feeling in the Eighteenth Century* (Oxford: Clarendon Press, 1990). More recently, Lynn Festa has described the ways in which "sentimental identification" became "the primary means of representing metropolitan relations with colonial populations," working both to create and complicate sympathy between colonizer and colonized. Lynn Festa, *Sentimental Figures of Empire in Eighteenth-Century Britain and France* (Baltimore: Johns Hopkins University Press, 2006), 3.
7. Bill Wandless, "Narrative Pain and the Moral Sense: Towards an Ethics of Suffering in the Long Eighteenth Century," *Literature and Medicine* 24, no. 1 (2005): 51–69.
8. Wandless, "Narrative Pain," 53.
9. Wandless, "Narrative Pain," 67.
10. Scholarship on Pratt's novel is still limited but has increased over the past ten years. Of the recent studies, one of the most interesting is Christopher Flynn, *Americans in British Literature, 1770–1832: A Breed Apart* (Burlington, VT: Ashgate, 2008). Flynn argues that the epistolary format of the novel allows for acts of reading that recreate sympathetic bonds between the characters and in the readers of the novel themselves. As Emma reads accounts

of warfare such as the Carbine fragment or views the battle scene in the painting in the library at Castleberry, she suffers and, Flynn writes, "presumably, the late eighteenth-century reader did as well" (27).

11. Trevor McMichael, "Gender, Neutrality, and the Nursing Father in Pratt's *Emma Corbett*," *The Eighteenth Century* 56, no. 3 (Fall 2015): 279.
12. Dror Wahrman, "The English Problem of Identity in the American Revolution," *American Historical Review* 106, no. 4 (October 2001): 1253. Wahrman's essay and subsequent book on the subject of national identity in the wake of the American Revolution is one of several that have been published over the past twenty years. The role of national literatures in the emergence of political identities in Britain and America is examined in Paul Giles, *Transatlantic Insurrections: British Culture and the Formation of American Literature, 1730–1860* (Philadelphia: University of Pennsylvania Press, 2001). For a discussion of the ways in which sensibility and masculinity were fused during the American Revolution to create a "transatlantic of masculine politeness" that was part of the soldierly code of conduct on both sides, thus diminishing difference based on nationality, see Sarah Knott, "Sensibility and the American War for Independence," *American Historical Review* 109, no. 1 (February 2004): 19–40.
13. Wahrman, "English Problem," 1253.
14. Wahrman, "English Problem," 1252.
15. Wahrman, "English Problem," 1251.
16. Bannet, *Transatlantic Stories*, 220.
17. Bannet, *Transatlantic Stories*, 219, 223.
18. Claudia L. Johnson, *Equivocal Beings: Politics, Gender, and Sentimentality in the 1790s* (Chicago: University of Chicago Press, 1995), 6.
19. Pratt, *Emma Corbett*, 118.
20. Pratt, *Emma Corbett*, 117.
21. Pratt, *Emma Corbett*, 136.
22. Pratt, *Emma Corbett*, 143.
23. See Bannet, *Transatlantic Stories*, 227, and McMichael, "Gender, Neutrality."
24. Kate Davies, *Catharine Macaulay and Mercy Otis Warren: The Revolutionary Atlantic and the Politics of Gender* (Oxford: Oxford University Press, 2005), 164.
25. Bannet, *Transatlantic Stories*, 216.

7

"THAT PERSON SHALL BE A WOMAN"

Matriarchal Authority and the Fantasy of Female Power in *The Female American*

Alexis McQuigge

The Female American (1767)—AN AUTOBIOGRAPHICAL tale purportedly written by a biracial, bicultural woman named Unca Eliza Winkfield, which is likely a pseudonym for a non-Indigenous person writing fiction—has been read as a text of female subordination, a proto-feminist and anti-patriarchal work, and a novel that results in the brief establishment of a "feminist colonial utopia."[1] The problem of authorship and the many and conflicting readings of this text point to a major difficulty readers face when approaching this work: the ideological complications of the text itself disrupt any attempt at a straightforward reading of it. Readers of this text have rightly read it as a work that ultimately promotes the British colonial drive and holds Britishness and Christianity as the utmost marker of civilization. Unca Eliza's attempts to convert Indigenous islanders during the later part of the text and her capitulation to her cousin's request for marriage and the surrender of her authority at the end of the novel model the Christian, European, colonizing ways of her father's culture. For instance, Unca Eliza is adamant about using the giant, hollow idol and its remarkable acoustics to "speak to the Indians from thence, and endeavor to convert them from their idolatry," rather than simply as a place to hide.[2] Likewise, she uses the authority that the islanders give this idol as a vehicle for both missionary work and a land grab: from inside the idol, she demands that the Indigenous people "do every thing she shall command [them]," "never hinder her," "do as she shall instruct [them], and never presume . . . to do any thing that she forbids."[3] The position of religious supremacy she assumes over her adopted Indigenous community is not in question in this reading of the text, nor is the dissatisfaction many readers experience when the novel ends with Unca Eliza being relegated to the position of the colonized wife of a missionary and becoming a bit player in her own story.

However, *The Female American* offers readers a fantasy of female autonomy that, despite Unca Eliza's Englishness, flourishes at key moments in the text. The ability to entertain this fantasy comes from Unca Eliza's matriarchal connection to the status of her mother and her aunt as Native American royalty, though the full realization of this fantasy is precluded by the heroine's commitment to the Christianity and culture of her father. Critics of the novel have frequently pointed to the heroine's hybridized racial identity, but fewer have sought out the moments when Unca Eliza Winkfield's English sensibilities, are, albeit briefly and fleetingly, dominated by the matriarchal traditions and power she draws on to achieve her colonial goals. These moments are ultimately overshadowed by the entrance of British authority in the person of her cousin and by Unca Eliza's own commitment to missionary work, but they allow readers—in particular white readers, some of whom are women—to envision what a life outside of the prescriptions of British culture might look like for the protagonist. These moments allow readers to reflect on the power she assumes when she aligns herself with her matriarchal rather than patriarchal heritage.

Scholars, such as Ann Beebe and Scarlet Bowen, have discussed the power that Unca Eliza's mother and aunt possess within their community, which in Bowen's words is "symbolically figured as a bow and arrow [Unca Eliza] receives from her aunt."[4] Bowen notes that Unca Eliza's mother and aunt have the right to "choose their husbands and propose marriage, the right to rule their tribes as 'queens,' and the ability to hunt using a bow and arrow."[5] In the middle section of the text, Unca Eliza's identification with this autonomy influences the way she employs her narrative to formulate a fantasy of female empowerment derived from her female forbearers. Even though *The Female American* certainly shows the protagonist behaving in ways inherited from her father's colonialist, Christian world—one bent on perpetrating coercion, subordination, and violence to literally gain ground through conversion—Unca Eliza's connection to her mother's heritage should be considered in light of the ways that it posits a briefly gained, but ultimately spectacularly lost, fantasy of female empowerment.

UNCA AND ALLUCA: MATRILINEAL ANCESTORS

As both Kristianne Kalata Vaccaro and Beebe have argued, Unca Eliza shifts her personas throughout the text. According to Vaccaro, Unca Eliza fulfills roles "ranging from author, narrator, and protagonist to historian, spiritual imperialist, and clergyman's wife," and Beebe notes that "she writes, directs, produces, and stars in an elaborate conversion scene worthy of any London playhouse."[6] Once marooned, Unca Eliza embraces more of the heritage personified by her mother and aunt in the early part of the novel, in spite of years of education in proper English femininity. While her notions of herself as a powerful woman with rights to self-governance are beyond those given to women in England, they are granted to women of her mother's lineage, and Unca Eliza embraces that autonomy to achieve her missionary goals. Though these traditions are no doubt based more on stereotypes of Indigenous people, rather than on factual representations, they influence how this novel negotiates Unca Eliza's, her mother's, and her aunt's autonomy. As Tim Fulford writes, for many people in England, Native American heritage "was reckoned through the matrilineal line."[7] Likewise, Bowen suggests that Britons believed that there was "gender egalitarianism present in many Native American cultures."[8] Unca Eliza's narrative draws on these beliefs to create a heroine who briefly exercises that egalitarianism, even if it is for rather unfortunate and disappointing goals. Unca Eliza, as authorial voice, signals that the expectations of this text are different from those of a domestic novel by noting that though "lives of women" are "commonly domestick," her narrative will not fit this profile.[9]

Bearing in mind the way the novel ends, readers should still consider the parts of the work where Unca Eliza's life differs from, rather than mirrors, that of a "commonly domestick" woman. During the "wonderful, strange, and uncommon" events of her life, one thing becomes clear: her cultural hybridity both grants her freedom to act in ways that Englishwomen were not encouraged to behave and opens the door to moments of power most women were not encouraged to experience. Unca Eliza declares that her life serves to "[effect] a more happy issue to [her] future adventures than could otherwise have happened" (46). Considering the reluctance Unca Eliza feels about marrying John and her position after they wed, these "future adventures" may not necessarily refer to her life at the end of the novel. Instead, we might read them in terms of a fantasy of female power in which Unca Eliza acts of her own accord, as did her mother and aunt. While for readers today this novel may preclude a satisfying conclusion to Unca Eliza Winkfield's "adventures," it, at the very least, allows her space to have them. Unca Eliza's maternal heritage is key to thinking about this work as a space in which women gain autonomy and exercise authority.

The relationship between Unca Eliza's father, mother, and aunt first suggests the possibilities that the text offers for female freedom. Early in the novel Unca Eliza's father, William, is taken captive by an Indigenous nation after a retaliatory raid on the Jamestown colony in Virginia. William faces beheading until, at the last minute, Unca (Unca Eliza's mother) chooses to save him. "Just as the executioner was about to give the stroke," a woman "who was one of the king's daughters" emerged, dressed in "jewels, diamonds, and solid pieces of gold and silver" (49).

The woman then "stroke[s] [Unca Eliza's] father with a wand" in an apparent "signal for deliverance" (49). That Unca Eliza's mother has the authority to save William from certain death at the hands of the men in her community suggests a culture radically different from the one in which eighteenth-century English readers of this text lived. It is also worth noting that though William is untied, he is not free. He is dressed in "a covering, like that the Indians wore," and "a kind of chain, formed of long grass" is put around his neck. With the "chain" around his neck, Unca "led him . . . to a bower" (49). The use of both "chain" and "led" in the text elicits clear signs of bondage and imprisonment. The power that Unca has over him in this moment is clear and foreshadows the power that Unca Eliza believes she holds over the islanders when she speaks to them from within the idol.

In the private moments between them, the power Unca has in the community is always clear. When Unca and William enter the bower, Unca "ma[kes] [William] sit" and then "seat[s] herself by him," where she "view[s] him with great attention from head to foot" and feels "his face and hands" (49). This act of surveying is an act of ownership (much like the moments when Unca Eliza surveys "her" islanders from within the idol), and their relationship unfolds in a series of commands Unca gives to William. When they enter the bower, she "ma[kes] a sign to him to lie down" and lays down her bow and "quiver filled with arrows" by the door (49). The reversal of the expected relationship between a white, European man and an Indigenous woman signals that this novel is approaching expectations of power differently than many texts of its time. The signs of authority Unca uses—looking upon him as a possession, commanding him to do things, carrying a weapon during their exchange—both highlight that William is the subordinate in this relationship and suggest that women are permitted to hold positions of power and can guarantee those positions with threats of violence. With death as his only alternative, the narrator tells us that William "compos[es] [his] mind" to do as Unca tells him, and his subjection to her desires continues as long as they live according to Indigenous rather than English custom (49). As Unca and her still-chained prisoner approach her father, Unca "present[s] the end of the chain she held to her father, who with much seeming affability return[s] it to his daughter. By this act [Unca Eliza's] father understood he gave him as a captive to his daughter" (50). Though Unca breaks the chain immediately after this exchange, leading William to "conceive her actions as declarative of his liberty," there is no suggestion that he will be allowed his freedom. His clothes "together with those of his less happy companions" are returned to him, but his freedom is not (50). William's dress in this moment becomes a sign of his status: he is literally wearing the clothes of his murdered friends, and his subjection can clearly be seen in his possession of them.

Impediments to this matriarchal control arise, however, as soon as William feels safe enough in the community (a privilege granted to him through his relationship with Unca) to assert the power he believes he holds as a Christian and an Englishman. After he lives within the community for months, Unca eventually proposes (or demands) their marriage (51). This proposal is a sign of her authority over William, yet in marrying, she loses command over him, herself, and her community. In response to her proposal, William demands Unca's conversion to Christianity, which ultimately forces her into the position of the culturally appropriate English housewife seen in so many novels of the period. Here we might see in Unca and William's relationship a likeness to the Pocahontas–John Smith story. Unfortunately, the circumstances of Unca's marriage ultimately leave her in the same position as Pocahontas and many Englishwomen, and in the position of her own daughter at the end of the novel: forced to surrender much of her identity and the power that comes with it to fit into her husband's life.

In addition to its depiction of Unca and William's relationship, *The Female American* offers a second representation of women's command—particularly in the character of Alluca, Unca's older sister. Having fallen in love with William, Alluca corners him and demands their marriage. William completely misreads the force of Alluca's demands, and this misreading suggests that within the boundaries of his own culture, William has not been taught to take female power seriously. When Alluca approaches William and confesses her love for him, her speech highlights the kind of influence that women—including Unca Eliza—are granted in this community. Alluca tells him, "It is our custom to be silent, or to speak what we think; we are of opinion that nature has given us the same right to declare our love as it has to your sex" (52). Here *The Female American* makes a progressive statement. Women have the same rights as men; they can speak their minds and choose their partners.

But women's power is also written as potentially destructive in this text, and any sign of it will need to be diffused for this text to be a proper English novel. Alluca's interactions with William are merely the first sign that, ultimately, this novel will simultaneously build, and then destroy, a fantasy of female power. William refuses Alluca's advances ("all he could say tended to provoke her anger"), and Alluca pronounces that if he will not agree to marry her, she will kill him (52). Clearly misreading the influence her commands and expectations hold, William is "not greatly alarmed, as [the words] were uttered by an unarmed woman, and which he conceived to be the effect of passion, and unluckily smiled" (52). William clearly takes for granted her authority, and this smirk enrages Alluca, who accuses him of "derid[ing]" her power. In defiance of his slight, she proclaims that she can dispense "love and death at her will," calls "six male Indians" to appear "from behind the trees," and shows William that "all power of defence or flight [has been] equally taken from him" (52). Alluca fulfills her promise to destroy him and poisons him nearly to death. The contradictions inherent in granting women power in this novel appear early on and indeed bring to light one of its major conflicts: a powerful woman is needed to convert the islanders in the second half of the text, but powerful femininity is also a dangerous and destructive force that must be given a wide berth.

Unca finds and saves William with her apparently instinctual "remarkable . . . knowledge of poisons . . . [and] antidotes," but Alluca's status as heir makes it impossible for the pair to stay in the community, and William and Unca move back to William's colony (53). While Unca takes "effectual care" for William's "security" temporarily, she consults with her father, who decides that the only way to protect William from Alluca is for the couple to marry and "set out instantly for the place of [his] abode" (54). The power that Alluca has in the community is able to dictate who lives among them, and William's misreading of and contempt for this power results in his and his wife's banishment and Unca's ultimate powerlessness in her new life.

Once William and Unca move to the English colony, Unca's status as powerful woman is converted into subjugated wife, which results in the abandonment of the external markers of her identity: her dress and her place in the community. Following their marriage, William and Unca are more aligned with European ways of life than Indigenous ones. They are married first by an "Indian priest" and then by an "English chaplain" in William's community (54–55). We see a turn in Unca's dress when readers are told by Unca Eliza, "My father had persuaded his wife to conform to the European dress" (55). Unca must surrender her status and her culture to do as William asks, and the adoption of English dress shows the power William has gained over his wife. The fact, though, that he is alive because of the remarkable power demonstrated by Unca and her position in the community serves as a constant reminder of the authority she once had and which will be passed down to her daughter.

In the novel's early chapters readers see that Unca's possession of William and also Alluca's threats to him emphasize women's power and men's relative powerlessness. This dynamic presages Unca Eliza's ability to act in ways that other Englishwomen would not be able to act and to have some control over her own fate, at least when it comes to her life before John joins it. Even after the death of her mother and aunt, Unca Eliza remains attached to them through the "bow and arrows, of exquisite workmanship" that her aunt had given her (57). This bow and arrow will remain with Unca Eliza as a symbol not just of her heritage, but also of her mother and aunt's culture and autonomy. That power, once realized, allows her freedom to act outside behavioral expectations for English women. This ability is what ultimately gives her the authority to convert the islanders she meets.

MAROONING AND UNMOORING

Though Unca Eliza moves from America to England and is raised as a wealthy Englishwoman, she still resists complete transculturation. Refusing to dress like an Englishwoman, Unca Eliza's clothing reflects her maternal heritage, and she carries her bow and arrow everywhere she goes. Unlike English ladies, she never "w[ears] a cap," and her "lank black hair is adorned with diamonds and flowers. . . . [Her] arms are also adorned with strings of diamonds, and one of the same kind surround[s] [her] waist." For fun, she "divert[s] [her]self with wearing the bow and arrow . . . [and] can shoot a bird on the wing."[10] As Chloe Wigston Smith writes, "Unca Eliza knows how to manage the gaze of her audience by manipulating her appearance and intercultural costume."[11] Unca Eliza's refusal to dress like a wealthy Englishwoman ultimately represents part of her early rejection of her mother's subordination to her husband and his culture. In the early parts of the novel—long before she is marooned and her cousin arrives on the island—we see Unca Eliza operating outside the boundaries of English cultural norms. As Marta Kvande has argued, "Using her Indian heritage—her physical prowess and her control of language—she asserts her independence and refuses to be subsumed into Britishness."[12] Like Unca and Alluca, but unlike an upper-class Englishwoman, she also feels free to speak on issues of marriage. She repeatedly "divert[s] herself" at the expense of her suitors, and in the face of her cousin John's importunities toward marriage she "always laughed at him, and answered in the Indian language, of which he was entirely ignorant; and so by degrees wearied him to silence on that head."[13]

Unca Eliza's marooning happens because her mother's culture has shown her that she has power to do what most Englishwomen do not: refuse marriage proposals without repercussion. This power is a large part of what marks her as different from heroines of eighteenth-century novels. When the captain hired to transport her enormous wealth after the death of her father tries to get her to agree to marry his son, she returns to her standard response and tells him that if his son can "shoot with [her] bows and arrows . . . as well as [she] c[an], [she] would have him." She quickly finds, however, that she is "too much in [the captain's] power" for that answer to suffice (62). The captain robs her and maroons her for her refusal. That Unca Eliza has misread her position in society is interesting: she assumes that the way she has been treated in England is a universal reaction to her status, while the captain's actions demonstrate that he sees her as powerless to act to save herself.

After the captain maroons Unca Eliza, we see two conflicting narrative strains begin to emerge more clearly. One is most closely linked to Unca Eliza's English upbringing and is based on her understanding of providence and her mission as a Christian. The other is more closely linked to her heritage and her connection to her mother and aunt. She knows, for example, that there are "Indian roots" for her to eat that would "serve instead of bread," and she knows the "look and taste" of wild grapes, which help to keep her fed (67). Her knowledge of natural elements mirrors her mother's expertise in saving her father from Alluca's attempted poisoning. She even carries a "small knife" in her pocket and knows how to use the "flint and steel" she finds in the hermit's cabin (69). These things are, decidedly, not the accessories of a wealthy Englishwoman, and Unca Eliza's possession of them indicates that she conceives of a life outside the realm of English femininity that is connected to her mother's knowledge of survival in nature. Her rejection of much of the advice given in the hermit's manuscript, including her refusal to even read most of it (she tells us she "had not patience to go through the whole history"), makes it clear that she feels herself to be free to act without consulting a man's opinion or drawing on his knowledge (81). When she does consult the opinion of a man, she has imaginary dialogues with her uncle. These conversations buoy her spiritually, but they do not help her to overcome many of the challenges of living on the island.

Though the Christian aspects of this novel and the words from Unca Eliza's uncle are never far from the surface in this work, moments that have been previously read as stemming from the novel's Christian ideology can be read in other ways. For instance, in the middle of the novel, Unca Eliza falls into a fever and is unable to eat or drink until she makes her way to a nearby river and falls in. This scene has been read as a kind of baptism, but it also reflects rebirth into her sense of entitlement to leadership that is represented by her mother and aunt, and it draws her further into the aspects of her Native American identity that had been put aside in favor of more British behaviors.[14] After she recovers, Unca Eliza spends her time "rambling" much as her parents did when they first met, a pastime completely opposite to her earlier declaration that she is "not fond" of the practice.[15] Her explorations lead her to the tombs of the "virgins of the sun" and to the golden idol's storehouse of finery, including a priest's cassock replete with "diamond buttons to fasten it" and rich bracelets "beset with precious stones."[16] Unca Eliza's realization that this garment, like her clothes in England, can be used to reflect the superiority she feels over the islanders is an essential process in this novel. Though she ultimately uses the status they grant her to rule over a new island, thus supplanting the leadership structures that existed before she arrived in a move reflective of her father's colonial goals, they also allow her to embrace her identity as a woman with power. In this case, it is her identity as a powerful woman that allows her to realize her primary goal: missionary work. That Unca Eliza believes she has the authority required to take on the characteristically male role of the missionary signals that the freedom and autonomy her mother enjoyed (including to explain her own religion to William) is something she also believes she can access. Her allegiance to her mother's culture and its tradition of commanding women is what makes the Christianizing mission of the last part of the novel possible. Thus, we can see that this novel's colonial successes can only happen because Unca Eliza possesses a sense of her own authority inherited from her mother and aunt. Her time alone on the first island reunites her with her matriarchal inheritance and allows a fantasy of power, even if, as Edward Simon notes, this inheritance is ultimately only tolerable briefly and only possible "in the realm of a literary artifact."[17]

MISSIONARY WORK, CONVERSION, AND FEMALE AUTHORITY

When Unca Eliza is faced with the danger the nearby Indigenous people might pose to her safety, she ultimately chooses to employ a solution that reflects her father's culture: colonization and conversion. She even uses her cultural knowledge of the Indigenous people to assume that they will be "docile" and "grateful" for her religious interventions. Trapped underground after an earthquake and facing the possibility of having to stay there permanently, she acknowledges that she must rely on her notion of English religious supremacy to force the islanders to be "the instruments of [her] deliverance."[18] Unlike the hermit who occupied the island before her, Unca Eliza uses the idol and the treasures in the tunnels below as a tool to this end. To execute this mission, though, she must draw on the authority she feels to approach them, instead of following the hermit's advice to hide from them. That she even believes she might be able to achieve this mission is a fantasy this novel perpetuates: a conventionally powerless mixed-race woman has the possibility of success.

As the Indigenous people approach the idol on their yearly worship trip, Unca Eliza dons the cassock, the gold and diamonds, and the crown and grabs a staff: here a symbol, like her bow and arrow, of her relationship to power.[19] In this moment, Unca Eliza channels the royalty of her mother and aunt, rather than the submission of women in her father's tradition. She reveals that, like the gifts of gold dust Alluca gives to atone for Unca's death, she will come bearing gifts to the islanders in the hopes her possession of these aligns her in their minds with their own notions of religious power. Unfortunately, it is in Unca Eliza's move to convert them that the fantasy playing out in the middle of this novel and the reality of its end diverge: Unca Eliza's decision to act as a missionary is a sign that she believes she has the authority to do so, but her decision turns the novel from a fantasy of female autonomy into a stereotypical novel of colonial conquest. As the novel progresses toward its inevitable conclusion, we see the influence of Unca Eliza's British, Christian heritage render her allegiance with her Native American culture little more than a tool with which to colonize.

THE ENGLISH INVASION AND THE CREATION OF A COMMUNITY

Unca Eliza's fantasy of female autonomy is allowed to continue, then, only as long as she is able to use it to colonial ends, and, more importantly, only as long as she remains the only representative of British culture on the island. The fantasy of female autonomy this novel entertains in its first half completely dissolves as her island is discovered by British men. Her reactions to her cousin John's arrival with a group of others on the idol's island demonstrates that she understands the threat that English culture poses to her new way of life. While she expresses her fears that the Indigenous people might be enslaved (or killed), readers must also see her fear as concern that her place in the community is about to be usurped.[20]

Believing that the only way she can maintain her power is by terrifying the British men into believing she is a supernatural being, Unca Eliza once again dons the priest's cassock, but this time she uses it to trick the Englishmen into believing that she is a "she-devil" (138). In the face of this invasion, Unca's only tool against European men is their own fear of powerful women. Unfortunately for Unca Eliza, her cousin John recognizes her, and almost as quickly as she gained it, her power begins to fade. As he joins the community, John takes on the role of colonist, not only of the islanders, but of Unca Eliza as well. Noting that it is compulsion rather than attraction that drives her to help John, Unca Eliza seemingly admits that she is only reluctantly rejoining English society and realizes the problems that causes for her. She says, "Better had it been never to have seen him again. . . . I might have concluded my life with ease and pleasure among the Indians" (139). When the men refuse to let John back on board their ship after their encounter with Unca Eliza, she rescues him and takes him to her island, knowing that because of the inhabitants' "implicit regard to every thing [she] said," he will be safe, even as an interloper (143). John immediately renews his earlier marriage proposals, and though Unca Eliza tries to get him to return to England, he is "determined to live and die" with her, an idea to which she is "strongly opposed" (145). In an acknowledgment of the surrender John's presence requires from her, she notes that she is "heartily sorry" that he intends to stay (146).

As John aids in the conversion of the islanders through sermons and baptisms, he also converts Unca Eliza to his own notions of what their community should look like. After repeatedly refusing his proposals—we must recall that she never considered him a suitable lover—she is finally "obliged" to marry him when he reminds her that in England and in the tiny England he is building their private talks together are improper outside the bounds of marriage (146–148). The moment she is persuaded, Unca Eliza gives up her position as subject of her own story. The displacement of her primary leadership is notable in her pronoun usage. For the rest of the novel, the first-person singular gives way to plural to include John as a co-leader and her equal, or worse, as having more power over her now that she is his wife. While I follow Bowen, Beebe, and Denise Mary MacNeil in arguing that John must modify his behavior to join her community, rather than the opposite, ultimately his capitulations to the demands of her society are much less severe than her capitulations to the demands of Englishness.[21] Beebe notes, "Three times she denies his importuning: she will not marry the John who cannot see and value her strengths and the life she has created with the Native Americans."[22] Though John must learn to have a great "understanding" of the "wonderfully comprehensive" Unca Eliza before he can take on a leadership role, he ultimately achieves this (and the total conversion of the islanders) with few complications.[23] Even Unca Eliza is forced to admit that the community has "a high opinion of [her] cousin, next to that they had for [her]."[24] Rochelle Raineri Zuck notes that this text "emphasizes women's ability to form relationships as a key component of their ability to . . . establish roots in a new community," but it also ultimately precludes women from all but the most domestic of tasks in these communities.[25] As John emerges as an authority figure, Unca Eliza's role changes from that of powerful woman to missionary's helpmate. MacNeil argues that "John is led by her, since he . . . has no cultural or social purchase with the islanders," but once he gains this social purchase through his religious practice the novel dissolves its fantasy of female power.[26]

As the text ends, we see the two narrative strains of this work diverge nearly irreparably. Unca Eliza still makes commands that are obeyed in the community, but John's role as priest and de facto leader lessens the authority she once had. His conversion of her ensures that she is committed to British notions of proper femininity. If there is a hopeful moment for readers disappointed with the end of the novel, it can be found in Unca Eliza's declaration that without a need for money she sends her own fortune home to be settled on John's sisters. That she chooses to bless them with her considerable fortune (and the economic freedom it represents) suggests that she believes in the possibility that economic stability represents a kind of freedom for them, even if this fortune will, no doubt, only make them appear more suitable as wives. Unlike earlier in the novel where Unca Eliza sees her role as community leader as the ultimate stable experience, the colonized Unca Eliza must tie stability to marriage. Unca Eliza traces her "adventures" to economic stability and Englishness. She may still believe in a fantasy of female power, even if she cannot access it herself, but that fantasy is ultimately tied up in conventional marriage plots—in this way, the novel mediates, even undoes, Unca Eliza's autonomy lest she appear too progressive to eighteenth-century readers, particularly women.

Although Unca Eliza's story sits primarily within the framework of a conversion narrative, *The Female American* still offers readers a fantasy of female empowerment where Unca Eliza is allowed, albeit briefly, to have uncommon adventures that other Englishwomen cannot have. The conversion work Unca Eliza does is real and problematic, but that she feels free to perform it signals that she maintains some ties with her mother's culture, at least until Britishness is imposed upon her again at the end of the novel. What this novel ultimately reveals, through its deep contradictions and confusion, is the value of maternal heritage and female power in women's lives. Even if those goals may seem repugnant to twenty-first-century readers and ultimately conventional to eighteenth-century ones, the text allows for them to be achieved through a nonconventional goal and posits the possibility of female intervention in colonial missions as a strategy for personal achievement.

NOTES

1. See Eve Tavor Bannet, *Transatlantic Stories and the History of Reading, 1720–1810: Migrant Fictions* (Cambridge: Cambridge University Press, 2011), 184; Victoria Barnett-Woods, "Models of Morality: The Bildungsroman and Social Reform in *The Female American* and *The Woman of Colour*," *Women's Studies* 45, no. 7 (2016): 619; and Ann Beebe, "'I Sent Over These Adventures': Women in *The Female American* and *The Widow Ranter*," *Women's Studies* 45, no. 7 (2016): 624.
2. Unca Eliza Winkfield [pseud.], *The Female American; or, The Adventures of Unca Eliza Winkfield*, ed. Michelle Burnham and James Freitas, 2nd ed. (Peterborough, ON: Broadview Press, 2014), 91.
3. Winkfield, *Female American*, 119.
4. Scarlet Bowen, "*Via Media*: Transatlantic Anglicanism in *The Female American*," *The Eighteenth Century* 53, no. 2 (2012): 201.
5. Bowen, "*Via Media*," 201.
6. Kristianne Kalata Vaccaro, "'Recollection . . . Sets My Busy Imagination to Work': Transatlantic Self-Narration, Performance, and Reception in *The Female American*,"

Eighteenth-Century Fiction 20, no. 2 (Winter 2007–2008): 133; Beebe, "'I Sent Over These Adventures,'" 628.

7. Tim Fulford, "Transatlantic American Indians," in *Transatlantic Literary Studies, 1660–1830*, ed. Eve Tavor Bannet and Susan Manning (Cambridge: Cambridge University Press, 2011), 106.
8. Bowen, "*Via Media*," 189.
9. Winkfield, *Female American*, 45.
10. Winkfield, *Female American*, 59.
11. Chloe Wigston Smith, "The Empire of Home: Global Domestic Objects and *The Female American* (1767)," *Journal for Eighteenth-Century Studies* 40, no. 1 (2017): 79.
12. Marta Kvande, "'Had You No Lands of Your Own?': Seeking Justice in *The Female American* (1767)," *Women's Studies* 45, no. 7 (2016): 690.
13. Winkfield, *Female American*, 60.
14. See Michelle Burnham and James Freitas, introduction to *The Female American; or, The Adventures of Unca Eliza Winkfield*, by Unca Eliza Winkfield [pseud.], ed. Michelle Burnham and James Freitas, 2nd ed. (Peterborough, ON: Broadview Press, 2014), 20; and Winkfield, *The Female American*, 67, 69.
15. Winkfield, *Female American*, 69.
16. Winkfield, *Female American*, 82, 87, 88.
17. Edward Simon, "Unca Eliza Winkfield and the Fantasy of Non-Colonial Conversion in *The Female American*," *Women's Studies* 45, no. 7 (2016): 654.
18. Winkfield, *Female American*, 97.
19. Winkfield, *Female American*, 122.
20. Winkfield, *Female American*, 122.
21. See Denise Mary MacNeil, "Empire and the Pan-Atlantic Self in *The Female American; or, The Adventures of Unca Eliza Winkfield*," in *Women's Narratives of the Early Americas and the Formation of Empire*, ed. Mary McAleer Balkun and Susan C. Imbarrato (New York: Palgrave Macmillan, 2016), 109–122.
22. Beebe, "'I Sent Over These Adventures,'" 635.
23. Winkfield, *Female American*, 50.
24. Winkfield, *Female American*, 148.
25. Rochelle Raineri Zuck, "New World Roots: Transatlantic Fictions, Creole Marriages, and Women's Cultivation of Empire in the Americas," in *Women's Narratives of the Early Americas and the Formation of Empire*, ed. Mary McAleer Balkun and Susan C. Imbarrato (New York: Palgrave Macmillan, 2016), 191.
26. MacNeil, "Empire and the Pan-Atlantic Self," 111.

8

"I AM DISAPPOINTED IN ENGLAND"

Reverse-Robinsonades and the Transatlantic Woman as Social Critic in *The Woman of Colour*

OCTAVIA COX

THE ABOLITION OF THE SLAVE Trade Act (1807) brought much self-congratulatory backslapping by the British, who celebrated it as a tremendous national achievement that showcased British compassion and morality.[1] A correspondent with the *Gentleman's Magazine*, the pointedly named "Benevolus," praised the "Justice and Benevolence" of Britain's "present enlightened Administration," remarking that the "Abolition of the Slave Trade . . . will do immortal honour to the Government."[2] Arguably, however, the gesture was motivated by lurking narcissism rather than humanitarian concern and offered symbolic change, not a genuine challenge to colonialist power structures.[3] *The Woman of Colour*, an epistolary novel published anonymously the subsequent year (1808), punctured English self-satisfaction at the abolition by exposing England as far from occupying the high ground regarding its transatlantic colonial subjects.[4] Forced to leave Jamaica for England, Olivia Fairfield, the eponymous biracial heroine, has high hopes of what she will discover across the Atlantic, having heard from her father that "in England, in his native country," there was "a more liberal, a more distinguishing spirit."[5] As the novel progresses, the author plays repeatedly on the difference between that which England projects itself to be and what Olivia experiences, exposing injustice within ostensibly enlightened English society; thus, Olivia becomes a female transatlantic social critic of England, designed to expose English bigotry. The narrative opens "At Sea," as Olivia is "LAUNCHED on a new world," ironically reversing "New World" and "Old World" labels.[6] From the novel's opening, then, readers should be alerted that traditional demarcations are going to be tested. The novel's primary purpose is to rupture England's self-regard toward its treatment of transatlantic subjects; seemingly paradoxically, its secondary aim is to encourage action from its (likely) young, female, English readers by promoting an idealized conception of English principles.

This essay argues that *Woman of Colour* is what I term a "reverse-Robinsonade": instead of depicting an enlightened European discovering an apparently uncivilized island and civilizing it, the reverse-Robinsonade takes an apparently uncultured native, in this case from Jamaica, to expose uncivilized aspects among apparently enlightened Europeans. Thus, the protagonist of a reverse-Robinsonade is a transnational social critic of a culture often imagined to be superior, exposing its flaws (sometimes via affected naïveté, other times using biting condemnation). Olivia is unusual in being a female transatlantic critic; this characterization enables the author to problematize the attitudes of English women to the institution of slavery, notably in the case of Mrs. Merton, who evinces no compassion for those humans whose misery facilitates her lavish lifestyle. Furthermore, Olivia, as a woman—and almost a paragon of virtue, an idealized English novelistic heroine—serves as an exemplar to female readers for how to contribute to slavery's amelioration, standing in contrast to the worldly Mrs. Merton and Lady Ingot, whose behavior should be eschewed. The author politicizes the private, domestic domain—that is, the sphere within the home and the family circle—by showing that abolition is not just an issue of (masculine) high politics, but concerns everyday (female) readers. The novel promotes the notion that women can contribute to the curing of social evils within the home, particularly through moral education of the young and of servants (often a woman's two prominent roles within her household were to manage her children and staff). It suggests that good men are most impressed with morality when it is articulated by an unimpeachable and impeccably proper woman of any color.

The author endeavors to persuade readers that slavery contravenes both the teachings of the Church of England, essentially kindness and charity, and ostensibly traditional English notions of liberty. The problem with present-day England, the text suggests, is that these ideals have been subverted: English society has become blind to what it should be; it needs to see things from an outside perspective. It is Olivia's task to re-teach English values back to the very English who have forgotten them. The mirror image of other long eighteenth-century transatlantic missionaries, like Robinson Crusoe and Unca Eliza Winkfield, Olivia spends much of the novel not converting natives of a "New World" but instead proselytizing English, Christian dogma back to the "Old World." While the novel awakens English readers to the plight of "poor blacks" overseas, the vision of change offered (perhaps influenced by the recent and notionally worrisome Haitian Revolution of 1804) is Burkean, advocating amelioration rather than revolution.[7] This is particularly evident in the author's treatment of Dido, whose attempts at self-agency are denied such that she remains trapped beneath Olivia's *benevolent* wing. Ultimately, for all its ostensible critique of England,

Woman of Colour both assumes and reinforces the putative superiority of English culture.

REVERSE-ROBINSONADES

The term "Robinsonade," derived from Daniel Defoe's transatlantic castaway in *Robinson Crusoe* (1719), came to mean a story about being marooned on a desert island or some similarly inhospitable place. Augustus Merton—Olivia's intended husband—refers to England as such a place, where Olivia is socially marooned, "a stranger in a strange country," and even proclaims that it would have been "better had she perished on the ocean, better had the tempestuous billows over-whelmed her, ere she set foot on this inhospitable shore!"[8] *Woman of Colour*'s author plays on Crusoean connotations of "being shipwreck'd" on an "*Island of Despair*" by having Olivia and Augustus use shipwreck imagery to describe their misery.[9] Augustus's despair renders him "like a shipwrecked mariner," while Olivia declares she does not want "to be the shipwreck of [Augustus's] happiness."[10] Immediately Olivia lands in England, she self-consciously quotes William Cowper's "Verses, Supposed to be Written by Alexander Selkirk during his Solitary Abode in the Island of Juan Fernandez" (1782).[11] Selkirk spent four years castaway on a South Pacific island and was a probable inspiration for Robinson Crusoe. Like Selkirk, Olivia longs to return to her "own native land" but comforts herself with "Religion" "more precious than silver and gold" and "all that this earth can afford."[12]

Woman of Colour reverses the traditional Robinsonade genre, in which the cultured European sallies forth abroad and teaches the unenlightened native a better way to live.[13] As Crusoe declares of Friday, "I . . . made it my Business to teach him every Thing," *Woman of Colour*'s "*Editor*" inverts this power dynamic; the narrative's stated purpose is for a "*despised native of Africa*" to "teach" the "*skeptical European*."[14] A contemporary reviewer in the *Monthly Review* sniped that the author "is too apt to 'express the jests' in italics," but the italicization here pointedly questions the validity of these categorizations.[15] Olivia's mother, Marcia, had been a "*slave*" on Olivia's father's plantation.[16] Olivia archly echoes the categories queried by the Editor in describing how, after converting to Christianity, Marcia enlightened Fairfield: "The scholar taught her master—The wild and uncivilized African taught a lesson of noble self-denial and self-conquest to the enlightened and educated European" (note how individual characters become allegorized as "The . . . African" and "the . . . European").[17] Three connotations of "master" come into play—as teacher, enslaver, and male—and the authority of all is contested. Furthermore, Marcia's teaching explicitly comes in the form of exposing how

England fails to embody the Christianity it purports to assume: "the *new* Christian [Marcia] pointed her finger at *him* [Fairfield], who, educated under the influence of the Gospel, lived in direct opposition to its laws!"[18] Like her mother before her, Olivia's role is to teach England to improve itself (throughout the novel "England" is used as a metonym for "the English"). The Black, feminine "scholar" must continue to teach the white, masculine "master."

Educating and Christianizing impulses run throughout Robinsonades.[19] Such is the case of Unca Eliza Winkfield, the transatlantic woman traveler in *The Female American* who presents readers with a female Robinsonade culminating in her conversion of Indigenous people and Englishmen.[20] Long before these travels, Unca Eliza's father, like many West Indian dwelling Englishmen, "determined to return to England" to "give [Unca Eliza] a better education."[21] Similarly, in *Woman of Colour*, Sophia Honeywood returned to England to educate young Charles at "an eligible school" because "she dreaded the tainted atmosphere of Jamaica."[22] Unca Eliza had "the religious part" of her "education" in England, and these "pious instructions" are of both "great comfort" and "highest use" to her castaway self.[23] Unca Eliza takes Church of England lessons, and spreads English constructions of virtue and morality transatlantically.[24] In calling on these religious teachings, Unca Eliza "employs transatlantic recollection in order to summon the religious authority of a wise and benevolent," manifestly English, "paternal figure."[25] Contrary to Unca Eliza, Olivia exposes the lack of English religious practice at home, which she attempts to rectify. The Ingots—East Indian "Nabobs," riddled with "folly, ostentation, and self-conceit"—and Miss Danby reject attending church because distinctions of wealth are not upheld: "The *breaths* of the greasy farmers is what I chiefly dread," Miss Danby laments.[26] Lady Ingot's "plan for a *little sequestration*" for the "family's accommodation at church" has alarming implications of profiteering.[27] The Ingots, as their name suggests, define themselves by wealth, and see the Church as a way of enriching their material means rather than their spiritual selves. Olivia, on the other hand, "not content with being *good* herself," "makes *others* so likewise" by insisting the Fairfield household "go to church on a Sunday."[28]

While we should consider the novel alongside Robinsonades, it may be better described as a reverse-Robinsonade: where a foreigner in England exposes English primitivism, criticizes social ills, and punctures England's idea of itself as the pinnacle of developed culture and civilization. A considerable tradition of using the "other," "foreign," and/or "peripheral" to critique a "home" society had emerged by the eighteenth century: Margaret Cavendish, in *Blazing World* (1666), and Jonathan Swift, in *Gulliver's Travels* (1726), for instance, invert the critical gaze squarely back to England from an imaginary other world. Reverse-Robinsonades go a step further: the "foreign" comes "home." In these texts, supposed colonial subjects visit the metropolis, apparently for education and/or cultural development, but the plots pivot to have the "native informant" focus on England's moral degradation.[29] As in *Woman of Colour*, in several reverse-Robinsonades it is "the gap between principles and actions which is threatening to destroy contemporary England."[30] Eighteenth-century reviewers did not use the term itself but describe the effects of the reverse-Robinsonade: in the words of the *Monthly Review*, reviewing Elizabeth Hamilton's *Letters of a Hindoo Rajah* (1796), the genre employs "an ingenious device . . . designed to place before the view of the English reader a picture of the prevalent manners and customs of his country," uncovering, according to the *Scots Magazine*, "that many of our practices, habits, and sentiments, depend entirely on custom, prejudice, and education," rather than on reason and morality.[31]

While some reverse-Robinsonades use a naïve foreigner, perplexed by what he or she finds, other criticisms were more arch. The scornful "Omiah," for instance, describes England as

> A world of prejudice, where Error rules,
> By Folly bred, and rear'd in Fashion's schools;
> Where on a gilded car in state she rides,
> Whilst custom draws, and ignorance misguides.[32]

Elsewhere, Oliver Goldsmith lambasted the arrogance of the English at their imagined intellectual superiority in *Citizen of the World; or, Letters from a Chinese Philosopher, Residing in London, to his Friends in the East* (1762): "Strange, say they, that a man, who has received his education at such a distance from London, should have common sense; to be born out of England, and yet have common sense! impossible! He must be some Englishman in disguise."[33] Olivia, also born out of England, aligns herself with "reason and common sense," and Augustus refers to Olivia as "the citizen of the world" (perhaps with an ironic nod to Goldsmith's work).[34] The author draws on Francis Bacon's seventeenth-century description: "If a Man be Gracious, and Curteous to Strangers, it shewes, he is a Citizen of the World; And that his Heart, is no Island, cut off from other Lands."[35] Compassion ought to be international, which Olivia embodies as a "citizen of the world, with a heart teeming with benevolence and mercy towards every living creature!"[36]

The year before *Woman of Colour*'s publication, Robert Southey produced the popular *Letters from England* (1807). Through a pseudonymous Spanish traveler, Don Manuel Alvarez Espriella, Southey presents England through fresh, skeptical eyes, quarreling with the disparity between rich and poor and arguing for greater class equality. Southey criticizes those, like the Ingots, who would see the "abominable custom" of maintaining social hierarchy even in church.[37] Not everyone approved of such foreigners criticizing England: Jane Austen, for one, condemned "Espriella's Letters" as "horribly anti-english [*sic*]."[38] While *Letters from England* has been described as "a repository for Southey's own, often inflammatory, opinions on society and politics," *Woman of Colour* overtly avoids being anti-English.[39]

ENGLISHNESS VERSUS OTHERNESS

Unlike figures presented as entirely foreign, the point is emphasized that Olivia is half English: genetically through her father and culturally through the tutoring of her English governess (Mrs. Milbanke). Olivia considers herself "more than *half* an English woman."[40] She occupies a position in which she is simultaneously outsider and insider. The author uses this dual perspective better to expose English society's corruption. On the one hand, readers encounter Olivia's unpleasant experiences at the hands of those who let England down by not living up to 'English' principles; on the other hand, Olivia has authority as an insider to criticize those people. Olivia complicates her English identity with her use of pronouns; others, too, use pronouns to exclude or include her. Olivia, having just set foot on English terra firma, refers to "our own dear Cowper" to align herself with English literary authority, but elsewhere to "our poor blacks" in Jamaica.[41] "'You speak like a *perfect* English woman,' said Lady Ingot [to Olivia]; 'I see you have already imbibed our air,'" which partially renders Olivia more English, but simultaneously demarcates her as being only *like* an English person, not *as* one.[42] The plural possessive pronoun establishes Lady Ingot as native, "our," and Olivia as assimilated, but essentially distinct, Other, "you."[43] Olivia responds, "It has always been my ardent wish to prove myself worthy of the *title*" of "English woman," playing on the "*title*" given to the Ingots.[44] England's misjudgment of its priorities in what it venerates is symbolized through the Ingots being given honor, a "title," by the establishment, becoming Sir Marmaduke and Lady Ingot.[45] Olivia's desire to "prove" herself a "worthy" "English woman" allows her to critique what she sees in England because she understands and respects what a proper English person ought to be: she reveres England, giving her license to criticize it for falling short of the standards it should expect of itself.

Sailing to England, Olivia pronounces, "The moment when I set my foot on your land of liberty, I yield up my independence," ironically reversing the notion, following Lord Mansfield's ruling, that England brings independence for all.[46]

Maria Edgeworth's "The Grateful Negro" (1804) articulates the conception: "The instant a slave touches English ground he becomes free. Glorious privilege!"[47] Earlier, Cowper's famous antislavery passage in *The Task* (1785), book 2, reads:

> Slaves cannot breathe in England; if their lungs
> Receive our air, that moment they are free.[48]

Despite its noble sentiment, Cowper's implementation of "our" and "their"/"they," like Lady Ingot, differentiates Englishness and Otherness. Cowper's poem forms the novel's epigraph: "He finds his brother guilty of a skin not colour'd like his own."[49] In Cowper's words, Mrs. Merton, with power to enforce the wrong, considers Olivia to be guilty of being colored differently from her own "alabaster" complexion and therefore her lawful prey.[50] The novel questions the assumed "mercy" of "Britain's power," undermines England's self-image as a "nation proud" of its compassion, and asks whether those in "our country" really are as "free" from "shackles" as Cowper supposes.[51] In juxtaposing "land of liberty" and "yield . . . independence," Olivia exposes, symbolically, the difference between England's pretensions and reality; "your" liberty, "my" lack of independence.[52] Readers are "invited" to realize that England is not the land of liberty some assume it to be.[53]

GENDER AND THE POLITICIZED DOMESTIC SPHERE

James Joyce, lecturing in Trieste in 1911/2, admiringly declared that Crusoe "is the true prototype of the British colonist," in whom one finds "the whole Anglo-Saxon spirit" complete with "manly independence."[54] Most reverse-Robinsonades follow this "manly" "prototype" and use male protagonists. Olivia, exceptionally, is a foreign *woman* entering and criticizing England: "*Woman of Colour* could be a rare female addition" to a "male tradition . . . designed to make readers see England anew through the rarely utilized eyes of a West Indian heiress."[55] *The Female American* had contested traditional identification of the adventure genre with masculinity, male protagonists, and defined-male writers.[56] *Woman of Colour* challenges the masculine perspective within reverse-Robinsonades. In fact, Olivia's power to convert others comes largely from her 'feminine' virtues. Olivia has "a sense of [her] sex's more exclusive feeling delicacy," and this quality enables her to unmask the everyday cruelties of others.[57] Precisely because she is "a woman,—a young—a tender woman" who bears but exposes unkindness despite having little power, she displays the "unexampled pre-eminence and virtue" that others are encouraged "to imitate."[58]

Olivia's homosocial relationships reveal how Englishwomen contribute to England's degradation.[59] The novel exposes how women, such as Mrs. Merton and Lady Ingot, participate in English society's degeneration through their engagement with Olivia as a "tropicopolitan": that is, "object of representation *and* agent of resistance."[60] Lady Ingot advocates, baldly, husband-hunting in Bengal for "an advantageous matrimonial connexion" as Olivia's "*colour* would be overlooked."[61] Mrs. Merton is a "city lady, whose ideas are all centered in self, and in money, as the grand minister to all her capricious indulgences" (76). Olivia's "feelings of humanity" and "principles of [Christian] religion" cause her to advocate for the "emancipation" of "slaves," a viewpoint not understood by avaricious Mrs. Merton, who presupposes that Olivia would put mercantile concerns before those of "humanity" and "religion" (80–81). As Mrs. Merton says, "Born, as you were, in the West Indies, your father a planter, I should have imagined that you would have entertained quite the contrary side of the question" (80–81). Readers see English people's worst behavior exemplified in these women, who assume Olivia would, like them, prioritize money over morals.

Problematical English conduct toward Jamaicans is seen to run throughout society, as in Abigail's mistreatment of Dido: "Mrs. Merton's maid treats me, as if me was her slave," Dido protests (100). Lady Maria Nugent, a nonfictional sojourner in Jamaica between 1801 and 1805, found that "the lower orders," with "conceit and tyranny," considered "the negroes as creatures formed merely to administer to their ease, and to be subject to their caprice"; indeed, she "found much difficulty to persuade . . . [her] white domestics, that the blacks are human beings, or have souls."[62] The noun "abigail" means "a lady's maid; a female servant or attendant."[63] Choosing the name "Abigail," then, suggests the author intended readers to view the character as representative, more broadly, of attitudes held by her society, that prejudice transcends socio-economic groupings. Unlike Lady Nugent, Mrs. Merton does not even attempt to educate her employees out of prejudice, just as she fails in her duty to educate her son.

However, Olivia converts little George Merton by using methods, ironically, espoused by the Society for the Propagation of the Gospel in Foreign Parts (SPG)—again, the "Foreign" is seen at 'home': she "appeal[s]" to his "Reason and Conscience . . . by the plain and most obvious Arguments."[64] Olivia uses little George to explain biblical equality, as exemplified in the King James Bible's rendering of Galatians 3:28 (the KJB being the authorized English translation for the Church of England, and the version from which Olivia quotes throughout *Woman of Colour*), which explicitly states the parity between "bond[ed] and free" people: "There is neither bond nor free, there is neither male nor female: for ye are all one in Christ Jesus."[65] Olivia argues, "The same God that made *you* made me . . . the poor black woman [Dido]—the whole world—and every creature in it! . . . God chose it should be so."[66] Through Church of England principles, Olivia teaches 'English' values, of tolerance and moral equality, back to those English who no longer exhibit them. Little George's mother remarks, acidly, "He is very backward in his *catechism*," but she "could not pretend to *teach* it to him."[67] Mrs. Merton pointedly ignores where Olivia actively attends: according to the SPG, those in positions of responsibility ought to "take a special Care, to lay a good Foundation . . . by Catechizing those under their Care, whether Children [such as little George] or other ignorant Persons [such as Abigail], explaining the Catechism to them in the most easie and familiar Manner."[68] All Abigails and Little Georges should be taught to imbibe, both in heart and in mind, the equality of all before God. Some contemporary readers found Olivia's religiose teachings offputtingly clunky; for instance, the *Critical Review* found that "Olivia is rather too methodistical; *providence* is for ever in her mouth; she indulges a little too liberal in her use of the *Most High*, and plumes herself too much on her religious duties, and her quotations from Scripture."[69] But the novel's political message is clear, and Olivia's moral lessons are drawn demonstrably from English establishment authority, the Church of England.

In focusing on women, the author shows how politics features in domestic settings, thus implying that progress is not simply a matter of high politics or lawmaking. Little George's lesson prompts Uncle George to raise the issue of abolition: "George, we shall have your sentiments on the abolition presently."[70] The connection between the domesticity of teaching a child and its relation to the political sphere's broader concerns is explicit. English domestic life affects ways in which England engages transatlantically.

Marcia's teaching through Christian principle continues in her daughter; Olivia teaches little George because his mother refuses to. Olivia is "not a little proud" of little George's lesson, as she "consider[s] it a conquest over prejudice!" (79). "Prejudices imbibed in the nursery are frequently attached to the being of ripened years," so "to eradicate them as they appear, is a labour well worth the endeavour of the judicious preceptor" (80). The author highlights the role that mothers have in eradicating the next generation's prejudices. Little George continues, referring to Jamaica, "black slaves are no better than horses over there" (80). Olivia argues that opportunity, not innate inequality, facilitates enslaved people's situations: "Those black slaves are, by some cruel masters, obliged to work like horses . . . but God Almighty created them *men*, equal with their masters, if they had the same advantages, and the same blessings of education" (80). Little George's reaction is in keeping with Percy Bysshe Shelley's notion of the moral imagination, later articulated in *A Defence of Poetry*: "The great secret of morals is Love; or a going out of our own nature, and an identification of ourselves with the beautiful which exists in thought, action or person, not our own. . . . The great instrument of moral good is the imagination."[71] Little George imagines how it would feel to be treated like a horse himself, asking what "*right*" "naughty masters" have to behave so: "I'm *sure* they can't like it—I shouldn't like to work like mamma's coach-horses, and stand shivering for hours in the wet and cold, as they do."[72] The repeated, but pointedly expanded, diction—"work like horses" and "work like mamma's coach-horses"—implicitly aligns Mrs. Merton with the "cruel masters." Little George does not like his mother's treatment of others, and so hopefully he will not subsequently replicate the same behavior. English attitudes to the plight of "slaves" is exemplified in his mother's affected indifference at and refusal to listen to little George's lesson: "Mrs. Merton now appeared to think the conversation as great a *bore* as making *tea*, and, walking to the further part of the room, she was patting her pug dog, and humming a tune at the same time."[73] Mrs. Merton chooses to ignore the very suffering that affords her the lifestyle she enjoys. The author imagines that the process of teaching Europeans to treat Africans better will have to be carried on over generations, and that women have a crucial role in disrupting the inheritance of prejudices.

OLIVIA'S ENGLISH CONFORMITY

Olivia's utter conformity to European standards, however, cannot be overlooked. She draws attention to her identity "as a stranger, and a mulatto West Indian," reminding readers that she is, apparently, an outsider, but her behavior conforms to English ideals of virtue, and her cultural authority is grounded in English literature.[74] Olivia speaks in perfect grammatical English, in a way that Dido does not (which demarcates Dido visually and aurally as Other).[75] The exposure of the myth of England's self-image is complicated by the text's reliance on English cultural authority and standards. Olivia performs the identity "Britons would least expect a black Caribbean woman to know well," that of 'English' feminine virtue.[76] She is "heavenly, heavenly Olivia!" whose "*mind* . . . is the seat of every *virtue*!"[77] She eschews "all the ceremonials of fashion and the tax which the arbitrary customs of the world has imposed so heavily upon reason and common sense" (125). Here "reason and common sense" with which Olivia aligns herself are by implication English qualities, which are eroded by the "world[ly]" taste of people like Mrs. Merton and Lady Ingot. In contrast, for Olivia, "the meretricious allurements of folly" are nothing to "the contemplation of virtuous simplicity!" (131).

Olivia embodies feminine resignation in line with the Editor's "*moral*" that "the mind" "imbued with the truths of our most *holy faith*" should "become resigned to its fate" (189); she vows, "It is part of my religious duty to endeavour to resign myself to the all-wise dispensations of the Most High" (154). The way in which Augustus responds to Olivia might serve as a guide for readers: initially he feels "disgust" at her "negro" "skin," but only "a very few hours served to convince" him that "her mind and form were cast in no common mould" (102). She is, indeed, "a superior being" (102). Augustus describes Olivia using characteristics familiar of the typical English novelistic heroine. "She has a noble and a dignified soul" and "is raised above the standard of her sex" (102). "She is accomplished and elegant," but not with "the superficial acquirements of the day" (103). Her "elegance is not the studied attitude of a modern belle, but the spontaneous emotion of a graceful mind" (103). Crucially, "The decision and promptitude with which she delivers her opinions, though accompanied by an air of modest timidity, prove that she has a spirit which will never suffer her to yield her principles or her sentiments, where her conscience tells her she is right: and that, though trampled upon, she will yet retain her native dignity of character!" (103). This virtuous, almost unrealistically ideal, description echoes, for example, the heroine of Samuel Richardson's behemothian *Clarissa* (1748–1749). Clarissa had, like Olivia, an air of modest timidity, but a spirit that would never suffer her to yield her principles, so much so that she starves herself to death. The third edition's postscript responded to readers' criticisms that "the character of our Heroine" is "not only improbable, but unattainable" by declaring that readers ought "to exert the like *humble* and *modest*, yet *steady* and *useful*, virtues" to "reach . . . the perfections of a Clarissa."[78] As it is supposed that Clarissa, as a perfect virtuous heroine, will serve as an exemplar to young female readers, so it is with Olivia.

Throughout *Woman of Colour*, admirable men lament that Olivia should be subjected to oppression and misuse: "Oh! why—why were you the *best* and gentlest of human beings? why were you the appointed victim of such unparalleled sufferings?"[79] Olivia epitomizes virtue by accepting suffering calmly, while refusing to allow her principles to be subdued: "They can never teach my heart to forego its nature, or my mind its principles" (66). As Lovelace writes of Clarissa, "She never *was* subdued," and indeed "her glory has been established by her sufferings!", so Mr. Lumley, "clergyman of the parish," declares of Olivia's behavior, "See here a conquest over *self*, which ye would vainly try to imitate!"[80] Like Clarissa, Olivia concentrates her "conquest" on governing her "*self*"; she is an example for English female readers "to imitate." Olivia's behavior and moral code is thus sanctioned by the novel's religious figure, described as an example of what makes England venerable.[81] Like Marcia before her, Olivia teaches "a lesson of noble self-denial and self-conquest to . . . European[s]" (55). Likewise, Olivia might convert readers as she had little George.

Olivia proves to be more English than many native Englishwomen (including Mrs. Merton, Miss Danby, and Miss Singleton). Charles Honeywood, as they are crossing the Atlantic, states: "Miss Fairfield, I know of no one like you—you will shame our English ladies—or rather, you are going where your virtues will not be known or appreciated!" (65). Olivia declares, ironically, that she "is no heroine" despite her conduct epitomizing one (61). In disavowing herself as heroine, Olivia is presented in contrast to Mrs. Merton, who had imagined herself heroine of "Augustus and Letitia, a novel, founded on facts"; so "she immediately fell *violently in love*" with Augustus, precipitating her "so novel-like" revenge upon him (175). Yet whereas Mrs. Merton had sought "the most silly novel[s]" "warm with the declaration of passion," *Woman of Colour* is not that kind of novel (173–174). Olivia's behavior, in line with conduct book heroines, is exemplary and unimpeachable, providing guidance for young female readers. This heroine is not "rewarded . . . with the usual meed of virtue—*a husband*," because "virtue, like Olivia Fairfield's, may truly be said to be its *own reward*" (189). Olivia is not presented as threatening, mollifying the potential threat of the message she carries with her. Augustus says to Olivia, "*Your* unparalleled sweetness and forbearance is what *I* must ever remember!" as should English female readers (126).

As well as religious quotation, Olivia copiously alludes to the male English literary canon—to William Wordsworth, Edward Young, William Shenstone, and Thomas Gray, among others—showing her thinking is steeped in English literature, implying that she possesses the cultural authority to criticize England. She quotes three of the canon's most prominent men: William Shakespeare, John Milton, and Alexander Pope. She adds to the pathos of Mr. Bellfield's "misfortunes" by aligning him with the words of *Romeo and Juliet*'s apothecary, "My poverty, but not my will, consents!"[82] She invokes Milton's *L'Allegro* to extol the active and cheerful life.[83] She quotes Pope's popular *Universal Prayer*, stating the "Power" of God has "taught" her to "feel another's woe."[84] To "feel another's Woe" enables one to "see" one's own "Fault[s]," "foolish Pride, / Or impious Discontent."[85] As the poem's title suggests, Pope advocates that God's laws apply universally, to all people, from all lands:

> FATHER of All! in every Age,
> In every Clime ador'd,
> By Saint, by Savage, and by Sage.[86]

Olivia draws on this very English authority to support her belief that all should be merciful to each other:

> That Mercy I to others show,
> That Mercy show to me.[87]

English luminaries support Olivia's perspective; she values English cultural authority, and English cultural authority argues for the equality before God, even of "Savage[s]."

The three Englishmen who, at the novel's close, embody Olivia's "veneration" for "England"—Lumley, Bellfield, and Augustus—typify 'English' virtue.[88] Lumley is "devout and impressive" (105). The Ingots refuse to interact socially with the Lumleys because Sir Marmaduke thought it "necessary to draw the line of separation *somewhere*" (123). Olivia, conversely, takes Caroline Lumley under her wing as "frequent . . . companion," and observes, "My behaviour surprises and charms her, as being contrasted with the foolish *hauteur* of other strangers" (123). The clergyman's family—with good, honest, unfussy Englishness—is preferred to the luxuriating East Indians: "The amiable simplicity and good-humoured frankness of the Lumleys, are well contrasted by the assuming pride and false consequence of the Ingots" (124). Bellfield, Sophia's uncle, is presented as a "good," "paternal" Englishman, as against Sophia's reckless "hot-headed West-Indian" husband: Sophia "sincerely wished she had never quitted those paternal arms which now sheltered her in their fond embrace!" (185–186). Augustus is "a lover of goodness and virtue" (104). Olivia experiences disappointment with many English people she encounters: "I am disappointed in England," she says, "I expected to meet with sensible, liberal, well informed and rational people, and I have not found them; I see a compound of folly and dissimulation" (88). Although her experience has been disappointing in some respects, England is still upheld as the seat of "sensible, liberal, well informed and rational people." Olivia realizes that "the circle of Mrs. Merton's friends" "is not the place to meet with the persons [she] expected" (88). Instead, she finds English goodness in the religious piety of Lumley, the kind patience of Bellfield, and the noble suffering of Augustus.

DIDO'S THWARTED AMBITION

Dido is also a transatlantic woman traveler with personal experiences of England. She, at least partially, follows in the tradition of Cervantes's Sancho Panza, the comic, practical, and faithful servant in *Don Quixote* who returns to his master's auspices after attempting self-governance. Lyndon J. Dominique optimistically assesses Dido's relationship with Olivia: "Dido's gratitude," apparently, is "discriminating" as she is "active in questioning the terms of freedom in England for people of African descent."[89] But "freedom" is not on Dido's agenda; instead, she hopes to ascend the established hierarchical system by being promoted to housekeeper. Dido is glad to "have a house and an establishment of [their] own": "Dido be *great* there," she says, "and housekeeper to her dear dearest lady."[90] Despite this apparent elevation, within the same breath, Dido maintains her position as subservient "to Massa Fairfield's daughter" (99). Olivia remarks, condescendingly, of Dido's new role, "Dido is delighted . . . and bears about the insignia of her office, in the bunch of keys at her side, and the *important* expression of her face" (105).

Dido's treatment at Olivia's hands is, of course, better than in the Merton household, where she was "'blacky,' and 'wowsky,' and 'squabby,' and 'guashy'" (100). When the Mertons visit New Park, Dido enjoys her upgraded status: "Thanks to my good lady,—Dido be Missee below stairs, and treated by all as if me was as good as another, for all me be poor negro wench!" (127). Dido "thanks" Olivia for being treated "as if" she was equal. Olivia commends Augustus's proper treatment of Dido, unlike Abigail, and states this will "win" Dido's affection: "But you know the honest heart of my faithful girl! Augustus treats her with that good-humoured kindness and freedom which is the sure way to win it" (100). For English people "the sure way" to "win" (with odd connotations of competition and triumph) the faithfulness of "slave[s]" is to treat them with "good-humoured kindness and freedom" (100). Clearly, suggesting Dido receive "good-humoured kindness and freedom" from whiter-skinned people is not objectionable, but the implication is that Black people ought to be encouraged to be "faithful" to whiter people. The status quo's hierarchy is not displaced by Dido; instead, readers are presented with her apparently willful enslavement. Augustus treating Dido with "freedom" will, oxymoronically, encourage her to be subservient to "her new beautiful Massa" (100).

Dido's fidelity to Olivia, and concomitantly Augustus, is more troubling than Dominique suggests. Olivia proclaims, "My faithful Dido" (151), "how grateful am I for her faithful attachment!" (181); as much as 'slaves' ought to be grateful for kind treatment by their 'masters/mistresses', 'masters/mistresses' should likewise be "grateful" for such "faithful[ness]." This does not suggest that the system should be overthrown, but instead conforms to Burkean conservative notions of each "little platoon" working for the benefit of all within it.[91] Lady Nugent described how "poor blackies . . . are all so good-humoured, and seem so merry" as they work.[92] *Woman of Colour* likewise presents Dido as merrily subservient to Olivia. At no point does the narrative suggest that Olivia seeks to free Dido, or that Dido might seek emancipation. In this respect, Olivia is as blind to her own conduct as those she chastises are to theirs. Dido exclaims she "was never slave but to her own dear Missee, and she was *proud* of that!"[93] That Dido is "*proud*" to be Olivia's "slave" troublingly endorses Edgeworth's "The Grateful Negro," which sentimentalizes 'slave/master' relations.[94] Dido is a grateful Caesar, not a vengeful Hector.

Dido develops some agency while in England. "Of her own inviting!" she engineers Honeywood's visit.[95] Dido promotes a scheme where Olivia marries Honeywood, which would enable her to retain her position as housekeeper. When this plan falls through, Dido declares (echoing Olivia's earlier disappointment in the Mertons' circle), "Me know nothing in this England town, but disappointments" (167). She is disappointed because her attempts to determine her own future have gone awry; she has not experienced the post-Mansfield emancipatory freedom supposed to exist for enslaved peoples on stepping foot in England. She had hoped for betterment in her position in England. Instead, she must return—under Olivia's auspices—to her Jamaican status. Olivia rebukes Dido's frustration: "Dido, how often must I tell you, that happiness is independent of situation" (168). This is easy enough for Olivia—who commands a position of relative privilege—to think, but Dido is decidedly less "independent of situation" than Olivia: she does not have the choices and autonomy available to her that Olivia does, and she has to submit to whatever Olivia decides. As Olivia makes apparent in the novel's final stages, when she "revisit[s] Jamaica" she will retain a privileged position and "shall again enjoy the society of [her] dear Mrs. Milbanke" (188). When Dido travels to Jamaica, her status will revert to that of "slave," and yet we learn in Olivia's penultimate missive that "Dido is already packing up with avidity," eager to return.[96] Brigitte Fielder articulates in her illuminating discussion of Olivia's and Dido's relationship that "inequality does not foreclose Dido's agency"; not entirely, but Dido's attempts at independence are ultimately thwarted.[97] The novel troublingly denies Dido agency to control her life and keeps her—chastened after her "disappointments"—in contended, even "avid," subservience.[98]

CONSERVATIVE AMELIORATION, NOT RADICAL REVOLUTION

Olivia perceives a different relationship to slavery in Bristol than in London. Bristol made its money in the slave trade, and so was frequently depicted in the long eighteenth century as a symbol of parvenu vulgarity and moral laxity. We might think here of Bristolian Mrs. Elton in Austen's *Emma* (1816), whose indecorousness and exploitativeness, especially through her references to Bristol, are mocked mercilessly.[99] The Mertons live in Bristol, although trading in London has contributed to their wealth. It is experiencing Bristol that makes Olivia "disappointed in England."[100] When she visits London (seat of lawmakers), however, her assessment of the nation shifts, and "England" becomes a symbol of "benevolence" (96). Depicting Bristol's corrupted culture and comparing it with London's allows the author to have her/his cake and eat it too: Bristolians embody the bad behavior that the author is trying to educate readers out of, but the author still manages in contrasting "compassionate" London to maintain the image of England as it likes to imagine itself (96).

Olivia "behold[s]" in Londoners a "boundless liberality in providing for the distresses of their necessitous fellow-citizens!"[101] The diction "fellow-citizens" recalls the French Revolution's admirable ideals: "citizens" possess civic rights and privileges, while "fellow" suggests equality. Contemporaries, such as Helen Maria Williams, had likewise considered principles spearheaded by the French Revolution as arguments against enslavement: "Europe is hastening towards a period too enlightened for the perpetuation of such monstrous abuses."[102] Williams, like Olivia, is "a citizen of the world."[103] *Woman of Colour* promotes some of the original ideals behind the French Revolution while cautioning against such violent action. Olivia sees the "compassionate eye" in London, and assumes this "benevolence" extends to enslaved people: "England is, sure, the favoured isle, where benevolence has taken up her abode! *Here* she dwells, here she smiles, while, towards my native island, she turns her 'far surveying,' her compassionate eye. She descries the sufferings of the poor negro, and promises benign assistance.—Yes! the cause of Afric's injured sons is heard in England; and soon shall the *slave* be free!"[104] The author quotes a phrase from Wordsworth's *Descriptive Sketches* (1793) to bolster the argument; the poem illustrates Wordsworth's "Wish for the extirpation of Slavery."[105] There is a direct echo in "compassionate eye" to the novel's stated "moral."[106] England's "benevolence" will lead to "*slave*[s]" being "free." Africa's "injur[y]" is a "cause" that "is heard" and "taken up" "in England." But crucially, Jamaica requires England's "benign assistance" to facilitate emancipation.

Although Olivia criticizes much of what she encounters in England, and her sojourn there leaves Dido and her "disappointed," the disappointment stems from the gulf between what she "expected" and "found."[107] Expectations of what England *should* be are, in fact, re-affirmed in the novel; the status quo is fulsomely supported, and reform rather than rebellion is espoused. Olivia's criticism of England concerns the practice not the principle. Indeed, one might read Olivia's and Dido's connection as embodying an idealized 'master/slave' dynamic, showing how amelioration could seemingly improve conditions and practices.

Olivia is conservative in her outlook; she argues that enslavement is wrong because it contradicts principles that England ostensibly holds dear—Christian charitability to others. Slavery corrupts 'English' Christian principles—it "hardens the heart, and deadens the feelings."[108] Dominique's buoyant reading claims that Olivia is "beleaguered but fiercely independent."[109] Olivia's thinking is not "independent," however. Burkean "just prejudice" is, in fact, what Olivia advocates in her employment of "old customs, and old notions."[110] Edmund Burke had argued that "prejudice is of ready application in the emergency"—pertinent for an author considering themes of emancipation in the wake of the recent alarming Haitian crisis—because "it previously engages the mind in a steady course of wisdom and virtue, and does not leave the man hesitating in the moment of decision, sceptical, puzzled and unresolved."[111] "Prejudice," for Burke, is "respect for the wisdom of others" who have gone before.[112] Dominique calls Olivia "a literal, subversive, and political threat sent to expose the dominant system of prejudice in England and to undermine it by associating with, and re-educating, Britons."[113] She is neither "threat[ening]" nor "re-educating" Britons with anything new, however; Olivia does not "undermine" the English "system." Instead, Olivia adheres to a Burkean "old scheme of things," eschewing the dangerous exotic "new" ideas represented via Lady Ingot.[114] Lady Ingot remarks to Olivia: "There is scarcely a female besides yourself in this neighbourhood, who has ever set her foot out of England. Conceive what narrow minded, prejudiced beings they must be? Not an idea but what was planted in them at their births and has been handed down by mothers and grandmothers, and great-grandmothers, through countless generations!"[115] Olivia rejects the assertion that someone must travel out of England to expand his or her mind; in fact, "*ideas*" handed down through countless generations are "worthy [of] retaining": "I confess, I think our mothers and grandmothers were sensible beings. I rather lean towards old customs, and old notions, and can trace one of *my ideas* as far back as the *Old* Testament" (110). Olivia shows female readers that you do not have to travel to learn: because "retirement seems the peculiar and appropriate station of our sex," "the enlargement of the mind, and the conquest of prejudice, is not always achieved, perhaps, by visiting foreign climes!" (111). The novel's purpose is for young female readers—who have not traveled abroad, and are unlikely to—to enlarge their minds and contest bigotry from the "retirement" of their own homes. Olivia has done their traveling for them. The author puts gender in the foreground; useful ideas are passed through the female line—through the "sensible beings" of "our mothers and grandmothers [and great-grandmothers]." The use of "our" here suggests that passing morality down through the generations is a collective enterprise.

In Marcia, Olivia sees that "the distributions of Providence are equally bestowed, and that it is culture not capacity, which the negro wants!" (55). The "culture . . . the negro wants" is assumed to be English. Felicity Nussbaum has called another reverse-Robinsonade, *Hindoo Rajah*, a "surreptitious" defense of

"British colonial[ism]," which also applies to *Woman of Colour*.[116] As with *Hindoo Rajah*, however, *Woman of Colour* defends "a version of colonialism which will work only if the English practice the Christian tolerance and mercy they preach."[117] Other reverse-Robinsonades, such as Anna Maria Mackenzie's *Slavery* (1792), where "European" "virtue" and "education" "polish" and "refine" "the savage" "of Africa," had advocated amelioration.[118] Likewise, at the novel's close, Olivia wants to return across the Atlantic to apply English values in order to "instruct" and "mend" "blacks."[119] In the penultimate paragraph, Olivia even uses the term "ameliorat[e]" about Jamaica: "I shall again zealously engage myself in ameliorating the situation" (188). Olivia's diction alludes to the 1798 Amelioration/Melioration Act, which was supposed to improve conditions for enslaved people in British Caribbean colonies.[120] Early in the novel, Olivia had used the same diction in explaining her preference for staying in Jamaica and "meliorating the sorrows of the poor slaves," rather than traveling to England.[121] Given the recent Haitian Revolution, the threat of "slave" insurgency continued to worry those wishing to maintain the status quo.[122] Lady Nugent, for example, was chastised for showing "unusual and extraordinary" "respect" to "slaves"; her associates "seemed to think the example dangerous" and might "even produce a rebellion in the island."[123] Likewise "Benevolus" of the *Gentleman's Magazine* warned that without attentive management of potential "insurrections," "it might make Jamaica like St. Domingo."[124]

"Is it, that I see through a magnifying glass to discover defects?" Olivia asks.[125] The author, unsubtly, alerts readers to Olivia's function, which is "to discover defects" and "magnify" them for readers to "see" more fully. English society's defects are exposed in order to put England right. Olivia is a foil through which the author reflects England back to itself. The focus is on pricking the consciences and changing the behavior of people in England, rather than on Olivia's subjectivity. The Editor makes clear that "the *moral*" of the work is expressly to "teach" the "*skeptical European*" to be more "compassionate" "towards the *despised native of Africa*."[126] It is irrelevant "whether Olivia Fairfield's be a *real* or an *imaginary* character."[127] The function of reverse-Robinsonades is to examine the home culture, and the novel's closing passage focuses not on Olivia herself, or even on Jamaica, the land she is returning to, but on "England, favoured Isle!—Happy country."[128] Olivia will "carry" her "veneration for [England's] name" back "over the world of waters"; she will keep in mind the "beautiful purity" of England's "laws," "arts," "sciences," and "religion" when she is "ameliorating" Jamaica (188). This transatlantic woman calls on readers to uphold and promote England's "benevolence" in the march toward emancipation (96).

NOTES

1. Joel Quirk, *The Anti-Slavery Project: From the Slave Trade to Human Trafficking* (Philadelphia: University of Pennsylvania Press, 2011), 49; Robin Blackburn, *The Overthrow of Colonial Slavery, 1776–1848* (New York: Verso, 1988), 314–315.
2. Benevolus, *Gentleman's Magazine: And Historical Chronicle* 77 (February 1807): 129, 128.
3. Lyndon J. Dominique, *Imoinda's Shade: Marriage and the African Woman in Eighteenth-Century British Literature, 1759–1808* (Columbus: Ohio State University Press, 2012), 236–237.
4. *The Woman of Colour, A Tale* (London: Black, Parry and Kingsbury, 1808). Quotations in this essay are from *The Woman of Colour: A Tale*, ed. Lyndon J. Dominique (Peterborough, ON: Broadview Press, 2008).
5. *Woman of Colour*, 58.
6. *Woman of Colour*, 53.
7. *Woman of Colour*, 188.
8. *Woman of Colour*, 102–103.
9. Daniel Defoe, *Life and Strange Surprizing Adventures of Robinson Crusoe (1719)*, vol. 1 of *The Novels of Daniel Defoe*, ed. W. R. Owens and P. N. Furbank (London: Pickering and Chatto, 2008), 109.
10. *Woman of Colour*, 103, 92.
11. *Woman of Colour*, 71; William Cowper, *The Poems of William Cowper*, ed. John Baird and Charles Ryskamp, 3 vols. (Oxford: Oxford University Press, 2014), 1:403–404.
12. Cowper, *Poems*, l:403–404, line 45; lines 25–28.
13. The vast majority of Robinsonades remained male-dominated, but female Robinsonades grew over the eighteenth century. See Jeannine Blackwell, "An Island of Her Own: Heroines of the German Robinsonades from 1720 to 1800," *German Quarterly* 58, no. 1 (Winter 1985): 5–26.
14. Defoe, *Robinson Crusoe*, 212; *Woman of Colour*, 189.
15. *Monthly Review; or, Literary Journal* 62 (June 1810): 212.
16. *Woman of Colour*, 53.
17. *Woman of Colour*, 54–55.
18. *Woman of Colour*, 54.
19. Maximillian Novak and J. Paul Hunter foreground *Robinson Crusoe*'s Puritan elements, arguing that the novel focuses on the experience of spiritual conversion. See Maximillian Novak, *Economics and the Fiction of Daniel Defoe* (Berkeley: University of California Press, 1962); and J. Paul Hunter, *The Reluctant Pilgrim: Defoe's Emblematic Method and Quest for Form in "Robinson Crusoe"* (Baltimore: Johns Hopkins University Press, 1966).
20. Note that the transatlantic traveler's gender is highlighted in the titles of both novels: *The Female American* and *The Woman of Colour*.
21. Unca Eliza Winkfield [pseud.], *The Female American; or, The Adventures of Unca Eliza Winkfield*, ed. Michelle Burnham and James Freitas, 2nd ed. (Peterborough, ON: Broadview Press, 2014), 57.
22. *Woman of Colour*, 186.
23. Winkfield, *Female American*, 52.
24. For more on projects of "New World" colonialism and religious conversion, see Michelle Burnham and James Freitas, introduction to *The Female American; or, The Adventures of Unca Eliza Winkfield*, by Unca Eliza Winkfield [pseud.], ed. Michelle Burnham and James Freitas, 2nd ed. (Peterborough, ON: Broadview Press, 2014), 9–32.
25. Scarlet Bowen, "*Via Media*: Transatlantic Anglicanism in *The Female American*," *The Eighteenth Century* 53, no. 2 (Summer 2012): 193.

26. *Woman of Colour,* 105, 119, 122.
27. *Woman of Colour,* 121; Denys Van Renen, "'The Temple of Folly': Transatlantic 'Nature,' Nabobs, and Environmental Degradation in *The Woman of Colour,*" in *Romantic Sustainability: Endurance and the Natural World, 1780–1830,* ed. Ben P. Robertson (Lanham, MD: Lexington Books, 2016), 155.
28. *Woman of Colour,* 121.
29. Victoria Barnett-Woods, "Models of Morality: The Bildungsroman and Social Reform in *The Female American* and *The Woman of Colour,*" *Women's Studies* 45, no. 7 (2016): 616 n4. Examples of reverse-Robinsonades include *The Spectator,* no. 50 (April 27, 1711), in Joseph Addison and Richard Steele, *The Spectator,* ed. Donald Frederic Bond, 5 vols. (Oxford: Oxford University Press, 2014), 1:211–215; *The Ranelean Religion Displayed. In a Letter from a Hottentot of Distinction, now in London, to his Friend at the Cape of Good-Hope* (London: W. Webb, 1750); Voltaire, *Le Huron, ou L'ingénu,* 2 vols. (Lausanne, 1767); Anna Maria Mackenzie, *Slavery: Or, The Times,* 2 vols. (London: G.G.J. and J. Robinsons and J. Dennis, 1792); Robert Bage, *Hermsprong; or, Man as He is Not,* 3 vols. (London: printed for William Lane, at the Minerva Press, 1796); and Elizabeth Hamilton, *Translation of the Letters of a Hindoo Rajah,* 2 vols. (London: Printed for G. G. and J. Robinson, 1796).
30. Pamela Perkins and Shannon Russell, introduction to *Translation of the Letters of a Hindoo Rajah,* by Elizabeth Hamilton, ed. Pamela Perkins and Shannon Russell, repr. with corrections (Peterborough, ON: Broadview Press, 2004), 22.
31. *Monthly Review; or, Literary Journal* 21 (October 1796): 176; *Scots Magazine* 59 (January 1797): 47. Neither review attempts to categorize or coin a term for the "ingenious device," but both helpfully describe the technique used by the reverse-Robinsonade genre.
32. Omiah, *An Historic Epistle, from Omiah, to the Queen of Otaheite; Being His Remarks on the English Nation* (London: T. Evans, 1775), 1, lines 5–8.
33. Oliver Goldsmith, *Collected Works of Oliver Goldsmith,* ed. Arthur Friedman, 5 vols. (Oxford: Clarendon Press, 1966), 2:142.
34. *Woman of Colour,* 125, 103. Goldsmith is quoted throughout the novel.
35. Francis Bacon, *Essayes or Counsels, Civill and Morall* (London: John Haviland for Hanna Barret, 1625), 70.
36. *Woman of Colour,* 103.
37. Robert Southey, *Letters from England,* by Don Manuel Alvarez Espriella [Robert Southey]. Edited by Carol Bolton (London: Routledge, 2016), 97.
38. Jane Austen, *Jane Austen's Letters,* ed. Deidre Le Faye, 3rd ed. (Oxford: Oxford University Press, 1995), 141.
39. Carol Bolton, introduction to *Letters from England: By Don Manuel Alvarez Espriella. Translated from the Spanish,* ed. Carol Bolton (London: Routledge, 2016), 7.
40. *Woman of Colour,* 111.
41. *Woman of Colour,* 71, 188.
42. *Woman of Colour,* 111.
43. Van Renen, "Temple of Folly," 151.
44. *Woman of Colour,* 111.
45. *Woman of Colour,* 187.
46. *Woman of Colour,* 66. Stephen Usherwood, "'The Black Must Be Discharged': The Abolitionists' Debt to Lord Mansfield," *History Today* 31, no. 3 (March 1981): 40–45.
47. Maria Edgeworth, "The Grateful Negro," in *Selected Tales for Children and Young People,* ed. Susan Manly (Basingstoke: Palgrave Macmillan, 2013), 179.
48. Cowper, *Poems,* 2:140, lines 40–41.
49. *Woman of Colour,* 51. The author slightly misquotes Cowper's "He finds his fellow guilty of a skin / Not colour'd like his own, and having pow'r / T' inforce the wrong, for such a

worthy cause / Dooms and devotes him as his lawful prey" (Cowper, *Poems*, 2:139, lines 12–15). In replacing "fellow" with "brother," the author perhaps conflates Cowper's poem and the antislavery campaign's slogan, "Am I not a Man and a Brother?"

50. *Woman of Colour*, 73; c.f. Cowper, *Poems*, 2:139, lines 12–15.
51. Cowper, *Poems*, 2:140, lines 41–47.
52. *Woman of Colour*, 66.
53. Sara Salih, *Representing Mixed Race in Jamaica and England from the Abolition Era to the Present* (London: Routledge, 2011), 71.
54. James Joyce, "Daniel Defoe," ed. and trans. Joseph Prescott, *Buffalo Studies* 1 (December 1964): 24.
55. Lyndon J. Dominique, introduction to *The Woman of Colour: A Tale*, ed. Lyndon J. Dominique (Peterborough, ON: Broadview Press, 2008), 40.
56. Burnham and Freitas, introduction to *Female American*, 13; Mary Helen McMurran, "Realism and the Unreal in *The Female American*," *The Eighteenth Century* 52, no. 3–4 (Fall–Winter 2011): 323.
57. *Woman of Colour*, 59.
58. *Woman of Colour*, 148.
59. Olivia's several homosocial relationships are revealing in other ways too, for example, with Mrs. Milbanke, Mrs. Honeywood, Caroline Lumley, and especially Dido (which I discuss later in the chapter). For a "queer" reading of *Woman of Colour*, which prioritizes Olivia's engagements with female characters, see Brigitte Fielder, "*The Woman of Colour* and Black Atlantic Movement," in *Women's Narratives of the Early Americas and the Formation of Empire*, ed. Mary McAleer Balkun and Susan C. Imbarrato (New York: Palgrave Macmillan, 2016), 174.
60. Srinivas Aravamudan, *Tropicopolitans: Colonialism and Agency, 1688–1804* (Durham, NC: Duke University Press, 1999), 4; Dominique, introduction to *Woman of Colour*, 31.
61. *Woman of Colour*, 150.
62. Maria Nugent, "Lady Nugent's Journal of Her Residence in Jamaica from 1801 to 1805," in *Travel Writing 1700–1830: An Anthology*, ed. Elizabeth A. Bohls and Ian Duncan (Oxford: Oxford University Press, 2008), 331.
63. *Oxford English Dictionary*, s.v. "abigail," accessed September 1, 2020, http://www.oed.com.
64. Society for the Propagation of the Gospel, *A Collection of Papers, Printed by Order of the Society for the Propagation of the Gospel in Foreign Parts* (London: Joseph Downing, 1706), 28. The SPG was a missionary organization of the Church of England.
65. Gal. 3:28. *The Bible: Authorized King James Version*, ed. Robert Carroll and Stephen Prickett (Oxford: Oxford University Press, 2008), 236.
66. *Woman of Colour*, 79.
67. *Woman of Colour*, 79.
68. Society for the Propagation of the Gospel, *Collection of Papers*, 28.
69. *Critical Review; or, Annals of Literature* 20 (May 1810): 109.
70. *Woman of Colour*, 81.
71. Percy Bysshe Shelley, *A Defence of Poetry*, in *Major Works*, ed. Zachary Leader and Michael O'Neill (Oxford: Oxford University Press, 2009), 682.
72. *Woman of Colour*, 80.
73. *Woman of Colour*, 80.
74. *Woman of Colour*, 92.
75. Dido says, for example, "Iss, iss, me think it be very pretty house" (*Woman of Colour*, 166). For more on Dido's "racialized dialect," see Fielder, "Black Atlantic Movement," 178.
76. Dominique, introduction to *Woman of Colour*, 25.
77. *Woman of Colour*, 154, 117.

78. Samuel Richardson, *Clarissa. Or, The History of a Young Lady*, 3rd ed., 8 vols. (London: S. Richardson, 1751), 8:298.
79. *Woman of Colour*, 161.
80. Richardson, *Clarissa*, 6:27; *Woman of Colour*, 105, 148.
81. *Woman of Colour*, 188.
82. *Woman of Colour*, 134; William Shakespeare, *Romeo and Juliet*, in *Royal Shakespeare Company Complete Works*, ed. Jonathan Bate and Eric Rasmussen (Basingstoke: Macmillan, 2008), 1734, act 5, scene 1, line 78.
83. *Woman of Colour*, 69.
84. *Woman of Colour*, 125.
85. Alexander Pope, *The Twickenham Edition of the Poems of Alexander Pope*, ed. John Butt, 11 vols. (London: Methuen, 1961–1969), 6:148, lines 33–38.
86. Pope, *Poems*, 6:145, lines 1–3.
87. Pope, *Poems*, 6:148, lines 39–40.
88. *Woman of Colour*, 188.
89. Dominique, introduction to *Woman of Colour*, 34–35.
90. *Woman of Colour*, 99.
91. Edmund Burke, *Reflections on the Revolution in France* (London: J. Dodsley, 1790), 68.
92. Nugent, "Journal," 328.
93. *Woman of Colour*, 100.
94. George E. Boulukos, "Maria Edgeworth's 'Grateful Negro' and the Sentimental Argument for Slavery," *Eighteenth-Century Life* 23, no. 1 (February 1999): 12–29; George E. Boulukos, *The Grateful Slave: The Emergence of Race in Eighteenth-Century British and American Culture* (Cambridge: Cambridge University Press, 2008).
95. *Woman of Colour*, 161.
96. *Woman of Colour*, 188. See Salih, *Representing Mixed Race*, 180 n20.
97. Fielder, "Black Atlantic Movement," 179.
98. *Woman of Colour*, 167, 188.
99. Gabrielle White, "*Emma*: Autonomy and Abolition," in *Jane Austen in the Context of Abolition: "A Fling at the Slave Trade"* (Basingstoke: Palgrave Macmillan, 2006), 52–72.
100. *Woman of Colour*, 88.
101. *Woman of Colour*, 96.
102. Helen Maria Williams, *Letters Written in France, in the Summer 1790*, ed. Neil Fraistat and Susan Lanser (Peterborough, ON: Broadview Press, 2001), 84.
103. Williams, *Letters*, 69.
104. *Woman of Colour*, 96.
105. William Wordsworth, *Descriptive Sketches. In Verse. Taken during a Pedestrian Tour in the Italian, Grison, Swiss, and Savoyard Alps* (London: printed for J. Johnson, 1793), iii. Olivia quotes Wordsworth's "But now with other soul I stand alone / Sublime upon this far-surveying cone" (27, lines 366–367).
106. *Woman of Colour*, 189.
107. *Woman of Colour*, 88.
108. *Woman of Colour*, 107.
109. Dominique, introduction to *Woman of Colour*, 39.
110. Burke, *Reflections*, 130; *Woman of Colour*, 110.
111. Burke, *Reflections*, 130.
112. Burke, *Reflections*, 130.
113. Dominique, introduction to *Woman of Colour*, 31.
114. Burke, *Reflections*, 130.
115. *Woman of Colour*, 110.

116. Felicity Nussbaum, *Torrid Zones: Maternity, Sexuality, and Empire in Eighteenth-Century English Narratives* (Baltimore: Johns Hopkins University Press, 1995), 171.
117. Perkins and Russell, introduction to *Hindoo Rajah*, 29.
118. Mackenzie, *Slavery*, 1:159; Adam Lively, *Masks: Blackness, Race, and the Imagination* (New York: Oxford University Press, 2000), 74.
119. *Woman of Colour*, 188.
120. Caroline Spence, "Ameliorating Empire: Slavery and Protection in the British Colonies, 1783–1865" (PhD diss., Harvard University, 2014).
121. *Woman of Colour*, 56.
122. Leonora Sansay, *Secret History; or, The Horrors of St. Domingo*, ed. Michael J. Drexler (Peterborough, ON: Broadview Press, 2007). Sansay's account examines the Haitian Revolution and was originally published in the same year as *Woman of Colour* (1808).
123. Nugent, "Journal," 332.
124. Benevolus, *Gentleman's Magazine* (February 1807), 129.
125. *Woman of Colour*, 108.
126. *Woman of Colour*, 189.
127. *Woman of Colour*, 189; Jennifer DeVere Brody, *Impossible Purities: Blackness, Femininity, and Victorian Culture* (Durham, NC: Duke University Press, 1998), 26.
128. *Woman of Colour*, 188.

9

CREOLE NATIONALISM, MOBILITY, AND GENDERED POLITICS IN *ZELICA, THE CREOLE*

Victoria Barnett-Woods

"Creole nationalism" appears as a contradiction in terms. From its earliest manifestations in the Caribbean, "creole" has referred to peoples of European descent who lived in the colonies and who predominantly considered themselves more culturally connected to Europe than to the colonial space where they spent a significant portion of their lives. In the nineteenth century, "creole" began to include those of mixed heritage as well as those born in the colonies. "Creolization" implies a cultural, racial, or ethnic mixing, or in the words of Edouard Glissant, of *métissage*, the "meeting and synthesis of two differences."[1] More broadly considered here, creolization refers to the multitudinous evolutions of peoples and languages, never tied to a singular national ideology, but perpetually open, aggregating and synthesizing a diverse range of cultural practices. "Nationalism," in contrast, is a term that reflects a systemic socio-political desire for homogeneity, for oneness. As Benedict Anderson has argued, nationalism is an ideological construct informed by a collective gathering of like-minded individuals and circulating print that consequently determines the racial, linguistic, and cultural boundaries of those included and excluded from a particular "imagined community."[2] When together, "creole nationalism" offers readers a new term for approaching the cross-cultural influences that shaped the long eighteenth-century Caribbean, especially at a time when the idea of an "imagined community" was amorphous and fluid on many of the islands. Within the context of this essay, "creole nationalism" refers to a cultural, economic, and emerging state system that defines itself by and through an aggregating multitude of languages, ethnicities, and cultural attitudes. At its core, "creole nationalism" functions under the assumption that a modern state can sustainably operate through collaborative efforts toward equitable justice, multilingualism, integration, and cross-cultural receptivity.

Naturally, the quixotic nature of this position is in need of a heavily poured dose of historical reality; the massive complex systems of colonization, enslavement, assimilationism, and eradication of Indigenous peoples that have irrevocably altered the Caribbean region point to the term's ideological challenges. Yet, as indicated by Laurent Dubois, events in the eighteenth- and nineteenth-century Caribbean, beginning with the Haitian Revolution, proved that there were emerging visions of a democratic system that excluded no one. The Haitian Revolution, for those who fought for its success, signaled a turn toward a fuller vision of democratized governance, a republic that embraced its citizens regardless of racial background. The story of the early post-emancipation Haiti is one of mutability and cultural flux, and entirely defiant of essentialist racial categorization.[3] It is within the space of quixotic hope and brutal tension that this essay examines two novels that focus on the Haitian Revolution at the time of its occurrence, the experimental musings of creole nationalism that emerged from the revolution, and Haiti's hemispheric ties to the early United States. Specifically, this essay argues that the novel *Zelica, the Creole* experiments with the notion of "creole nationalism" and interrogates early American (U.S.) naturalizations of race and gender hierarchies derived from white and male ideological formations of the "New World."[4] The lead heroine's mobility, cultural and linguistic fluidity, and strength of character complicate the seeming authority of homogeneity within the construction of the nation-state in the circum-Atlantic world. In using the more well-known work of Leonora Sansay's *Secret History; or, The Horrors of St. Domingo* as a springboard for my discussion of the revisionist narrative of *Zelica*, I draw my conclusions about the literary demonstrations of creole nationalism as it is represented in these two novels.[5] For its part in an edited volume that examines women's travel, this essay provides a way to think through the representations of travel in the early nineteenth-century Atlantic. The character of Zelica, and to a lesser extent Clara from *Secret History*, demonstrates that women's hemispheric travel and cultural exchange played an active role in the construction of early hemispheric American literary history. The types of heroines in these novels offer insight into the imaginative collective social thought of those who existed within the real world. Novels that meant to reflect the truth of people's lives also participated in the creation and solidification of that truth, and *Secret History* and *Zelica* are no exception.

The scholarly foundation for my claim comes from the works of Sean Goudie and Eve Tavor Bannet. Goudie's *Creole America* discusses the North American strategies of hemispheric difference, as the United States attempted to sever all national ties to the West Indies, particularly with the aftermath of the Haitian Revolution in the early nineteenth century. Goudie writes, "The shadowy presence of creole American identities underlies anxious efforts to construct exceptional

U.S. 'American' identities and literary and cultural traditions."[6] Yet, as Goudie convincingly argues, attempts at U.S. exceptionalism belied the notion that there were undeniable cross-permeations, cultural and linguistic exchanges, and sites of *métissage* between the new modern nation of the United States and the Caribbean. In his words, the "Hamiltonian empire for commerce" generated an "instability wherein West Indian and Anglo-American cultures and commodities circulate in ways that resist U.S. attempts to sustain hierarchical distinctions between them."[7] One such commodity of resistance that circulated within the circum-Atlantic system of cultural exchange was the novel. Many scholars have tied the circulation of the novel with the meta-narrative of a nation's history, particularly with the rise of bourgeoisie culture and print technology.[8] However, as Eve Tavor Bannet articulates in *Transatlantic Stories*, long eighteenth-century prose writing predicated on historical fact at times struggles with History's (capital H) narrative. The figures in many novels, instead of regurgitating the desire of a homogeneous nation-state structured by strategies of exclusion, actually "reflect very variously upon [historical facts], measuring themselves against diverse genres and subject-positions, and repeatedly demonstrate for the ignorant or unwary how many different stories could be hung on the same facts."[9] The Atlantic novel, much like Glissant's discussion of creolization, was a form riddled with recontextualizations, reformulations, reprints, rewrites, abridgements, edits, and cross- and inter-generic histories. In understanding the inherent instability of the novel form in the eighteenth and early nineteenth centuries, so too does it become easier to understand the meta-narrative dimensions of the history of the Atlantic itself.

Bannet's and Goudie's shared claim that narratives of "fact" and representations of historical "truth" were in constant flux in the long eighteenth-century Atlantic world lays the foundation for this essay's claim that creole nationalism and hemispheric mobility shape the representation of evolving gender and racial politics in *Zelica, the Creole*. The "re-writing" of Sansay's 1808 *Secret History* to include Zelica's narrative in the 1820 revisionist novel is a testament to the shifting range of political views of the French-Haitian struggle for power in the years between 1804 and 1820. As such, the concept of creole nationalism gestures toward possible circum-Atlantic acceptance of an influential and modern Black republic in the Western Hemisphere. The Haitian Revolution and victory over French attempts to reclaim Haiti proved that the European formation of the citizen-subject was a naturalized construct, an ill-fitting fiction when contextualized by a circum-Atlantic environment.

Though the concept of creole nationalism is shared between *Secret History* and *Zelica*, it is important to note that there exists some debate as to whether Sansay is the definitive author of the latter novel. In 1992, Phillip S. Lapsansky, in his rediscovery of *Zelica*, assuredly confirms that Sansay penned the 1820 anonymously published novel, citing a notice for "forthcoming books" in two British periodicals that attribute *Zelica* to "'Madame de Sansée.'"[10] More recently, scholars have questioned Sansay's authorship of *Zelica*. Marlene Daut posits that the novel is not "immediately tied to Sansay's own autobiographical writing [as is done deliberately in *Secret History*]."[11] Daut, who sees *Zelica* as "derivative" of *Secret History*, locates the novel in the categorical genre of historical fiction, not entirely reflective of Sansay's actual accounting of her time spent in Haiti between 1802 and 1804. Michael J. Drexler also pauses on giving the authorial credit of *Zelica* to Sansay, noting the stark differences between it and *Secret History* in terms of generic form (epistolary versus third-person narrative) and plot outcome for the characters.[12] However, what is important for the discussion in this essay is tracing the concept of creole nationalism from the historical figure of Sansay to *Secret History* and, most importantly, to *Zelica*. It is possible that Sansay is the author of both works, as she contemplated and in many ways embodied hemispheric creole nationalism. Twelve years separate the publication of *Secret History* and *Zelica*, potentially allowing the visceral experiences of the Haitian Revolution to be revisited and re-written. Notwithstanding the question of authorship, the intertextual relationship between *Secret History* and *Zelica* can supply a great deal for a reader interested in researching the intersections of race and gender in early American literature and history. Each of the literary heroines, as with the historical Sansay, navigates a male-dominated maritime environment and claims a place within it.

To grasp the full extent in which *Zelica, the Creole* represents a complex critique of Eurocentric formations of nationalism, offering, instead, a mixed-race woman as a symbol of evolving and synthesizing creole nationalism, it will be important to first discuss *Zelica*'s literary antecedent and its author: Sansay's *Secret History*. In the historical accounts of Sansay's life, much can be gleaned about the gendered identity politics and social mobility inherent to her character. Born Mary Hassal in 1773, she married Louis Sansay, an émigré French creole planter who came to her home city of Philadelphia to escape the "horrors" of the Haitian Revolution of the 1790s. When he decided to reclaim his plantation in 1802, she agreed to accompany him. With this decision, she appears to give little regard for the maintenance of her tavern, which she inherited in her youth upon the death of her stepfather. A site of stable commercial business, the tavern would have provided a steady source of income, especially given its known popularity among politicians. But it would have also restricted Sansay to stay in Philadelphia, quite possibly for the entirety of her life.[13] Choosing to marry Louis Sansay offered her an escape (possibly from public scandal associated with her affair with Aaron Burr) and opened the opportunity for a more creolized life abroad; it meant that Sansay would no longer have to toil away in a metropolitan tavern, attending to the thirsting needs of others.[14] Before her departure, Sansay created a social safeguard by going to Washington, D.C., and acquiring letters of introduction and protection, allowing her social mobility while in Haiti and physical mobility should she need to leave Haiti on her own. Despite the social restrictions of being a French planter's wife, Sansay determined the conditions of her travel and stay. For her, as well as for her protagonist Clara in *Secret History*, it was not merely about traveling abroad, but rather about independently determining the circumstances of that travel. In securing those circumstances, Sansay becomes arguably a more cosmopolitan figure, pushing the boundaries of gendered protocols for traveling freely between the French West Indies and the U.S. mid-Atlantic. While not distinctly emblematic of creole nationalism, the move to Haiti in a pinnacle moment in its history helps to place Sansay in a position where she can actively contribute to a more inclusive modern republic (even if it is mediated through her husband's actions).

Turning to the novel, *Secret History* represents an on-the-ground experience during the Napoleonic invasion of Haiti/Saint Domingue and of brutal violence between Haitians and French soldiers. For many scholars, the historicity of the novel is under debate, as Sansay's personal biases and subjective interpretation could have clouded a truthful recording of the historical event. According to Drexler, the narrative, while "clearly adapted from her own experience," also uses the fluidity of novelistic techniques to "envision a world where women's happiness seems all but circumscribed by violent masculinity."[15] The perforated line between fiction and fact is what allows Sansay the authorial mobility to record the historical "horrors of Santo Domingo" within the novel form. Since Joan Dayan's groundbreaking reading of the work, many scholars have maintained that *Secret History*, while subject to the healthy skepticism that comes with reading first-person accounts, can be treated as a historical document.[16] Considering the historical influences and Sansay's own experience, the text then offers a unique insight and sharp critique of the patriarchal constructions of nationalist subject-formations. Both Elizabeth Maddock Dillon and Tessie P. Liu have written that the work's gendered representations of Louis Sansay and General Jean-Baptiste Donatien de Vimeur, comte de Rochambeau, intersect with the political discourses of the racialized conflict in dynamic ways. Though writing from different angles of the text, both scholars conclude that *Secret History* presents a creole novel that addresses the impotency of white male rule, where "extramarital struggles become entwined with warfare and counterinsurgency."[17] Dillon's claim that the work is an attempt to write a creole novel is of particular importance. She asserts that while *Secret History*'s collapse of romance and horrific physical violence may be "jarring initially," it eventually unfolds its hemispheric realities to the reader: "Just as striking as the initial disparity between the narrative of domestic intrigue and that of anti-colonial revolution is the extent to which the two strands of narrative cross, re-cross, and displace one another."[18] The interstitial spaces of the intertwining narrative threads of both domestic and racialized tensions make this work an early example of a creole novel as well as an early generic motion toward the representation of a creole nationalist subject. At its core, *Secret History* struggles with issues related to both gender and racial equality in an uncertain colonial state, assessing and critiquing structures of patriarchal control that inhibit an inclusive republic.

Much like Sansay's historical life, *Secret History*'s protagonist Clara carefully navigates troubled political and social waters to liberate herself from the draconian forces of patriarchal power and enforced homogeneity. Between the two narratives of political violent engagement and equally volatile domestic relationships, there is a consistent dichotomy established between imprisonment and white female creole mobility. The male characters in *Secret History* utterly fail as exemplary nationalistic subjects because of their roles as social jailers. For example, intermittent references to St. Louis (Clara's husband) describe him as "jealous," quick to "rage," and "ill-humored," among other unsavory characteristics that suggest a resentful and puerile man.[19] Clara also hints in a letter to her sister that St. Louis would regularly force himself upon her during their time spent in Saint Domingue, and all she could do was "oppose to his brutality with [her] tears and [her] sighs" (137). General Rochambeau represents another kind of patriarchal imprisonment, imposing his world view of power acquired through fear, manipulation, and violence, thereby implying his connection to the French Reign of Terror. Descriptions of his character suggest he is a manipulative, unctuous man, "a Bacchus-like figure, which accords neither with [Clara's] idea of a great General nor a great man" (73). His corruptive behavior, gravitating toward luxury at the expense of his military operation is also a point of critique: "He gives splendid balls, and elegant parties; but he neglects the army and oppresses the inhabitants" (91). Historical accounts of the general testify to his penchant for excessive spending and a luxurious lifestyle.[20] As noted by Melissa Adams-Campbell, the male characters in this work, best exemplified by Rochambeau and St. Louis, consciously abuse their power as a symbolic gesture to maintain control over their "property."[21] As early formations of U.S. American nationalism were tied to property rights and ownership (including the enslavement of other humans), these men and their behavior signal the cracks of this European ideology, particularly when another human is classified as property within its terms.[22] As abolitionists fought to maintain that those of African descent cannot be enslaved because of their race, Clara's encounters with St. Louis and Rochambeau actively criticize the notion that women are the property of men simply because of their sex.

To take the claim of destabilizing white male power informed by European and colonial assumptions of property ownership one step further, Sansay's *Secret History* not only critiques this model, but also provides an alternative. The work suggests that creole nationalism is best symbolized in the liberated, mobile, and hemispheric woman. Adams-Campbell contends that as white male power crumbles in *Secret History*, women of all colors gain social strength and self-determinacy, thereby revolutionizing the domestic politics of the feminine subject at the same time that a war wages for political sovereignty. The creole woman, specifically the *white* creole woman of republican virtue, unfettered to the systems of patriarchal imprisonment, generates a new model of creole nationalism in the novel.

However, in *Secret History*, the concept of creole nationalism is restricted to that of the hemispherically mobile white creole woman. Though Adams-Campbell discusses the interpolated story of a Black female insurgent on the brink of execution calling out her husband's cowardice as a point of female empowerment, the Black subjects still get executed.[23] Her discussion of the "mulatta figure" is of even more interest. In *Secret History*, Sansay (according to Adams-Campbell) distinguishes between white and mixed-race women by making the mixed-race woman comparatively freer as she functions outside the European normative social structure of woman-as-property. However, that freedom is only acquired through the sexual economies of prostitution: "Unlike Clara and other married women who are divested of control over their bodies, . . . *ménagéres* maintain some control over their bodies by retaining the rights to exchange those bodies on the free market."[24] In other words, in having the power to commodify their bodies, earning a profit through prostitution, mixed-race creole women have more economic and social freedom than their married white creole counterparts. Adams-Campbell, in this rendering of the mixed-race woman in the Caribbean, is working from the established trope of the "tropical temptress," whose sexual powers and financial autonomy had, in the words of Kimberly Manganelli, "undermined the patriarchal social order in the colony and threatened the imperial project." Kimberly Snyder Manganelli writes.[25] The trope of the "tropical temptress" is a familiar one to travel narratives, treatises, histories, and works of fiction set in the Caribbean. While both Adams-Campbell and Manganelli see the "tropical temptress" as a figure of female empowerment, she is still forcibly relegated to the outskirts of a given national formation, ostracized for being a prostitute.

Zelica, the Creole is a novel that upsets the dichotomy between white and mixed-race women established in *Secret History*, as it introduces a mixed-race woman who embodies the complex formations of creole nationalism. The eponymous heroine maintains a physical and social mobility that is built upon her republican values, not her bodily commodification. She complicates the sexual trajectory of the mixed-race woman by critiquing the trope of the "tropical temptress" and offering new modes of mobility that are predicated on an educated background, cultural fluidity, and linguistic aptitude. Further, over the course of the novel, Zelica proves that the West Indian woman of color is just as capable as any white creole woman to reject the male-dominated structures of authority that would otherwise restrict a woman's autonomy. She is a globally and racially mindful subject, self-determined and deftly successful at navigating the cultural differences across the Atlantic. Zelica expresses alternative forms of ascendency for mixed-race women through her republican virtues, even illuminating the fact that the creole nationalist subject is not one who vies for social rank or distinction, but rather believes in gender and racial equality at the genesis of a nation.

Though *Zelica* follows the same general narrative plot as *Secret History*, its approach to the historical accounts of the Haitian Revolution offers a stark contrast. *Zelica* begins with equal focus to the capacity and dignity of the Black insurgency and the devastation incurred by the white planters with the arrival of the French military.[26] The novel immediately establishes Haiti as a site of violence, a beautiful landscape conquered by war's atrocities: "The mountain was strewed with severed limbs, blackened bodies, and disfigured heads—the survivors had not the last mournful satisfaction of weeping over the remains of the object most dear to them, for their remains were not distinguishable. Groans of agony, cries of anguish, and shrieks of despair resounded *on every side*; the wounded claimed the compassion of those who had, as if by miracle, escaped unhurt" (1:21; my emphasis). Both Clara and the reader are introduced to Haiti through this horrific tableau, which also then coordinates the tone of the novel—a tone that posits that the racialized warfare on the island will be a perpetual threat to the physical and moral integrity of the characters. It looms large and violates indiscriminately, as "on every side" indicates in the passage. Clara is not immune to the violence in *Zelica*, indicated by the fact that, nearly at the moment of their arrival, she and her husband, St. Louis, are captured and taken up a hill to be executed by the Haitians. Zelica, a stranger with "large black eyes that swam in melty languor," intervenes and saves the captives' lives (1:46). At the point of their departure, with the St. Louis couple en route to their home, an unspoken kinship between Zelica and Clara develops; it is one that "united their souls" and binds the two women for the duration of the novel (1:93). In nearly every episode of warfare, the mixed-race Zelica rescues Clara from either death or capture by the insurgent Glaude, who is obsessively transfixed by Clara's beauty. Each time Clara is removed from harm's way Zelica reiterates, "If I can save you, I shall not have lived in vain" (1:177). In both words and actions, Zelica appropriates the ostensibly male role of perpetual protector while also cementing a cross-cultural alliance with Clara. As men slaughter one another, Zelica, who ideologically believes in Black Haitian rule and aligns herself militarily with the Haitians, devotes herself to protecting Clara. Throughout the novel, Zelica reinforces the notion that while rebellion may be necessary for claiming sovereignty, not everyone is to be sacrificed for its cause. More peaceful operations are possible in the transition between the French colony and the Haitian nation-state. In protecting Clara, Zelica is also protecting foundational tenets of creole nationalism: the embrace of ethnic difference and equanimity.

The masculinized tensions produced by war are contrasted with a sense of female sorority and empowerment, not unlike what is seen in *Secret History*. What differs between the novels is the inclusion of Black and mixed-race women into the female creole collective. Not only is Zelica a survivalist figure who forges a companionship with Clara, but also the introduction of the obeah woman Madelaine in the novel complements the story with a character of Black female force. Madelaine is St. Louis's enslaved woman, but is often perceived as a symbol of power and admiration in Haiti: "Madelaine was revered by them, and indeed by all the people of colour in the city, as being gifted in supernatural powers. She was of the Ebo race, extremely intelligent, and supposed to possess all the knowledge and all the art of a sorceress; there was not a negro in the country who did not believe firmly that she could cause them the severest tortures, force from them their most secret thoughts, and even destroy them by her magical powers; therefore in proportion for the fear she inspired, was the respect shown her" (3:102). Madelaine, though an enslaved subject, invokes her power within the Haitian community to execute her will with impunity. Much like Zelica, Madelaine's affections for Clara also lead her to be a guardian. Though ideologically a defender of the Haitian cause, Madelaine's loyalty to Clara and her security throughout the novel humanizes the "sorceress," and again speaks to a female creole collective that supports one another against the rash of male-driven warfare. In order to be a protector, however, Madelaine must be physically and socially mobile. Zelica's military connection is what grants her the opportunity to move about Haiti without question. For Madelaine, it is the community's belief in her preternatural powers that gives her social mobility. In neither instance is social movement predicated on male characters granting privileges or concessions. For the novel as a whole, it is the women of mixed or African ancestry on the island who have the greatest amount of power, and with that power they choose to protect other women. Coursing through the island to the most devastated parts of Haiti to ensure Clara's safety, both Madelaine and Zelica channel the strength of sorority, versatility, and the intelligence of republicanism.

In *Zelica*, there is also a pattern of physically and emotionally stronger Haitian women contrasted with weaker, self-centered white creole women. For example, Zelica's consistent feats of heroism inspire Clara to move to philanthropic action. After meeting with the mother superior of the recently destroyed nunnery, Clara pleads to Rochambeau to invest money in its rehabilitation. The nunnery and church rebuilt with funds provided by Rochambeau and Clara are lauded by the entire white creole population (2:254). Yet, a significant distinction exists between the formations of sisterhood represented by Zelica and Clara. While Clara sought to help the Catholic sisters of Saint Domingue, the money donated toward the church's rehabilitation was given by Rochambeau (who was motivated by his attraction to Clara) (2:238). Zelica, by contrast, consistently navigates the military terrain through diplomacy and subterfuge. During a Haitian skirmish, for example, Zelica goes incognito to rescue Clara from her intended kidnappers, a feat that included scaling a wall and multiple disguises (3:81–84). Male characters in the novel are not the means of achieving a specific goal for her; rather, they are the obstacle that she must overcome. Zelica sustains a disinterested approach to men and, while physically beautiful, does not employ that beauty to garner favor. Unlike the representations of creole and mixed-race women of the Caribbean who continually manipulate their sexuality to acquire wealth and social mobility, *Zelica* actively critiques it by contrasting its eponymous heroine with the white Clara. Clara's actions grant her relative creole mobility in the novel but are completely contingent on the decisions made by male characters. Zelica, independent of the male-driven politics of sex and power, is a model of feminine self-determinism and creole mobility that contributes a newfound identity of the modern woman.

Typically, generic conventions of the novel introduce a heroine's history early on. However, in the case of *Zelica*, the reader does not gain insight into her character, motivations, and history until the middle of the third volume. Until that point, it is Zelica's actions that define her creole character. However, after yet another harrowing rescue, Clara begs her defender to share her story. The reader learns that Zelica is the daughter of a white French creole planter and his mixed-race wife. Her father, De la Riviére, grew invested in the amelioration of the conditions of both the enslaved and free people of color on the island, his zeal gaining strength with each passing year (3:125). At the age of five, Zelica was sent to France "to be educated; but chiefly, as [her] father declared, to keep [her] from imbibing the prejudices of [her] country against [her] maternal ancestors" (3:126). While in France, Zelica fell in love with the Frenchman Lastour, claiming that, from her mother, "I inherited the fervor of the children of the sun—I loved, as only those born in burning climes can love" (3:127). As a young adult, Zelica is then called back to Saint Domingue by her father, who then communicates that she has been betrothed to the Haitian rebel leader Henri Christophe as a token of De la Riviére's loyalty to the rebellion. At hearing of her objectification, mediated through an exchange between Christophe and De la Riviére, she notes, "I rejected the conditions they offered me with the most violent indications of horror. 'Death,' I exclaimed; 'death would be a thousand times preferable,'" and she vows to kill herself before she would marry Christophe (3:130–131). It is because of the alliance between her father and the Haitians that she operates within the ranks of the insurgency, and her father's allegiance grants her some military sway. However, Zelica disavows the patriarchal system designed to objectify and immobilize her. Similarly found in *Secret History*, the gendered issues of domestic imprisonment are conflated with the race-based hierarchies conditioned by slavery. Zelica deliberately points out the inherent hypocrisy of her father's demands of forced marriage by declaring that "devoting" his daughter as property to another directly conflicts with his seemingly fervent position as an "advocate of freedom" and "an enemy of oppression" (2:205). Zelica is a proponent of a Black Haitian nation-state and its position as a possible power in the Atlantic. She is also a proponent of the politically engaged and autonomous modern woman. Her refusal to accept the conditions established by her father and Christophe, and her decision to protect other women from the violence of state warfare, stems from her outright rejection of patriarchal systems of authority garnered by European notions of republican motherhood. At no point does Zelica claim dependency on a male character, including her own father; she employs De la Riviére's connections (not De la Riviére) to keep Clara safe.

Zelica's proto-feminist self-perception and pro-revolutionary sensibility are uniquely informed by her transatlantic travels. In part, ten years spent in a post-republic France as well as her organic companionate relationship with Lastour granted Zelica a set of principles that ideologically guided her toward both gender and racial equality in Haiti. Her transatlantic cultural background also underpins her condemnation of her father's decision to force her hand into marriage with Christophe, especially as she recognizes that her parents were joined in a companionate marriage. Zelica is a woman of mixed cultural heritage, but she is also an embodiment of transnational *métissage*. She has "all the beauty of her mother" and all "her father's firmness," speaks multiple languages, and determines the circumstances of how and where she travels once her father betrayed her trust and she lost her sense of filial obligation to him (2:202). Travel not only shapes Zelica's world view, but the conditions of travel contribute to how characters perceive their social roles in a war-torn Haiti. Both men and women travel in the novel, either across the Atlantic or hemispherically between Haiti and the United States. Yet, it is the women of *Zelica* who represent the creole nationalism so foundational to the novel's structure and argumentative positioning. Zelica travels between France and Haiti; Clara journeys to Haiti from the United States with her husband; and Madelaine was brought to the colony as a saltwater slave. In each of these circumstances, these journeys were conditioned by a system of patriarchal authority. The women, who have traveled under the circumstances of either duty or slavery, are now in a state on the brink of political independence, with the sense of gendered freedom already hinted at through Zelica's and Madelaine's physical mobility around the island. The female characters best embrace the cross-cultural *métissage*, synthesizing their experiences of travel, heightened personal liberty, and voluntary sorority and protection. Though the white male characters have traveled over the Atlantic as well, they have also been conditioned by the metropolitan politics of capitalism, property ownership, and imperialism. Consequently, they are written as too blinded by their own ambitions and sense of power to embrace the creole nationalism so critical to the sustainability of Haiti's political independence and participation on the global stage.

With the conflict rising between the Haitian insurgents and French white creoles, it no longer becomes safe for Clara and St. Louis to stay on the island. Zelica, with the help of her father (who has recognized at this point that the violence between the two groups has escalated out of control), coordinates their departure on a British vessel bound for North America. As Clara is passed into English hands, Glaude, who had been observing the midnight exchange from a distance, yells out "traitor!" and plunges a sword into De la Riviére's heart. During the scuffle, an unsheathed sword stabs Clara through the chest and she "expired without a groan" (3:293). Overwhelmed by what she has just witnessed, Zelica plunges into the ocean, only to be rescued by her love interest, Lastour, who had come to Haiti in search of her. Lastour, Zelica, and St. Louis embark safely on the vessel and wait for an opportune time to leave Haiti for the United States. The novel ends with their departure, while Clara's body remains in Haiti, cared for by Madelaine (3:309). This episode has been the subject of much critique from scholars. Carroll Smith-Rosenberg has written that Clara, who symbolizes American republican principles of commercial investment, dies passively at the hands of Haitian violence; her character represented the United States' decreased commercial interest in collaborating with the Haitians.[27] Respecting Zelica's survival, Daut contends that the novel's ending can be read as entirely pessimistic: "Given all of the uncertainty about the possible fates awaiting Zelica both on her journey to the US and upon landing on its shores, the ending of the novel seems to me to merely punctuate the anxiousness of non-violent attempts to espouse abolitionist thought, which were wholly complicated not simply by the material facts of slavery and revolution themselves, but by the vastly divergent gendered and 'racial' identities through which anti-slavery and revolutionary ideas could be narrated."[28] Daut concludes that Zelica's trip to the United States is rife with ambiguity. Given that slavery was still legal in the early nineteenth century, Zelica's mixed-race background may have threatened her status as a free woman. Further, anti-miscegenation laws would have prohibited her marriage to Lastour, regardless of whether Zelica was able to "pass" for white. According to Daut, within the novel's historical context, Zelica would have left one set of challenges for an entirely new set once in the United States.

My reading of the novel's end is a bit more optimistic than those provided by Daut and Smith-Rosenberg, though it no way discredits their more historically oriented claims. My reading is derived from the novel's renderings of creole mobility and republican values that have been the focus of this essay. As discussed earlier, Zelica and Clara represent two different formations of creole nationalism: though they both desire independence from the tyranny of male-dominated systems of oppression, only Zelica can act upon this desire. Clara is bound to her uninteresting and flagrantly cheating St. Louis and the manipulative General Rochambeau until her death; even in her death, she is a casualty of male-to-male violence. Zelica, by contrast, is free from her patriarchal chains and vows to remain as such despite her father's demands. At the novel's end, Zelica is united with Lastour, and the two feasibly can enter into a companionate marriage should it be wanted by both partners. With Clara's death and Zelica's survival, there is a symbolic gesture toward a social evolution of creole subjectivity. If Zelica is the allegorical embodiment for all that is the modern Atlantic creole—independent, mixed-race, female, survivalist, educated, and politically engaged—then her departure for the United States marks her as a progressive avatar of idealized creole nationalism. In the words of Anderson, she is a "creole pioneer" for a post-revolutionary Atlantic world.[29]

Her departure for the United States also marks Zelica as hemispherically mobile, an important composite feature of the creole nationalist subject. Throughout the novel, she remains geographically unrestricted, and while she does not find herself attracted to Christophe, or any other Black man, for that matter, she recognizes the strength of the Haitian insurgents: "They may be swept form the surface of the earth,—they may be overpowered by numbers and perish, but they will never be reduced to slavery. Their souls are fired by a love for liberty; their arms are nerved by a desire of vengeance—a desire cherished and nurtured in their hearts' closest folds, for wrongs that have pressed on them for ages. You may exterminate, but you will never conquer them."[30] Much like the Haitians with whom Zelica was ideologically allied, she, too, was never to be conquered, always opting for death over being subjugated. Her impassioned sentiments as she shares these thoughts with white creoles echoes that of Patrick Henry's famous quotation, "Give me liberty, or give me death!," proclaimed during the peak of the American Revolutionary War. She does not agree with the level of violence occurring during the French military occupation, but she also recognizes that it is a necessary evil to acquire personal and political freedom, just as it had been for Haiti's North American predecessors. Several additional moments in the novel continue to draw a direct parallel between the revolutionary wars of Haiti and the nascent United States. For example, a connection is made between François Dominique Toussaint L'Ouverture and George Washington: though Toussaint "was not so propitious as that of the immortal hero he wished to imitate," he "had desired to emancipate permanently the people of colour from the bonds of slavery, and establish them [with] the rights to which they have been deprived."[31] The political hemispheric bonds between the United States and Haiti contribute to the overall optimistic reading of Zelica's hemispheric mobility. Ideologically, Haiti represented a revolutionary shift between old and new views, much as the United States had done in the years prior. In leaving for the United States from Haiti, Zelica symbolizes a plausible avenue of hemispheric unification where Black and white revolutionary creoles who provincialized European colonialism could join in a shared political hemispheric history.

The concept of creole nationalism can be observed and critiqued in both *Secret History* and *Zelica, the Creole*. The character of Clara in *Secret History* initiates a projection of the idealized creole national subject through formations of international sisterhood. *Zelica* further expands the boundaries of creole nationalism with the introduction of its transnational mixed-race heroine. In politically aligning herself to an evolved creole nationalism divested of its male-driven motifs of commercial slavery and military dominance, Zelica demonstrates the hemispheric possibilities of both gender and race equality in the circum-Atlantic world. Also, as an embodiment of Glissant's concept of *métissage*, Zelica synthesizes her experiences in France and Haiti to generate an idealized creole national who supports tolerance and racial equality in Haiti, the second Atlantic republic. As a figure of global citizenship, unfettered to the concept of a singular "American" nation-state, Zelica respects the efforts of Haitian independence as she travels to the United States at the novel's end. Written by "an American" to an international transatlantic audience, the novel offers a revitalized conceptualization of what it means to an American hemispherically, not just nationally. As the title of the novel also suggests, a "creole" can be a traveling woman of color who pioneers gender and race equality across the Atlantic. In giving new definitions to "creole" and "American," *Zelica, the Creole* offers a different kind of narrative possibility for the formation of the globally minded nation-state.

NOTES

1. Edouard Glissant, *Poetics of Relation*, trans. Betsy Wing (Ann Arbor: University of Michigan Press, 2010), 34.
2. Benedict Anderson, *Imagined Communities: Reflections on the Origin and Spread of Nationalism* (New York: Verso, 2006).
3. Laurent Dubois, *Avengers of the New World: The Story of the Haitian Revolution* (Cambridge, MA: Harvard University Press, 2004), 6–7.
4. *Zelica, the Creole; A Novel, by an American*, 3 vols. (London: William Fearman, 1820). The nomenclature of "New World" is in reference to the European views of the Western Hemisphere at the time of colonization. The term itself is Eurocentric and assumes a monodirectional flow of knowledge, technology, and cultural influence. For an insightful discussion of this term and its value within Atlantic studies, see Anibal Quijano, "Coloniality of Power, Eurocentrism, and Latin America," *Nepantla: Views from South* 1, no. 3 (2000): 533–534.
5. Leonora Sansay, *Secret History; or, The Horrors of St. Domingo* (1808), ed. Michael J. Drexler (Peterborough, ON: Broadview Press, 2007).
6. Sean Goudie, *Creole America: The West Indies and the Formation of Literature and Culture in the New Republic* (Philadelphia: University of Pennsylvania Press, 2006), 9.
7. Goudie, *Creole America*, 174.
8. Anderson, *Imagined Communities*; Ian Watt, *The Rise of the Novel: Studies in Defoe, Richardson, and Fielding* (Berkeley: University of California Press, 2000); Michael McKeon, *The Origins of the English Novel, 1600–1740* (Baltimore: Johns Hopkins University Press, 2002).
9. Eve Tavor Bannet, *Transatlantic Stories and the History of Reading, 1720–1810: Migrant Fictions* (Cambridge: Cambridge University Press, 2011), 230. Lennard J. Davis, in discussing the generic collapse of the early novel with printed news, makes a similar argument in his book *Factual Fictions: The Origins of the English Novel* (Philadelphia: University of Pennsylvania Press, 1996), 56. There is a paradox between the factual "news" that one gives (such as that found in a biography or memoir) and the fictional story of an unreal hero. The desire for the "authentic narrative" is, in part, what drives the factuality of fictional narratives. There is a final authority of truth found in the observations of a detached "editor" as found in many of the works of the eighteenth and nineteenth centuries.
10. Phillip S. Lapsansky, "Afro-Americana: Rediscovering Leonora Sansay," in *The Annual Report of the Library Company of Philadelphia for the Year 1992* (Philadelphia: Library Company of Philadelphia, 1993), 29.
11. Marlene Daut, *Tropics of Haiti: Race and the Literary History of the Haitian Revolution in the Atlantic World, 1789–1865* (Liverpool: Liverpool University Press, 2015), 261.
12. Michael J. Drexler, introduction to *Secret History; or, The Horrors of St. Domingo*, by Leonora Sansay, ed. Michael J. Drexler (Peterborough, ON: Broadview Press, 2007), 36.
13. By that time, public scandal had directly connected Aaron Burr with Leonora Sansay. With further detail given in the introduction to *Secret History*, Drexler explains that the two had been friends as early as 1796 and, quite conceivably, lovers. The marriage to Louis Sansay was at Burr's suggestion, but it appeared clear that Burr and Sansay were intimately connected. Louis Sansay feared that if he left for Saint Domingue without his wife, he would surely be cuckolded. For additional details, see Drexler, introduction to *Secret History*, 28–33.
14. Drexler alludes to a potential romantic affair in his introduction to *Secret History*, 44, 46. While speculated, Drexler has no primary source material that can verify that the two were involved in a sexual extramarital relationship.
15. Drexler, introduction to *Secret History*, 32–33.

16. Joan Dayan, *Haiti, History, and the Gods* (Berkeley: University of California Press, 1995), 156–182.
17. Elizabeth Maddock Dillon, "The Secret History of the Early American Novel: Leonora Sansay and Revolution in Saint Domingue," *Novel: A Forum on Fiction* 40, no. 1 (Fall 2006): 77–103; Tessie P. Liu, "The Secret beyond White Patriarchal Power: Race, Gender, and Freedom in the Last Days of Colonial Saint-Domingue," *French Historical Studies* 33, no. 3 (Summer 2010): 387–416, quotation on 390.
18. Dillon, "Secret History," 78.
19. Sansay, *Secret History*, 75, 85, 88.
20. Dayan corroborates Sansay's account of Rochambeau's cruelty of character with historical documentation in *Haiti, History, and the Gods*, 158–161.
21. Melissa Adams-Campbell, "Romantic Revolutions: Love and Violence in Leonora Sansay's *Secret History, or The Horrors of St. Domingo*," *Studies in American Fiction* 39, no. 2 (Fall 2012): 130.
22. It is important to note that in the first drafted Haitian Constitution of 1801, property rights were "sacred and inviolable." Every person had equal right to property that he could purchase, and no other individuals were allowed on that property without a specific purpose: "Anyone who attempts to deny this right shall become guilty of crime towards society." For the detailed modes and protections for securing individual property rights, see Titles V, XII, and XIII. The idea of "owning" land, protected by law in Haiti, has a direct connection with French property law and the North American (United States and Canada) value of individual rights over land. See "Haitian Constitution of 1801," The Louverture Project, October 10, 2007, accessed January 21, 2020, https://thelouvertureproject.org/index.php?title=Haitian_Constitution_of_1801_(English).
23. Adams-Campbell, "Romantic Revolutions," 131. The scene Adams-Campbell refers to appears in Sansay, *Secret History*, 91–92.
24. Adams-Campbell, "Romantic Revolutions," 137.
25. Kimberly Snyder Manganelli, *Transatlantic Spectacles of Race: The Tragic Mulatta and the Tragic Muse* (New Brunswick, NJ: Rutgers University Press, 2012), 24.
26. *Zelica*, 1:4–11.
27. Carroll Smith-Rosenberg, "Black Gothic: The Shadowy Origins of the American Bourgeoisie," in *Possible Pasts: Becoming Colonial in Early America*, ed. Robert Blair St. George (Ithaca, NY: Cornell University Press, 2000), 264. For an interesting historical examination of American commercial interests in Haiti during the nineteenth century as it relates to Sansay's work, see Dillon, "Secret History," 96–98.
28. Daut, *Tropics of Haiti*, 285.
29. Anderson, *Imagined Communities*, 47–65.
30. *Zelica*, 1:86.
31. *Zelica*, 1:209.

10

FEMININE NEGOTIATIONS WITHIN THE COLONY

Aphra Behn's *Oroonoko* and Phebe Gibbes's *Hartly House*

KATHLEEN MORRISSEY

APHRA BEHN'S 1688 *OROONOKO* IS CONSIDERED a blueprint for the novel, the crowning contribution of the first professional female dramatist in the English language, and an early literary depiction of the transatlantic slave trade. *Oroonoko* remains in the literary conversation for many reasons, one of which is because it is a composite of genres; it can be read as a heroic tragedy, a novella, and a courtly romance. More than a royalist allegory with potentially progressive identity politics, *Oroonoko* takes cues from other styles to articulate a woman's nuanced representation of the colonial setting. Unlike early fictional travel texts, such as *Robinson Crusoe*, *Oroonoko* provides a colonial voice that is not masculinist. While it is useful to compare Behn's work to her male contemporaries', we should also place *Oroonoko* in the context of later novels in the period, specifically those focused on women and colonial travel writing. Even in the many novels written within and largely focusing on the domestic space of England, the colonies shape the outlines of the setting. As noted by Edward W. Said, the tailored gardens of *Mansfield Park* cannot be disentangled from the violence of colonialism and slavery.[1] In addition to eighteenth-century works, *Oroonoko* belongs in a conversation about early nineteenth-century female-centric novels, such as Jane Austen's, and in the colonial travel text genre.

Oroonoko showcases the subversive strategies of women in the colonial setting, which prefigures later women's colonial writing in the eighteenth century, such as the British Indian travel novel *Hartly House, Calcutta: A Novel of the Days of Warren Hastings*. Phebe Gibbes offers readers an example one hundred years after Behn's novella. In a 1789 novel veiled as a travel narrative, Gibbes reinvents colonial identity through a sentimental heroine. After being relocated to join her father, Sophia writes letters portraying India in a positive light. By comparing the lessons of Hinduism to Christianity, she criticizes the conduct of the British at home. In her observations on widowhood, Sophia establishes a similitude between Indian women and British women. She also develops a platonic romance with "her" Brahmin, a man who educates her on Vedic philosophy.[2] By acclimatizing to the environment, Sophia undoes the construct of the stoic British subject in the colonial space.

Like Behn, Gibbes portrays an unmarried daughter who enters the colonial space due to filial devotion and uses the colony as a zone of critique for home. The transatlantic woman's experience sets up a convergence of feminine resistances, making it compatible with the representations of eastern travel texts in the context of eighteenth-century British imperialism. When the two texts are placed in conversation, *Hartly House* reads like an Orientalist reinvention of the transatlantic sentimental heroine introduced by Behn. While an understudied novel by a minor author written later than the Restoration is not an obviously intuitive text to pair with it, a comparative reading reveals the literary legacy of Behn's colonial heroine's tropes. Although fictional representations, *Oroonoko* and *Hartly House* provide insight into the at-home subject's imagination of the colonial setting. The women addressed in this essay occupy the imagined headspace of the traveler and are able to look back at England and critique it from an authoritative, external position. In the case of the colonies, fictional travel writing is uniquely insightful in understanding how female subjects could write with authority and familiarity about places such as Surinam and India without ever journeying there; it is a kind of literary colonization, one that allows the woman British subject to make sense of seemingly exotic cultures through thought experimentation.

FEMININE STRATEGIES: IMOINDA AND BEHN'S NARRATOR

While *Oroonoko* has been praised as a proto-feminist novella due to the narrator's (implicitly identified as Behn's) travels and impulse to use writing as a tool of patriarchal critique, the discussion is often centered on the white narrator rather than the Black female characters in the text. Critics, such as Pumla Dineo Gqola, argue that Imoinda's body is a mere plot point for Behn's narrator to wax on the tragedy of the men in the text, thus making Imoinda's representation a critical failure in the text's feminist vision, if it can be deemed to have one.[3] Imoinda's beauty, virginity, and death are agonized over by male characters, but never discussed from her own perspective. As Gqola notes: "That Imoinda's is the difficult position is inconceivable to Behn's narrator. This inability to sympathise with a woman trapped in a system which treats her as property is ironic given that Behn's novella is said to be a critique of the oppression of women through the institution of marriage. Faced with a woman commodified by society, Behn instead glorifies patriarchal power."[4] As evidenced by the harem scene, the narrator does not often empathize with Imoinda, even in moments of crisis, and instead lingers on how Imoinda affects the men. Imoinda's tactics of diversion against the king and Trefry are only effective because they appeal to the men's honor. Imoinda is, as Gqola argues, constantly described as sophisticated and royal, but she is used by the white narrator to further humanize male characters, especially Oroonoko.

Although Gqola rightly points to the narrator's unsympathetic portrayal of Imoinda's suffering, Basuli Deb reserves the possibility that Imoinda displays some agency in the text.[5] Deb points to proto-feminist features of the text related specifically to the heroine, including her thwarting of the African king's sexual violence, as well as that of the white colonists', and Imoinda's co-decision to abort her own and her child's life. What ultimately preserves Imoinda from sexual violence in Africa is the taboo of incestuous bloodlines, not her careful maneuverings. Nonetheless, Deb interprets Imoinda's reference to the taboo as a deliberate exploitation of a masculinist tradition. By invoking the taboo, Imoinda escapes the immediate threat of rape, but unfortunately she is sold into slavery. This turn of events is not a feminist victory, but a demonstration of the tragic inevitability of male dominance in spite of a woman's resistance.[6]

Despite Behn's emphasis on the men's feelings, the narrator shows Imoinda weaponizing her femininity against the men. Upon Trefry's attempt to rape her, Imoinda "disarms" him with a display of feminine virtue: "I have been ready to make use of those advantages of strength and force nature has given me," he says, "but oh! she disarms me with that modesty and weeping, so tender and so moving that I retire, and thank my stars she overcame me."[7] Even though this scene is designed to demonstrate Trefry's honorable character as a man of feeling, it also demonstrates how Imoinda can momentarily overcome a colonizer-rapist through hyperfeminine performance. By rendering herself a caricature of a weeping damsel, Imoinda reinforces that she is not merely a slave-object, but rather a woman-subject who will resist unwanted sexual advances.

Despite the narrator's apparent lack of sympathy for Imoinda, she is somewhat similar to her in the sense that they are both women who make significant, self-determined choices notwithstanding the restrictions placed on them by the masculinist colonial setting. The narrator participates in the dehumanization of Imoinda, but she is also commodified under the long reach of male proprietorship, albeit to a vastly different degree. The institution of slavery makes Imoinda the constant object of male violence. Conversely, the narrator's freedom is evidence of her position as a legible white subject within the colony. Even so, the colony is not a safe place, even for a distinguished daughter like herself. She lacks the protections of a husband or a father in an unfamiliar space where violent insurrections occur and white male power prevails over women. Because of this precarity, the narrator also employs a feminine performance to protect herself. She leaves after the failed rebellion and reflects on her last interaction with Oroonoko/Caesar: "His Discourse was sad; and the earthly smell about him so strong, that I was persuaded to leave the Place for some time; (being myself but sickly, and very apt to fall into Fits of dangerous illness upon any extraordinary melancholy)" (98). Curiously, the narrator did not fall ill with melancholy when she wrote about his horrific death with great detail. By writing about his death, she exercises the horrors of regicide on the Black body as a cautionary demonstration for English readers. The narrator's delicate feminine nature is a useful device when she needs to remove herself. Her flight allows her to identify with Oroonoko as a king and simultaneously condemn Caesar as a criminal-rebel. By leaving, the narrator can end her association with Oroonoko/Caesar, make use of him for political effect, and avoid being at odds with the male colonizers in her precarious position.

Though the narrator avoids responsibility for the many tragedies in Surinam, her lamentation after Caesar's whipping reveals that she is keenly cognizant of not only her mobility, but how her freedom is evidence of her colonial complicity. She recalls, "While we were away, they committed this cruelty; for I suppose I had Authority and Interest enough there, had I suspected any such thing, to have prevented it" (92). After some interrupting conditional clauses, the narrator supposes that if only she suspected anything, she could have used her authority to stop the brutality. She excuses her inaction by pointing to her location and her lack of awareness to obfuscate her sense of responsibility. By leaving at critical times, she can ultimately decide how involved she is. However, the narrator's complicity cannot be fully absolved with her negotiable involvement no matter how she acts.

Unlike the narrator, Imoinda lacks the ability to move away from conflict. Instead, she must face conflict head on and fight valiantly. This is played out in the battle scene, which captures the pluralism in the text's feminine representation. The narrator juxtaposes Imoinda against the governor's "Indian mistress," who sucks the poison out of his wound inflicted by Imoinda's arrow (92). An enslaved royal African woman, an Indigenous woman, and a white Englishwoman are all players in the same conflict with varying stakes. The Indian mistress does not want to lose her governor (so the text would suggest), Imoinda does not want to continue living as an enslaved person, and, in a far less affected position, the narrator wants to see natural kingship succeed. None of the women have the same stakes, nor are they on the same side; they are all opposed on an axis of identity even though they are all compromised on a spectrum of femininity. In the liminal space of this axis is Imoinda, where she is somewhat associated with the other female characters, but is unapproachable, alien, and ultimately isolated due to her ambiguity. For example, the Indian mistress and Imoinda could be paired for their disempowered status, but their desires are not aligned; one is a rebel attempting to overturn enslavers' power, and the other an intimate partner of the colonizer, willing to use her body as a receptacle for the revenge taken against him. The narrator could also be thought of as a pair with Imoinda, as she is also a woman who sides with Caesar. However, she is different from Imoinda in terms of visibility. As the narrator, she dictates how and when she is seen. Imoinda is always hypervisible as an exoticized object. The Indian mistress's debut in the story, spectacular as it is, is a jarring reminder that there are actors made invisible by the narrator.

Despite the narrator's ability to reveal or hide herself, she does momentarily place herself under the same kind of visual scrutiny experienced by the other women. The narrator travels to the Indian town to learn more about the place. The Indians touch her clothes and hair, and question if the "thing[s] can speak" (82). They use the language of the Enlightenment to assess her by inquiring whether or not the white colonists possess enough "sense and wit" to discuss the "affairs of life and war" (82). This scene turns the colonial gaze inward in a moment that Mary Louise Pratt would identify as the reciprocity of the imperial eye; the European subject becomes the eager object of the "Other." However, in Pratt's assessment, the imperial gaze is reversed to show the "Other" approving of the colonizer, which subtextually condones the colonial mission.[8] Behn's narrator is functioning in the same fashion as colonial male travelers, but she is not necessarily seeking approval from the Indians. Rather, she uses their point of view to critique herself as an object of scrutiny. This is a strategy that is also later employed in the late eighteenth and the early nineteenth centuries: European writers used colonized figures as mouthpieces for domestic criticism in fiction. For example, Elizabeth Hamilton uses Sheermaal's voice to criticize institutions such as the transatlantic slave trade in her fictional text *Translation of the Letters of a Hindoo Rajah*. This technique allows the narrator to critique the colonial subject writ largely through herself as self-deprecating woman. She is exploiting any bias against a woman writer by directing it toward an anticolonial sentiment. By inviting scrutiny as a seen object, the narrator is establishing symmetry between herself and the other women who lack the same narrative control over their bodies.

In a final gesture that illuminates the symmetry between the women in the text, the narrator gives Imoinda the very last word of acknowledgment after praising Oroonoko: "Thus died this great Man, worthy of a better Fate, and a more sublime Wit than mine to write his Praise: Yet, I hope, the Reputation of my Pen is considerable enough to make his glorious Name to survive to all Ages, with that of the brave, the beautiful and the constant *Imoinda*."[9] On the surface, this statement may appear to be a dismissive, obligatory gesture to Imoinda. The narrator favorably compares Oroonoko to herself in a vaguely modest way; his wit is more than her own, making her effort to memorialize him nearly futile. She interestingly does not clarify that Imoinda is too glorious for her to document. By not doing so, the narrator implies that she is uniquely qualified to write about her. This subtle but important nod of acknowledgment reminds the reader of women's marginalized position in the stories of men.

The value of the transatlantic heroine lies in her ability to negotiate in the colonial space as a woman vulnerable to violence. Despite being sold as a slave to colonial men, Imoinda is able to temporarily resist through calculated employments of femininity, specifically through the act of weeping and expressing virtue. The narrator has to make significantly less severe decisions as a legible white subject, but she makes negotiations in the same spirit; she uses the stereotypical fainting gesture to avoid participating in the battle over Caesar, evades marriage, and escapes violence despite being associated with a rebel. In the larger recovery project of women's travel literature, there is a tendency to imbue the works of women, including Behn's, with an optimistic narrative of progress, one that may overlook the tragic nuances of colonial women's betrayals and compromises. Behn's narrator ultimately exists in the colonial space to participate in the undoing of Imoinda and women like her. She spares little mercy for women in a text that serves to glorify men. However, beneath her praises of men and her inability to fully sympathize with Imoinda, Behn's narrator reveals the uncomfortable reality that, in varying degrees, all women in the colony are peripheral in their own stories. Despite her failings as an ally, Behn's narrator portrays her compromises alongside Imoinda's inevitable suffering to highlight the incessancy of male domination within the colonial institution.

HARTLY HOUSE: ORIENTALIZING THE TRANSATLANTIC HEROINE

The colonial critique of the British subject predates the pro-colony pushback against nationalistic debates in the late eighteenth century. While some of the colonizers depicted in *Oroonoko* are brutish and violent, there is still the possibility of nonviolent cultural exchange within the text, making Behn's stance on colonialism ambiguous. Behn presents two types of colonial figures: the corrupt and the open-minded. Though there is a considerable lapse of time between the publication of *Oroonoko* and the British Empire's peak involvement in eastern colonies, these seemingly oppositional colonial personalities were at the heart of the polemical debate about the ramifications of the East India Company.

The debate reached a zenith in the failed impeachment trial of Warren Hastings, governor-general of India in 1788. The rhetoric against him mirrors the governor in *Oroonoko,* as Hastings was described as a cruel figure. Edmund Burke argued before Parliament that "all the Commons of England [resented], as their own, the indignities and cruelties that are offered to all the people of India."[10] However, Hastings advocated for a somewhat tolerant colony; he "maintained the pre-existing system of an Islamic criminal law, while governing Hindus and Muslims each according to their own civil laws."[11] At the core of Burke's critique is a kind of anti-transnationalism; though he made appeals to the cruel treatment of India's people and condemned specific, corrupt members of the company, it was the tolerance of Eastern cultures that he mainly contested. For him, the stoic, superior British male subject was being threatened by "Eastern corruption."[12]

In the midst of this contentious political climate, a novel spoke directly to this divide between hybridity and nationalism. *Hartly House, Calcutta: A Novel of the Days of Warren Hastings* is a vindication of British India from the perspective of a silly but sharp girl named Sophia. Within the novel, Sophia undoes the stoic British subject by constantly praising the virtues of Calcutta. For example, she values native philosophies over Christianity. She says, "Their manners are highly interesting, from their *simplicity* and liberal mindedness; and I blush to feel how superior to all that Christianity can boast, of peace and good-will towards men."[13] Despite its backhanded racial essentialism, Sophia's praise, like Behn's narrator's praise of Indigenous practices in Surinam, is imbued with domestic criticism. These moments of self-criticism, coupled with high praise of other traditions, are made possible through a transnational exchange of culture.

The narrators in both *Hartly House* and *Oroonoko* romanticize the death of wives in their descriptions of the cultural customs. For them, the act of an individual wife marks an occasion to describe the people as a whole. Additionally, both speakers emphasize the voluntary nature of the woman's death as an act of virtue. For Sophia, the self-immolation of a widow inspires a reflection on virtuous womanhood: "Those wives, who, with a degree of heroism, that, if properly directed, would do honour to the female world, make an affectionate and voluntary sacrifice of themselves upon the funeral pile of their departed husbands:—it is true, there have been instances of their shewing reluctance,—but those instances seldom occur. No bride ever decked herself out with more alacrity or elegance, than the woman about to give this last proof of conjugal attachment—and they are, no doubt, sanctified to all intents and purposes by their priest's fiat, and pass immediately into the presence of Brumma, to receive their reward."[14] Sophia's interpretation of the suttee practice focuses on the brides' affectionate sacrifice for their husbands and their immaculate, elegant dress. This high praise is quite antithetical to the commonly understood imperial perspective on suttee. As Gayatri Chakravorty Spivak explains, suttee was the practice that justified the idea of "white men saving brown women from brown men": the British male colonial powers abolished it for seemingly good intentions.[15] However, the treatment of the female body became the final excuse to entirely dismiss Hindu culture as barbaric and decidedly institute "civilized" British domination. Spivak explains that suttee was not universally practiced, but was nevertheless the subject of male-dominated discourses about British India. The discourse was equally hijacked by Indian nativists who claimed that the woman desired death; both arguments never attempt to acknowledge or articulate "the testimony of the woman's voice consciousness."[16] Sophia's attempt to praise the women, while also making note of the instances of reluctance, demonstrates a shallow but tolerant perspective alternative to the imperial or nativist narrative.

Similar to suttee, the death pact between husband and wife in Behn's *Oroonoko* raises problems around consent and coercion from a woman's perspective. Namely, Oroonoko explains to Imoinda that escape was impossible and proposes to mercifully kill her to prevent their unborn child from the horror of slavery. She volunteers to die by his hand: "He found the heroic wife faster pleading for death that he was to propose it, when she found his fixed resolution; and, on her knees, besought him not to leave her a prey to his enemies."[17] The narrator describes her as heroic, but also describes how the fate of wives is always determined by their husbands: "for wives have a respect for their husbands equal to what any other people pay a deity; and when a man finds any occasion to quit his wife, if he love her, she dies by his hand; if not, he sells her, or suffers some other to kill her."[18] The emphasis on "any occasion" indicates a lack of indiscrimination: a woman's minor mistakes or grave offenses are equally subject to her husband's highest punishment. This inequity, alongside the wife's expected, godlike reverence for the husband, reveals how a woman's willingness to die by her husband's hand is at best a coerced inevitability. At worst, it could be understood as a last ditch effort to avoid brutality by a stranger. Behn's narrator upholds the heroism of Imoinda's decision to die while also highlighting the oppressive male forces that undermine her control. The narrator's critical perspective on the marriage culture could be read into the way she describes Imoinda's overzealous eagerness to die. She is, after all, a model wife, kneeling on the ground in front of her husband. However, the narrator uses the terminology of Imoinda's culture to honor her death: "[Imoinda was] sent into her own country (for that's their notion of the next world) by him she so tenderly loved."[19] This last sign of respect demonstrates a willingness to understand Imoinda's experience. Similar to Spivak's perspective on the masculinist discourse around suttee, Behn's narrator does not justify colonial intervention on behalf of the sacrificial wife; she problematizes the wife's willingness by delineating the patriarchal culture that limits women's options.

Both Behn's narrator and Sophia use their vantage point as white female subjects to observe good wives, notably women of color, dying for their husbands. Sophia does not describe the good wife's voiced positionality, but instead interprets the act of suttee as a paragon of universal femininity; the good wife does honor to the "female world" by being a hero. Sophia's exultation is bifurcated between the dutiful wife trope and a high-minded understanding of women's ability to choose their fates. She shows the duality of her adoration by highlighting the feminine, elegant bride ensemble alongside the abstract goal of heroism. She does not hear the "subaltern speak," but sees the subaltern as the epitome of womanhood for all of the "female world," thus establishing a connection between herself and the wife.[20] However, the act of viewing is not impartial; it calls attention to Sophia's and the narrator's own limitations as spectators. They can document their sympathy and praise for the woman, but they cannot stop the act from happening. They are exempt from the duty to die, but as figures in the female world, they are also limited in the ways they can exert their will and deny their obligations to men. Their efforts to document these deaths can be seen as an attempt to approximate a nascent transnational feminism that considers nonwhite women, but the promise of this universalism is undercut by the particularity of their colonial position.

Sophia's status as an early representative of this brand of feminism, however, is problematic due to her superficiality. In a brief review of *Hartly House*, Mary Wollstonecraft criticizes the narrator's vapid personality, the novel's non-English vocabulary, and the shallow mystique of the setting: "A few words and expressions, have an air of ignorance or affectation; indeed they are not English; however, excepting these trifling blemishes on the face of it, the style is easy, and the reflections pertinent: particularly those which contrast the uninterrupted round of gaudy pleasures,—pleasures which are most apt to fascinate thoughtless minds, with the swift stroke of death, that sweeps without distinction all ages to the tomb, nor warns them by previous decay."[21] In a single paragraph, Wollstonecraft dismisses the novel's emphasis on "gaudy pleasures," which are only fascinating to "thoughtless minds." This contradicts the interests of Sophia, who loves to discuss the British-Indian lifestyle of palanquins, dances, and social outings. From Wollstonecraft's perspective, traditional femininity, as embodied by Sophia, oppresses women and guarantees their subordinate status to men. Sophia's unabashed interest in the pleasures of Calcutta appears oppositional to the idea that women are capable, rational beings worthy of rights. Wollstonecraft's condemnation of Sophia's girlish pleasures reflects an early feminist principle that femininity is an irredeemable construct designed to shackle women's intellect.

However, as demonstrated by Sophia, Behn's narrator, and Imoinda, feminine performance is a useful tool in a heroine's repertoire. In the same vein as Samuel Richardson's Pamela, Sophia is able to secure a marital arrangement by thwarting male advances with feminine virtue; specifically, she avoids the nabobs interested in her, marries a respectable heir, and remains uncorrupted by new wealth. In the case of *Oroonoko*, Behn's narrator would have been less safe if she did not tactically use her femininity to avoid melancholic situations. Imoinda, who suffered the most dire circumstances, uses feminine performance to preserve herself from sexual defilement. It is important to note that across these examples, the women's circumstances are entirely defined by men. Their femininity, one of the only tools afforded to them, permits some ability to manipulate their conditions. While these heroines could be read as rehearsing a feminine sensibility that, in the words of Wollstonecraft, confirms women's exclusion from true moral and intellectual virtue, I argue that they are too limited in their agency to be fully complicit in patriarchal oppression.

In *Hartly House*, this limitation is most obvious in Sophia's father's stance on her marital status. Sophia's experience, like the women's in *Oroonoko*, is undercut by constant sexual negotiations, which are always finalized by men's decisions. After Sophia's father accepts an arrangement with a rich widower, he forces her to make a marital decision. Up until this point, she has thwarted every romantic advancement. In response, Sophia dramatically weeps. She explains: "I wept aloud, Arabella—embraced my father—besought his pity and his pardon; and all this without his discovering of my motive—for, unconscious of deviating in a single thought from what was excellent and amiable in his character, it never once occurred to him, that little mean suspicions occupied my breast."[22] This performance masks her "suspicions" as she attempts to manipulate her father's "pity." However, her weeping proves fruitless, and her fate concludes with her father's wishes fulfilled. She weds Doyly upon her return to England. Despite this inevitability, Sophia manages to delay engagement until Doyly conveniently becomes an heir to a fortune. Her hyperfeminine behavior is the only way she can achieve any consolation.

Sophia's silliness should not be written off as a useless aspect. In the same way that Behn's narrator uses self-deprecation to criticize the colonial subject, Sophia's girlishness softens her condemning opinion of British customs and colonial practices. If these women were to embody the masculinist discourse of reason, they would not so definitively criticize the colonial project. If the expectation of early feminists is to exemplify empowerment beyond the framework of patriarchy, then these examples of femininity as a device of colonial critique would be excluded from proto-feminist discourse. With her excitable sensibilities, Sophia is capable of seeing the value of cross-cultural exchange. In fact, she enthusiastically accepts that India will change her from the minute she lands. She proclaims, "My foolish heart was in the *bugero*, before my father, at the earnest solicitations of his friends, and a look of desire from me, assisted me to descend from the ship: but as I descended, my astonishment and delight so abundantly increased at each step, that the European world faded before my eyes, and became *orientalised* at all points."[23] In one of the earliest uses of the word "orientalised" in English literature, Sophia captures the effect of travel beyond Europe as a self-aware woman of the eighteenth century. Before she has even entered India, she has already transformed, using expressions that were previously foreign to her. It is within the sensationalized self of the feminine woman that the national subject becomes unraveled.

One of the major marks of change for Sophia is her life-altering romantic relationship with a native Brahmin. For the transnational heroine, contact and reciprocity open up a cross-cultural world view. In the same vein as Behn's narrator, who allows the Indigenous people to study her, Sophia desires to be seen by the Brahmin in a feminized reversal of the imperial gaze. Vision is a mode of reciprocity in the colonial environment; the Indigenous inhabitant returns the gaze, which legitimizes the colonizer's presence in a kind of "anti-conquest."[24] After the Brahmin is introduced, he politely compliments the women in the room. Sophia wishes his compliment uniquely flattered her above the other women in attendance: "I would have given more than I shall mention to have known my Bramin had distinguished me from the rest of the company, but was not so happy."[25] Sophia respects the Brahmin as a high-caste person and tries to validate herself with his approval. Although they never consummate their love, their eventual courtship is defined by an intense emotional intimacy.

Interracial relationships were common in the British colony, but they were most often not between British women and Indian men. As explained by Joan Mickelson Gaughan, the directors of the East India Company rescinded the ban on British women in the seventeenth century as a way to prevent more interracial unions. Nearly half of all marriages were mixed: several men married "castees, mustees, French women, and Georgians."[26] The issue of these interracial marriages, which were generally tolerated, had to do with the company's shareholding: "such marriages were not legal in England and succession to family property and honours depended on legitimacy," Gaughan reminds us.[27] Therefore, the company intentionally imported British wives to solidify inheritance rights. A British wife was often more expensive to maintain, but was necessary to ensure legitimate heirs. Therefore, British women like Sophia were status symbols for wealthy men in the colony.

Sophia enjoys the same freedom of courtship that British company men often exercised, but without the compromising factor of sex, which would jeopardize her material value as a British woman. The Brahmin legitimizes her presence by doting on her, and she uses him as a source of emotional comfort. In an intimate conversation, she asks the Brahmin what she would be transformed into if she died, prompting him to explain the tenets of reincarnation. After flirtish banter, she writes, "He promised me to observe every *lovely* creature, (that was his word) if he survived me, in order to accomplish my wish, and render himself happy by being useful to me."[28] However, later in the story, he is not the one who survives—*she* lives on. Much like the conclusion of *Oroonoko,* the male figure's death is technically a convenience, as it resolves the plot without any specific negative consequences on the white transnational heroine; the narrator does not get murdered for treason, and Sophia avoids the consequences of an illegal love marriage. It also settles the love triangle between Sophia, the Brahmin, and her father's choice; she gains the Brahmin's love as an approval of her presence as an imperial subject and secures a traditional marital choice. However, despite her secured status, she is permanently changed by her transnational experience and must go on living as a surviving witness of the cross-cultural experience.

After the Brahmin's death, Sophia declares herself as the living testament to him: "I will raise a pagoda in my heart, that shall endure till that heart beats no more" (246). She feels he was taken from her right as she "felt [herself] becoming a Braminate" (200). By defining herself as the Brahmin's woman, she recognizes herself as not only as his unofficial wife, but also an extension of him. She orientalizes the female British subject by living as his widow. She resigns herself to marrying her father's choice, but reinvents him with Gentoo instruction; she declares that he "shall figure away as my Bramin" (276). He is a white, acceptable stand-in for the love marriage she actually wanted, turning the white male body into an inscribed object. In this act, she reverses the sexual commodification of the marriage contract. He, a hybridized British man, is a status symbol for the cosmopolitan female traveler.

Though she manages to fulfill her duties while securing a Brahmin-like husband, Sophia laments a painful ambivalence in her remodeling of Doyly. This demonstrates the ultimately tragic condition of the transnational heroine, who can never fulfill her desires within the limited framework of patriarchy. As a Brahminate, she must be a gentle person who sees her partner as an equal, but as a colonial subject, she must impose her will. To her friend she writes: "Did you ever imagine your friend would make so magnificent a conquest?—Poor Doyly, how small he has felt ever since!—forgive my folly—I recollect my Bramin, and am myself again" (286). By remembering the Brahmin, Sophia becomes "herself." Sophia's identity is fractured, and her consciousness exists within an uncomfortable in-between state engulfed by the Brahmin's world view, but left to survive in the Western world's marriage market.

Gibbes, like Behn, further expands upon the precarious nature of national identity through the transnational heroine. The distinctions between the texts are differences of setting, not differences of vision; *Oroonoko*'s transatlantic women prefigure Gibbes's orientalized heroine. Across both texts, the transnational women work against the masculinist forces that they inevitably encounter. Their receptiveness, as demonstrated by Sophia's love and the narrator's interactions with the Indigenous people, favorably shows the unraveling of the colonial European subject as a changeable conception. Their stereotypical femininity informs the early feminist conceptions of Wollstonecraft as they redeem it to establish some control in their compromised positions and reject the sanctity of British identity, making room for a hybridized selfhood. Ultimately, despite their victories against male figures, they are connected by their tragic failures to actualize their desires in spite of their efforts. Their concessions offer a valuable critique of the historically male-dominated colonial setting, which simultaneously gave women some freedoms at the cost of their valuable autonomy.

NOTES

1. Edward W. Said, *Culture and Imperialism* (New York: Alfred A. Knopf, 1993).
2. Throughout the essay, I use the contemporary spelling of the term "Brahmin" in reference to the Hindu caste. In *Hartly House*, Gibbes uses the spelling "Bramin," which was a commonly used version by the administration of the British Raj. See Phebe Gibbes, *Hartly House, Calcutta*, ed. Michael J. Franklin (New Delhi: Oxford University Press, 2007).
3. In Behn's text, Imoinda is also referred to as Clemene (the name her enslavers gave her) and Oroonoko as Caesar. In this essay, I refer to Imoinda by her African name and Oroonoko by both his African name and his enslaved name, to distinguish the way he is viewed in the story.
4. Pumla Dineo Gqola, "'Where There Is No Novelty, There Can Be No Curiosity': Reading Imoinda's Body in Aphra Behn's *Oroonoko or, the Royal Slave*," *English in Africa* 28, no. 1 (2001): 109.
5. Basuli Deb, "Transnational Complications: Reimagining *Oroonoko* and Women's Collective Politics in the Empire," *Frontiers: A Journal of Women Studies* 36, no. 1 (2015): 33–56.
6. Deb, "Transnational Complications," 33.
7. Aphra Behn, *Oroonoko; or, The Royal Slave*, ed. Catherine Gallagher with Simon Stern (Boston: Bedford/St. Martin's Press, 2000), 71.
8. Mary Louise Pratt, *Imperial Eyes: Travel Writing and Transculturation* (London: Routledge, 1992), 80.
9. Behn, *Oroonoko*, 100.

10. Edmund Burke, *The Speeches of the Right Honourable Edmund Burke on the Impeachment of Warren Hastings: To Which Is Added a Selection of Burke's Epistolary Correspondence* (London: George Bell and Sons, 1877), accessed January 21, 2020, https://archive.org/details/speechesofrighth02burk.
11. Jenny Sharpe, "The Violence of Light in the Land of Desire; or, How William Jones Discovered India," *Boundary 2* 20, no. 1 (1993): 32.
12. Burke, *Speeches*, 439.
13. Gibbes, *Hartly House*, 132; emphasis added.
14. Gibbes, *Hartly House*, 183.
15. Gayatri Chakravorty Spivak, "Can the Subaltern Speak?," in *The Post-Colonial Studies Reader*, ed. Bill Ashcroft, Gareth Griffiths, and Helen Tiffin, 2nd ed. (London: Routledge, 2006), 33.
16. Spivak, "Can the Subaltern Speak?," 50.
17. Behn, *Oroonoko*, 100.
18. Behn, *Oroonoko*, 95.
19. Behn, *Oroonoko*, 95.
20. Spivak, "Can the Subaltern Speak?"
21. Mary Wollstonecraft, *Analytical Review, IV*, in *The Works of Mary Wollstonecraft*, ed. Janet Todd and Marilyn Butler (London: Pickering and Chatto, 1989), 7:111.
22. Gibbes, *Hartly House*, 114.
23. Gibbes, *Hartly House*, 11.
24. Pratt, *Imperial Eyes*, 80.
25. Gibbes, *Hartly House*, 129.
26. Joan Mickelson Gaughan, *The 'Incumberances': British Women in India, 1615–1856* (Oxford: Oxford University Press, 2014), 50.
27. Gaughan, *'Incumberances,'* 46.
28. Gibbes, *Hartly House*, 185.

AFTERWORD

Eve Tavor Bannet

EXHIBITION OF THE HIGHLY MEDIATED character of the source texts and demonstration of the importance of men even to our reconstruction of women's agency in the Atlantic world are two of the most striking, and indeed admirable, methodological features of the essays in this collection. As their authors indicate, these frequently connected features affect the historicity of female subjects in diverse ways, and these, in turn, distribute them along a spectrum between history and fiction in which there are no pure exemplars of either extreme. This spectrum, which has implications for our scholarship, warrants closer inspection and further reflection. I propose to begin that process here.

At or close to the history end of the spectrum, we might place the texts of women like Falconbridge, Tristan, Calderón, and Merian who deployed the travel narrative as what Shelby Johnson calls "a generic ecology" that linked writers and readers throughout the Atlantic world, while transforming it generically into a political pamphlet, or in Merian's case into a scientific tract, that successfully inserted itself into contemporary masculine print controversies or scientific debates. As we saw, these women adapted predominantly masculine genres and made their adaptations publishable in male-dominated print cultures and disputes by creating what Diana Epelbaum frames as a performance linked to gender—for instance, focusing on domestic and philanthropic issues that had already been "feminized" in Britain or on topics such as dress styles, religion, and women's lives that formed part of "the discourse of femininity" in Peru and Mexico, or intimating that they were only publishing to defend a husband or themselves against unjust public attacks. In describing what they saw in the Americas, these women writers offered far-reaching critiques of their ubiquitously colonizing patriarchal cultures, but they also mitigated the threat their work posed by enveloping their innovations and critiques in layers of indirection. They folded their own oppression into that of colonized Others or offered colonial Others as examples of "strong and resilient women" who exercised "female agency and power." They inserted their perceptions into "complex" and "sometimes contradictory messages," allowing their representations of the evils of colonial society or of the flora and fauna in the Americas to reflect back on practices and policies in the mother country. They also couched their critiques in literary devices, such as Calderón's use of reported conversations and of satire, Merian's deployment of the exemplarity narrative, or Falconbridge's iteration of what Ian Haywood describes as typically Romantic representations of "spectacular violence."[1] One might therefore say that these women writers acquired agency by intelligently negotiating patriarchal cultures and by variously employing, exploiting, and circumventing patriarchal expectations and constraints. As Grace A. Gomashie emphasizes, therefore, such travel narratives cannot be taken as autobiographical or as reflecting women's real perceptions and experiences in any "straightforward" sense. Each text's relation to its author's life and experiences was qualified and shaped not only by gender and generic considerations, but also by its author's social position, the circumstances in which she traveled or published, the print market into which her text was inserted, and any omissions, embellishments, and changes voluntarily or involuntarily introduced prior to publication. Consequently, though in principle such texts occupy the history-truth-and-reality end of the spectrum, there are interesting questions to be asked about when, where, and how (if ever), these women's travel descriptions and observations came to figure as straightforward truth—as Calderón's did when William H. Prescott (a man who had never been there) integrated her accounts of the country into his *History of the Conquest of Mexico.*

At or close to the fiction end of the spectrum, we might place Bonny and Read, the cross-dressing female pirates, and the ladies of Newfoundland—once-living women who are known to us now only as portrayed by a man and absorbed into a masculine imaginary. Emphasizing both the absence of facts about the "real-life" Bonny and Read and that we are only looking at representations, Ula Lukszo Klein shows that Charles Johnson's *General History of the . . . Pyrates* drew on generic *topoi*—primarily woman-warrior archetypes from popular balladry and Romance—as well as on laboring-class values to construct a "fantasy of female empowerment." In Johnson's fantasy, cross-dressing female pirates "transcend gender and sexual expectations," "take advantage of the freedom of the sea in spectacular and seductive ways," and enjoy "a variety of options for mobility and independence" that were generally unavailable to eighteenth-century women. This was a masculine fantasy of absolute freedom, as well as a "white romance of piracy" defined against racial exclusions. And we are a long way here both from the short, brutish lives of mariners, privateers, and pirates and from cross-dressing women's own more necessity-driven accounts of their lives as soldiers and sailors. Pam Perkins, for her part, shows how, in his journals and private papers, Governor Cochrane made women "central to the imaginative construction of a recognizably British identity for Newfoundland colonists" and to "imagin[ing] Newfoundland as part of a transatlantic British world." Since the Enlightenment, "the gentler sex" had embodied, symbolized, and supposedly performed the civilizing function; indeed, in stadial history, the stage of civilization that a society had reached was demonstrated by the condition and treatment of its women. Consequently, for Cochrane, it was not real women's presence or their individual identities so much as their collective enactment of British gentility (through displays of genteel British dress and manners, and attendance at genteel British-style entertainments) that would elevate Newfoundland from a "way station for fishermen" into a respectable outpost of empire. Indeed, as Perkins shows, Cochrane had no interest in women who could not be co-opted into his fantasy. We are a long way here from Janet Schaw's *Journal of a Lady of Quality*, to say nothing of Aphra Behn's *Widow Ranter*. One might therefore say that the women in Klein's and Perkins's essays derive their agency from what they stand for in men's minds, and their significance from the highly idealized characters and roles attributed to them in men's imaginaries. Here, which facts about women's real lives are recorded or omitted is determined, overlaid, and colored by the imaginary on which their functions for, and utility to, men depend.

The essays dealing with novels that were "founded upon fact" fall somewhere between these two extremes. Kathleen Morrissey's interpretation of Behn's *Oroonoko* and Phebe Gibbes's *Hartly House* and Alexis McQuigge's reading of Unca Eliza's maternal Indian heritage in *The Female American* place them closer to Falconbridge, Merian, Tristan, and Calderón on the spectrum. Like the latter, these novelists show their narrators and heroines exploiting feminine stereotypes to acquire agency, or projecting "powerful femininity" onto native others, and "use the colony as a zone of critique for home." All three novels also intervened in debates about colonial administration contemporary with their publication. Morrissey treats Behn's and Gibbes's writings as fictions that testify to their authors' imaginative abilities because they are no longer believed to have visited the colonies themselves, and this helps her to uncover a female tradition in travel writing, stemming from Behn, that challenged masculine exemplars of the genre. The elements of this female tradition, as she lays them out, include the valorizing of cultural learning; "unraveling of the colonial European subject as a changeable conception"; exploration of hybrid or dual female identities and of the critical potential of subaltern gazes; comparisons of women's subjection to patriarchal violence across racial lines; and giving white women some "victories against male figures" in narratives that terminate in heroines' "tragic failures to actualize their desires in spite of their efforts." McQuigge runs counter to most scholars in offering a utopian reading of matriarchal power in *The Female American*, but her description of the novel otherwise fits quite well into Morrissey's female tradition, and it also seems possible to describe Falconbridge's, Tristan's, and Calderón's writings along these lines.

By contrast, Jennifer Golightly's and Octavia Cox's respective analyses of *Emma Corbett* and *The Woman of Colour* place these novels closer to the imaginary end of the spectrum. Golightly shows how Samuel Jackson Pratt used spectacular representations of female suffering to "humanize" violent, warlike men and images of women's inert or lifeless bodies "enshrined in male memory" to return men to domestic bonds and transatlantic fellowship from the conflict and brutality of war. Here again women derive their significance from what they stand for in a masculine imaginary—as Golightly says, Pratt made "women embody the suffering and anguish caused by the war." We are a long way here from the active and practical roles that women actually played in war as farmers and managers of estates in men's absence, as nurses, cooks, and camp followers to armies, or as wives of ships' captains at sea.[2] In light of the other essays in this volume, we might also construe Pratt's images of Emma saving herself from danger while disguised as a man or as a Native American by revealing her sensibility, and thus her gender, through tears and faints, as derogatory and dismissive allusions to women writers' versions of hybrid female characters and to their strategic deployment of traditional femininity as an instrument of female agency. It seems that for Pratt, women and women's representations of women were both best dead. Cox, for her part, reads the anonymously authored *Woman of Colour* as a "reverse-Robinsonade" in which the biracial heroine not only exposes the racial prejudice in England, but also, by embodying "almost unrealistic" English ideals of female virtue and Christian conduct, demonstrates how far England falls short of its own ideals. The novel thus "promot[es] an idealized conception of English principles," and a "conservative amelioration" of society that leaves servitude, traditional hierarchies, and the status quo intact, and discourages women from leaving their domestic "retirement" to "travel to learn." Given the novel's allusions to a purely male canon (women authors typically invoked other women authors instead or as well), and given the heroine's embodiment of such "old ideas," this account of the novel suggests that here again the heroine derives her significance from highly idealized roles reserved for good women in masculine imaginations.

What should we make of this spectrum? We might, of course, take it as an illustration of the idea, current among us since Lennard J. Davis's *Factual Fictions*, that the lines between history and literature, fact and fiction, were still blurred during this period.[3] But it would be more useful, and a more accurate representation of the work accomplished by the essays in this volume, to view this spectrum as an illustration of the observation of contemporaries such as Isaac Watts and David Hume, who insisted that *all* narratives are mixtures of fact and fiction, whether they present themselves as "true history" or not.[4] The task of feminist scholarship as demonstrated in these essays is to try to disentangle the facts from the fictions in primary texts that do not reflect women's thinking or experience in any straightforward sense—some of which contain more fact than imagination and fiction, and some more imagination and fiction than fact. At the same time, these essays demonstrate that we can no longer confine "facts" and "reality," as nineteenth-century documentary realism and much twentieth-century scholarship did, to reflections within a text of recognizable characteristics of the real world. For these essays show that such factors as the content of public debates, generic conventions, men's expectations and representations of women and native people, the idealized roles assigned to genteel white women in extant patriarchal social and political imaginaries, colonialism, the character of the political regime, and nationally acceptable interpretations of Christianity all formed part of the reality with which women travel writers contended as they wrote and published their work. Such realities were reflected in their writings too, helping to determine the selections and omissions in their text, as well as to shape its arguments, form, point of view, manner of expression, or modes of affirmation.

This expanded sense of reality, which encompasses the relations in which writers and texts stood to other people (husbands, patrons, booksellers, officials, readers, subaltern women, et alia), is doubly important, because prior to the ideological dominance of liberalism sometime in the middle of the nineteenth century, identities were viewed not as individual, but as relational. Independence did not mean the freedom to express oneself as a unique individual by doing whatever one liked. From John Locke and Mary Astell to Mary Wollstonecraft and beyond, this was characterized as licentiousness. Independence meant freedom to think for oneself and, with it, the ability to govern one's own conduct in accordance with moral, social, and statutory laws to which everyone had consented—as opposed to being forever subject to the arbitrary will and opinions of an enslaver, governor, or monarch, and forced to obey others in all things. Independence was thus the agency of social beings intensely conscious of their relations to others who understood that the "social good" or well-being of society as a whole depended on the virtuous or mutually useful and beneficial character of people's relationships to others, and who saw it as the task of every rational being to "improve" and perfect themselves, their relationships, and the societies, large and small, public and private, of which they formed part. Michel Foucault sweepingly condemned independence of this sort for making people "docile bodies" and "the principle of [their] own subjection."[5] Ironically, however, this was precisely the kind of independence that invented "critique" and gave the politically powerless agency: it produced all those Enlightenment critiques of the ancien régime that imagined, initiated, and promoted change, as well as all those critiques of modernity signed by Foucault. This bears directly on historical women. For as many of the essays in this volume show, women writers lived, wrote, and were portrayed in travel narratives and novels as imbricated in, and struggling with, a web of social relationships with men and other women, many of which they showed to be dangerous or unsatisfactory. Women demonstrated their agency and independence of thought as writers by critiquing and endeavoring to correct and improve the ways in which men, enslavers, and governors related to women and native people, while skillfully using ideas and manners of presentation to which men in principle consented, to gain a hearing and get their points across. One might add that, according to some twentieth-century feminists, relational thinking remained characteristic of "women's ways of knowing" at least until the "me generation."[6] In historical scholarship, relational thinking and the now largely unfamiliar kinds of agency and independence predicated upon it are not things to be discounted and sweepingly dismissed.

The spectrum that these essays create can also be viewed as illustrating Hume's observation that the difference between history and fiction lies principally in how we read a text: when we think we are reading history, he says, we regard the narrative's content with more seriousness, and give it more credulity and weight, than we do when we read the same text as fiction. One of the strengths of this volume is that contributors are cognizant of this issue too, and handle it in a variety of ways. The stakes for scholarship are most fully laid out by Victoria Barnett-Woods at the beginning of her essay on *Zelica*. As she explains, both *Zelica*'s historicity and its genre are affected by current uncertainty about whether Leonora Sansay—whose *Secret History* is believed to describe her real experience of Haiti during the slave revolt—was also the author of *Zelica*. *Zelica*, if she did not write it, cannot be read as Sansay's revision and recycling of historical facts and personal experiences initially conveyed in her *Secret History*. *Zelica* becomes just another fiction, a minor and not altogether successful exemplar of the genre "historical fiction" that is of little interest to us now. Barnett-Woods acknowledges the debate on Sansay's authorship of *Zelica*, but proceeds on the assumption that Sansay is the author based on the two texts' "intertextual relationship." This was the decision required to permit this essay on *Zelica* to be written and comparisons between it and *Secret History* to be made.

Other contributors show that history versus fiction was not the only generic choice they had to make about how to read all or parts of a primary text. Morrissey tells us that *Oroonoko* is "a composite of genres"—a heroic tragedy, a novel set in the Americas, a classical romance, a royalist allegory—which her essay will treat as belonging to the "colonial travel" literature genre. McQuigge tells us that *The Female American* is a travel narrative of Native American "female empowerment," which results in the brief establishment of a "feminist colonial utopia." Generic decisions such as these make an even greater difference to texts than do decisions about their historicity or fictionality. *The Female American* appears an almost entirely different story when McQuigge focuses on the biracial heroine's Native American half to read it as a narrative of female and Native American cultural empowerment and when Cox focuses on Olivia's English half to read it as a reverse-Robinsonade. *The Woman of Colour* likewise appears an almost entirely different narrative when its biracial heroine's white half is highlighted by Cox's reading of it as a reverse-Robinsonade and when her Jamaican half is highlighted by Lyndon J. Dominique's reading of it as a Caribbean novel in the introduction to the Broadview edition.[7] Even more disconcerting is the way texts that are read *as* "a composite of genres" affect the genre "travel narrative" and what we have assumed about what Shelby Johnson calls "the experiential differences that distinguished 'travelers' from 'immigrants.'" When a text reformulates travel tropes taken from the travel narrative to evaluate different models of population removal and control, or presents itself as a composite of a colonial settler's journal and travel narrative, is its author still a traveler, its genre still "travel"? If an enslaved woman like Imoinda in *Oroonoko* (or, indeed, like Mary Prince in her coauthored *Life*) or an Indian convert and missionary like Unca Eliza can be construed as a "transatlantic traveler," what does the confluence of "slave narrative" and "travel narrative," or of "travel narrative" and "spiritual (auto)biography," in the same text do to our conceptions of either genre? Are composites of genres still travel narratives? Are they only partly travel narratives? Do they deconstruct the genre? Or perhaps, the better question is the larger question of whether these questions, which assume pure genres, are the useful questions to ask.[8]

I am inclined to view *mixta genera*, as well as mixtures of fact and fiction, as intrinsic to travel writing during this period, as well as to other popular eighteenth- and early nineteenth-century genres such as the novel, the periodical, and the magazine. This makes *mixta genera* and mixtures of fact and fiction formal signifiers of the historicity of certain texts and certain genres. Like modern scholars such as Ralph Cohen, Rosalie Colie, or Alasdair Fowler, whose work is underappreciated now, contemporary authors for the popular market whom Isaac Disraeli called "miscellanists" never tired of defending *mixta genera* against what was then only a tiresome new wave of university-trained belletrist and neoclassical critics who constituted themselves as taxonomists and promoters of pure genres.[9] Miscellanists argued that *mixta genera* was the older and more familiar tradition—was not the Bible itself (to say nothing of individual books within it) a composite of diverse genres? Was not *mixta genera* what French neoclassical critics held against Shakespeare? British miscellanists also argued that *mixta genera* was best suited to the entertainment and instruction of the "unlearned"—the merchants and shopkeepers, idle gentlemen and clerks, artisans and servants, women and young people, who increasingly populated the vernacular market for print. Since subject matter was intimately linked to genres, *mixta genera* made it possible to include and explore a variety of subjects, and thus to appeal to a wider variety of readers, as well as to hold the attention of readers with mostly short attention spans who needed frequent changes of topic, perspective, and pace to keep them interested. Since new and different mixtures were allowable, *mixta genera* prevented texts from becoming formulaic, to offer readers, in addition to the pleasure of variety, all the pleasures of novelty and surprise. Above all, by multiplying and intermixing the perspectives that different genres provided, *mixta genera* did what texts in "pure genres" that created "a single unified impression" did not—they permitted individual readers to pursue and extract from it whatever part(s) or perspectives they found valuable, memorable, or applicable to their own lives, experiences, and concerns.[10] Rather than demanding that a reader determine a work's true meaning, *mixta genera* invited, validated, and justified different, partial, and even conflicting readings of the same text. Viewed in this light, the *mixta genera* of the texts considered here both invite and validate readings that make different choices about what to extract—for instance, either the Native American parts of *The Female American* or the white European ones—just as they invite and justify the choices we make about genre—permitting us, for instance, to read *Oroonoko* as a travel narrative, a heroic tragedy, a novel set in the Americas, a classical romance, and/or a royalist allegory. However, for an academic reader, considered as "the person supposed to know," this view of matters raises questions of its own.

NOTES

1. Ian Haywood, *Bloody Romanticism: Spectacular Violence and the Politics of Representation, 1776–1832* (Basingstoke: Palgrave Macmillan, 2006).
2. See, for instance, Karen Hagemann, Gisela Mettele, and Jane Rendall, eds., *Gender, War and Politics: Transatlantic Perspectives, 1775–1830* (Basingstoke: Palgrave Macmillan, 2010); Joan Druett, *Hen Frigates: Wives of Merchant Captains under Sail* (New York: Simon and Schuster, 1998); Suzanne Stark, *Female Tars: Women aboard Ship in the Age of Sail* (Annapolis, MD: Naval Institute Press, 1996); Holly A. Mayer, *Belonging to the Army: Camp Followers and Community during the American Revolution* (Columbia: University of South Carolina Press, 1996); and Joan R. Gundersen, *To Be Useful to the World: Women in Revolutionary America, 1740–1790*, rev. ed. (Chapel Hill: University of North Carolina Press, 2006).
3. Lennard J. Davis, *Factual Fictions: The Origins of the English Novel* (Philadelphia: University of Pennsylvania Press, 1996). See also Mark Phillips, *Society and Sentiment: Genres of Historical Writing in Britain, 1740–1820* (Princeton, NJ: Princeton University Press, 2000); and Charles Batten, *Pleasurable Instruction: Form and Convention in Eighteenth-Century Travel Literature* (Berkeley: University of California Press, 1978).

4. Isaac Watts, *Logick: Or, The Right Use of Reason in the Enquiry after Truth*, 2nd ed. (London: John Clarke et al., 1725); David Hume, *A Treatise of Human Nature* (London: John Noon, 1739–1740).
5. Michel Foucault, *Discipline and Punish: The Birth of the Prison*, trans. Alan Sheridan (New York: Vintage Books, 1977), 203.
6. Mary Field Belenky, *Women's Ways of Knowing: The Development of Self, Voice, and Mind* (New York: Basic Books, 1986); Nancy Rule Goldberger, ed., *Knowledge, Difference, and Power: Essays Inspired by Women's Ways of Knowing* (New York: Basic Books, 1996).
7. Lyndon J. Dominique, introduction to *The Woman of Colour: A Tale*, ed. Lyndon J. Dominique (Peterborough, ON: Broadview Press, 2008), 11–42.
8. For current views of the travel genre, see Tim Youngs, ed., *The Cambridge Introduction to Travel Writing* (Cambridge: Cambridge University Press, 2013); Barbara Korte, *English Travel Writing from Pilgrimages to Postcolonial Explorations* (Basingstoke: Palgrave Macmillan, 2000); Carl Thompson, *Travel Writing* (London: Routledge, 2011); Julia Kuehn and Paul Smethurst, eds., *Travel Writing, Form, and Empire: The Poetics and Politics of Mobility* (London: Routledge, 2009); and Alfred Bendixen and Judith Hamera, eds., *The Cambridge Companion to American Travel Writing* (Cambridge: Cambridge University Press, 2009).
9. Ralph Cohen, "History and Genre," *New Literary History* 17, no. 2 (January 1986): 203–218; Rosalie Colie, *The Resources of Kind: Genre Theory in the Renaissance* (Berkeley: University of California Press, 1973); Alasdair Fowler, *Kinds of Literature: An Introduction to the Theory of Genres and Modes* (Cambridge, MA: Harvard University Press, 1982); Isaac Disraeli, *Miscellanies; or, Literary Recreations* (London: T. Cadell and W. Davies, 1796), 5.
10. See Eve Tavor Bannet, *Eighteenth-Century Manners of Reading: Print Culture and Popular Instruction in the Anglophone Atlantic World* (Cambridge: Cambridge University Press, 2017).

BIBLIOGRAPHY

Adams-Campbell, Melissa. "Romantic Revolutions: Love and Violence in Leonora Sansay's *Secret History, or The Horrors of St. Domingo*." *Studies in American Fiction* 39, no. 2 (Fall 2012): 125–146.

———. "Writing Pocahontas: Romantic Women Writers and the Transatlantic Rescuing Indian Maiden." In *Transatlantic Literature and Transitivity, 1780–1850: Subjects, Texts, and Print Culture*, edited by Annika Bautz and Kathryn N. Gray, 69–90. New York: Routledge, 2017.

Addison, Joseph, and Richard Steele. *The Spectator*. Edited by Donald Frederic Bond. 5 vols. Oxford: Oxford University Press, 2014.

Adey, Peter. *Mobility*. London: Routledge, 2010.

Agosín, Marjorie, and Julie H. Levison, eds. *Magical Sites: Women Travelers in 19th Century Latin America*. Buffalo, NY: White Pine Press, 1999.

Aljoe, Nicole N. *Creole Testimonies: Slave Narratives from the British West Indies, 1709–1838*. New York: Palgrave Macmillan, 2012.

Allen, Walter, comp. *Transatlantic Crossing: American Visitors to Britain and British Visitors to America in the Nineteenth Century*. London: Heinemann, 1971.

Allewaert, Monique. *Ariel's Ecology: Plantations, Personhood, and Colonialism in the American Tropics*. Minneapolis: University of Minnesota Press, 2013.

Almeida, Joselyn M. *Reimagining the Transatlantic, 1780–1890*. London: Routledge, 2011.

Anderson, Benedict. *Imagined Communities: Reflections on the Origin and Spread of Nationalism*. New York: Verso, 2006.

Anon. "Weekly Record." *Boston Weekly Magazine* 2, no. 46 (August 1, 1840): 367.

Anspach, Lewis Amadeus. *A History of the Island of Newfoundland*. London: printed for the author, 1819.

Aravamudan, Srinivas. *Tropicopolitans: Colonialism and Agency, 1688–1804*. Durham, NC: Duke University Press, 1999.

Austen, Jane. *Emma*. Edited by James Kinsley. Oxford: Oxford University Press, 2008.

———. *Jane Austen's Letters*. Edited by Deidre Le Faye. 3rd ed. Oxford: Oxford University Press, 1995.

Bacon, Francis. *Essayes or Counsels, Civill and Morall*. London: John Haviland for Hanna Barret, 1625.

Bage, Robert. *Hermsprong; or, Man as He Is Not*. 3 vols. London: printed for William Lane, at the Minerva Press, 1796.

Bailey, Brigitte. *American Travel Literature, Gendered Aesthetics, and the Italian Tour, 1824–1862*. Edinburgh: Edinburgh University Press, 2018.

———. "Introduction: Transatlantic Studies and American Women Writers." In *Transatlantic Women: Nineteenth-Century American Women Writers and Great Britain*, edited by Beth L. Lueck, Brigitte Bailey, and Lucinda L. Damon-Bach, xiii–xxviii. Durham: University of New Hampshire Press, 2012.

Bannet, Eve Tavor. *Eighteenth-Century Manners of Reading: Print Culture and Popular Instruction in the Anglophone Atlantic World*. Cambridge: Cambridge University Press, 2017.

———. *Transatlantic Stories and the History of Reading, 1720–1810: Migrant Fictions*. Cambridge: Cambridge University Press, 2011.

Bannet, Eve Tavor, and Susan Manning. "Introduction: British and American Genres." In *Transatlantic Literary Studies, 1660–1830*, edited by Eve Tavor Bannet and Susan Manning, 1–9. Cambridge: Cambridge University Press, 2012.

———, eds. *Transatlantic Literary Studies, 1660–1830*. Cambridge: Cambridge University Press, 2012.

Barker-Benfield, G. J. *The Culture of Sensibility: Sex and Society in Eighteenth-Century Britain*. Chicago: University of Chicago Press, 1992.

Barnett-Woods, Victoria. "Models of Morality: The Bildungsroman and Social Reform in *The Female American* and *The Woman of Colour*." *Women's Studies* 45, no. 7 (2016): 613–623.

Bassler, Gerhard P. *Vikings to U-Boats: The German Experience in Newfoundland and Labrador*. Montreal: McGill-Queen's University Press, 2006.

Batten, Charles. *Pleasurable Instruction: Form and Convention in Eighteenth-Century Travel Literature*. Berkeley: University of California Press, 1978.

Bautz, Annika, and Kathryn N. Gray, eds. *Transatlantic Literature and Transitivity, 1780–1850: Subjects, Texts, and Print Culture*. New York: Routledge, 2017.

Beebe, Ann. "'I Sent Over These Adventures': Women in *The Female American* and *The Widow Ranter*." *Women's Studies* 45, no. 7 (2016): 624–637.

Behn, Aphra. *Oroonoko; or, The Royal Slave*. Edited by Catherine Gallagher with Simon Stern. Boston: Bedford/St. Martin's Press, 2000.

Belenky, Mary Field. *Women's Ways of Knowing: The Development of Self, Voice, and Mind*. New York: Basic Books, 1986.

Bendixen, Alfred, and Judith Hamera, eds. *The Cambridge Companion to American Travel Writing*. Cambridge: Cambridge University Press, 2009.

Benedict, Barbara M. *Curiosity: A Cultural History of Early Modern Inquiry*. Chicago: University of Chicago Press, 2001.

Benevolus. *Gentleman's Magazine: And Historical Chronicle* 77 (February 1807): 128–130.

The Bible: Authorized King James Version. Edited by Robert Carroll and Stephen Prickett. Oxford: Oxford University Press, 2008.

Blackburn, Robin. *The Overthrow of Colonial Slavery, 1776–1848*. New York: Verso, 1988.

Black Sails. Aired 2014–2017, on Starz.

Blackwell, Jeannine. "An Island of Her Own: Heroines of the German Robinsonades from 1720 to 1800." *German Quarterly* 58, no. 1 (Winter 1985): 5–26.

Bohls, Elizabeth A. *Women Travel Writers and the Language of Aesthetics, 1716–1818*. Cambridge: Cambridge University Press, 1995.

Bolton, Carol. Introduction to *Letters from England*, by Don Manuel Alvarez Espriella [Robert Southey], 1–78. Edited by Carol Bolton. London: Routledge, 2016.

Boulukos, George E. *The Grateful Slave: The Emergence of Race in Eighteenth-Century British and American Culture*. Cambridge: Cambridge University Press, 2008.

———. "Maria Edgeworth's 'Grateful Negro' and the Sentimental Argument for Slavery." *Eighteenth-Century Life* 23, no. 1 (February 1999): 12–29.

Bowen, Scarlet. "*Via Media*: Transatlantic Anglicanism in *The Female American*." *The Eighteenth Century* 53, no. 2 (Summer 2012): 189–207.

Bowers, Toni, and Tita Chico, eds. *Atlantic Worlds in the Long Eighteenth Century: Seduction and Sentiment*. New York: Palgrave Macmillan, 2012.

Braidwood, Stephen J. *Black Poor and White Philanthropists*. Liverpool: Liverpool University Press, 1994.

Braunschneider, Theresa. "Acting the Lover: Gender and Desire in Narratives of Passing Women." *Eighteenth Century: Theory and Interpretation* 45, no. 3 (2004): 211–229.

Brenton, Mary Elizabeth. Unpublished letter to Sir William Jackson Hooker, October 20, 1832. Directors' Correspondence 61/54, f. 2. Library and Archives at Royal Botanic Gardens, Kew, London. Accessed September 1, 2017. http://plants.jstor.org/stable/10.5555/al.ap.visual.kusdc152.

Brody, Jennifer DeVere. *Impossible Purities: Blackness, Femininity, and Victorian Culture.* Durham, NC: Duke University Press, 1998.

Burke, Edmund. *Reflections on the Revolution in France.* London: J. Dodsley, 1790.

———. *The Speeches of the Right Honourable Edmund Burke on the Impeachment of Warren Hastings: To Which Is Added a Selection of Burke's Epistolary Correspondence.* London: George Bell and Sons, 1877. Accessed January 21, 2020. https://archive.org/details/speechesofrighth02burk.

Burnham, Michelle, and James Freitas. Introduction to *The Female American; or, The Adventures of Unca Eliza Winkfield,* by Unca Eliza Winkfield [pseud.], 9–32. Edited by Michelle Burnham and James Freitas. 2nd ed. Peterborough, ON: Broadview Press, 2014.

Burwick, Frederick, and Manushag Powell. *British Pirates in Print and Performance.* New York: Palgrave Macmillan, 2015.

Byrd, Alexander X. *Captives and Voyagers.* Baton Rouge: Louisiana State University Press, 2008.

Cabañas, Miguel A. "North of Eden: Romance and Conquest in Fanny Calderón de La Barca's *Life in Mexico.*" *Studies in Travel Writing* 9 (2005): 1–19.

Calderón de la Barca, Frances Erskine Inglis. *Life in Mexico during a Residence of Two Years in That Country.* 2 vols. Boston: Charles C. Little and James Brown, 1843.

Carson, William. *Reasons for Colonizing the Island of Newfoundland, in a Letter Addressed to the Inhabitants.* Greenock, Scotland: William Scott, 1813.

Carter, Alexandra E. "William H. Eagar: Drawing Master of Argyle Street, Halifax." *Journal of Canadian Art History* 7, no. 2 (1984): 138–155.

Cartwright, George. *A Journal of Transactions and Events, during a Residence of Nearly Sixteen Years on the Coast of Labrador.* 3 vols. Newark, England: Allen and Ridge, 1792.

Centro de la Mujer Peruana Flora Tristán. "Misión y visión." Accessed March 5, 2020. http://www.flora.org.pe/web2/index.php?option=com_content&view=article&id=198&Itemid=27.

Chappell, Edward. *Voyage of His Majesty's Ship* Rosamond *to Newfoundland and the Southern Coast of Labrador.* London: J. Mawman, 1818.

"Chappell's Voyages to Hudson's Bay and Newfoundland." *Monthly Review,* n.s., 87 (September 1818): 66–74.

Charke, Charlotte. *A Narrative of the Life of Mrs. Charlotte Charke.* Edited by Robert Rehder. London: Pickering and Chatto, 1999.

Chazal, André. *Mémoire à consulter pour M. Chazal contre Madame Chazal.* Montmartre: Imprimerie de Cosson, 1838.

Clifford, Mary Louise. *From Slavery to Freetown: Black Loyalists after the American Revolution.* Jefferson, NC: McFarland, 1999.

Cochrane, Matilda, Lady. Commonplace Book 1813. MS 2485. National Library of Scotland, Edinburgh.

Cochrane, Thomas. "Selections from Thomas Cochrane's Newfoundland Journal." Compiled and edited by Pam Perkins. In "Thomas Cochrane and Newfoundland in the 1820s," by Pam Perkins. *Journal of Newfoundland and Labrador Studies* 29, no. 1 (Spring 2014): 117–168.

———. Unpublished journal, November 12, 1824–September 20, 1826. MS 2590. National Library of Scotland, Edinburgh.

———. Unpublished letter to Lord Bathurst, May 1, 1827. MS 2370, fol. 43. National Library of Scotland, Edinburgh.

Cohen, Margaret. *The Novel and the Sea.* Princeton, NJ: Princeton University Press, 2010.

Cohen, Ralph. "History and Genre." *New Literary History* 17, no. 2 (January 1986): 203–218.

Coleman, Deirdre. Introduction to *Maiden Voyages and Infant Colonies: Two Women's Travel Narratives of the 1790s*, edited by Deirdre Coleman, 1–42. London: Leicester University Press, 1999.

———. *Romantic Colonization and British Anti-Slavery*. Cambridge: Cambridge University Press, 2005.

Colie, Rosalie. *The Resources of Kind: Genre Theory in the Renaissance*. Berkeley: University of California Press, 1973.

Cowper, William. *The Poems of William Cowper*. Edited by John Baird and Charles Ryskamp. 3 vols. Oxford: Oxford University Press, 2014.

Crabtree, Sarah. "Navigating Mobility: Gender, Class, and Space at Sea, 1760–1810." *Eighteenth-Century Studies* 48, no. 1 (Fall 2014): 89–106.

Craft-Fairchild, Catherine. "Cross-Dressing and the Novel: Women Warriors and Domestic Femininity." *Eighteenth-Century Fiction* 10, no. 2 (1998): 171–202.

Critical Review; or, Annals of Literature. Vol. 20 (May 1810): 108–109.

Daut, Marlene. *Tropics of Haiti: Race and the Literary History of the Haitian Revolution in the Atlantic World, 1789–1865*. Liverpool: Liverpool University Press, 2015.

Davies, Kate. *Catharine Macaulay and Mercy Otis Warren: The Revolutionary Atlantic and the Politics of Gender*. Oxford: Oxford University Press, 2005.

Davis, Lennard J. *Factual Fictions: The Origins of the English Novel*. Philadelphia: University of Pennsylvania Press, 1996.

Davis, Natalie Zemon. *Women on the Margins: Three Seventeenth-Century Lives*. Cambridge, MA: Harvard University Press, 1995.

Dayan, Joan. *Haiti, History, and the Gods*. Berkeley: University of California Press, 1995.

Deb, Basuli. "Transnational Complications: Reimagining *Oroonoko* and Women's Collective Politics in the Empire." *Frontiers: A Journal of Women Studies* 36, no. 1 (2015): 33–56.

Defoe, Daniel. *Life and Strange Surprizing Adventures of Robinson Crusoe (1719)*. Vol. 1 of *The Novels of Daniel Defoe*, edited by W. R. Owens and P. N. Furbank. London: Pickering and Chatto, 2008.

Dekker, Rudolf, and Lotte van de Pol. *The Tradition of Female Transvestism in Early Modern Europe*. New York: St. Martin's Press, 1989.

Descartes, René. *Principles of Philosophy*. London: D. Reidel, 1983.

Dillon, Elizabeth Maddock. "The Secret History of the Early American Novel: Leonora Sansay and Revolution in Saint Domingue." *Novel: A Forum on Fiction* 40, no. 1 (Fall 2006): 77–103.

Disraeli, Isaac. *Miscellanies; or, Literary Recreations*. London: T. Cadell and W. Davies, 1796.

Dolan, Brian. *Ladies of the Grand Tour: British Women in Pursuit of Enlightenment and Adventure in Eighteenth-Century Europe*. New York: HarperCollins, 2001.

Dominique, Lyndon J. *Imoinda's Shade: Marriage and the African Woman in Eighteenth-Century British Literature, 1759–1808*. Columbus: Ohio State University Press, 2012.

———. Introduction to *The Woman of Colour: A Tale*, edited by Lyndon J. Dominique, 11–42. Peterborough, ON: Broadview Press, 2008.

Donato, Clorinda. "The Peregrinations of Two 'Péruviennes': Travel, Gender and Sexuality in the Transatlantic Crossings of Mme de Graffigny's Zilia and Flora Tristan." *Revista de Humanidades*, no. 27–28 (October 2010): 37–60.

Doyle, Laura. *Freedom's Empire: Race and the Rise of the Novel in Atlantic Modernity, 1640–1940*. Durham, NC: Duke University Press, 2007.

Drexler, Michael J. Introduction to *Secret History; or, The Horrors of St. Domingo*, by Leonora Sansay, 10–37. Edited by Michael J. Drexler. Peterborough, ON: Broadview Press, 2007.

Druett, Joan. *Hen Frigates: Wives of Merchant Captains under Sail*. New York: Simon and Schuster, 1998.

Dubois, Laurent. *Avengers of the New World: The Story of the Haitian Revolution*. Cambridge, MA: Harvard University Press, 2004.

Dugaw, Dianne. "Female Sailors Bold: Transvestite Heroines and the Markers of Class and Gender." In *Iron Men, Wooden Women: Gender and Seafaring in the Atlantic World*, edited by Margaret S. Creighton and Lisa Norling, 34–54. Baltimore: Johns Hopkins University Press, 1996.

———. *Warrior Women and Popular Balladry, 1650–1850.* Cambridge: Cambridge University Press, 1989.

Duncan, James. "A Memoir of Maria Sibilla Merian." In *Lives of Eminent Naturalists, with Engraved Portraits Accompanying Each*, 2:17–46. Edinburgh: W. H. Lizars; London: S. Highley; and Dublin: W. Curry, 1840.

Dunscombe, Elizabeth. Unpublished letters to Sir Thomas Cochrane, March 13 and 15, 1827. MS 2350, fols. 15–18v, 22–23. National Library of Scotland, Edinburgh.

Easton, Fraser. "Covering Sexual Disguise: Passing Women and Generic Constraint." *Studies in Eighteenth-Century Culture* 35 (2006): 95–125.

———. "Gender's Two Bodies: Women Warriors, Female Husbands, and Plebeian Life." *Past and Present* 180 (2003): 131–174.

Edgeworth, Maria. "The Grateful Negro." In *Selected Tales for Children and Young People*, edited by Susan Manly, 175–194. Basingstoke: Palgrave Macmillan, 2013.

———. *The Longford Edition: Tales and Novels.* 10 vols. London: George Routledge and Sons, 1893.

Equiano, Olaudah. *Public Advertiser*, April 6, 1787, 3.

Etheridge, Kay. "The Biology of *Metamorphosis insectorum Surinamensium*." In *Metamorphosis insectorum Surinamensium*, by Maria Sibylla Merian, 29–39. Facsimile ed., edited by Marieke van Delft and Hans Mulder. Tielt, Belgium: Lannoo Publishers, 2016.

———. "Maria Sibylla Merian: The First Ecologist?" In *Women and Science, 17th Century to Present: Pioneers, Activists and Protagonists*, edited by Donna Spalding Andréolle and Véronique Molinari, 35–54. Newcastle upon Tyne: Cambridge Scholars Publishing, 2011.

Falconbridge, Anna Maria. *Two Voyages to Sierra Leone.* In *Maiden Voyages and Infant Colonies: Two Women's Travel Narratives of the 1790s*, edited by Deirdre Coleman. London: Leicester University Press, 1999.

The Female Soldier; or, The Surprising Life and Adventures of Hannah Snell. 1750. Augustan Reprint Society, publication no. 357. Los Angeles: William Andrews Clark Memorial Library, University of California, 1989.

Festa, Lynn. *Sentimental Figures of Empire in Eighteenth-Century Britain and France.* Baltimore: Johns Hopkins University Press, 2006.

Fielder, Brigitte. "*The Woman of Colour* and Black Atlantic Movement." In *Women's Narratives of the Early Americas and the Formation of Empire*, edited by Mary McAleer Balkun and Susan C. Imbarrato, 171–185. New York: Palgrave Macmillan, 2016.

Flynn, Christopher. *Americans in British Literature, 1770–1832: A Breed Apart.* Burlington, VT: Ashgate, 2008.

Foucault, Michel. *Discipline and Punish: The Birth of the Prison.* Translated by Alan Sheridan. New York: Vintage Books, 1977.

———. *Security, Territory, Population: Lectures at the Collège de France, 1977–1978.* Edited by Michel Senellart. Translated by Graham Burchell. New York: Picador, 2004.

Fowler, Alasdair. *Kinds of Literature: An Introduction to the Theory of Genres and Modes.* Cambridge, MA: Harvard University Press, 1982.

Fulford, Tim. "Transatlantic American Indians." In *Transatlantic Literary Studies, 1660–1830*, edited by Eve Tavor Bannet and Susan Manning, 106–123. Cambridge: Cambridge University Press, 2011.

Fyfe, Christopher. *A History of Sierra Leone.* London: Oxford University Press, 1962.

———. Introduction to *"Our Children Free and Happy": Letters from Black Settlers in Africa in the 1790s*, edited by Christopher Fyfe, 1–19. Edinburgh: Edinburgh University Press, 1991.

———, ed. *"Our Children Free and Happy": Letters from Black Settlers in Africa in the 1790s.* Edinburgh: Edinburgh University Press, 1991.

———. *Sierra Leone Inheritance.* London: Oxford University Press, 1964.

Gallagher, Catherine. "The Caribbean in the Triangular Trade." In *Oroonoko; or, The Royal Slave,* by Aphra Behn, 3–25. Edited by Catherine Gallagher with Simon Stern. Boston: Bedford/St. Martin's Press, 2000.

Gaughan, Joan Mickelson. *The 'Incumberances': British Women in India, 1615–1856.* Oxford: Oxford University Press, 2014.

Gerzina, Gretchen. *Black London.* New Brunswick, NJ: Rutgers University Press, 1995.

Gibbes, Phebe. *Hartly House, Calcutta.* Edited by Michael J. Franklin. New Delhi: Oxford University Press, 2007.

Gilbert, Alan. *Black Patriots and Loyalists: Fighting for Emancipation in the War for Independence.* Chicago: University of Chicago Press, 2012.

Giles, Paul. *Transatlantic Insurrections: British Culture and the Formation of American Literature, 1730–1860.* Philadelphia: University of Pennsylvania Press, 2001.

Glissant, Edouard. *Poetics of Relation.* Translated by Betsy Wing. Ann Arbor: University of Michigan Press, 2010.

Goldberger, Nancy Rule, ed. *Knowledge, Difference, and Power: Essays Inspired by Women's Ways of Knowing.* New York: Basic Books, 1996.

Goldsmith, Oliver. *Collected Works of Oliver Goldsmith.* Edited by Arthur Friedman. 5 vols. Oxford: Clarendon Press, 1966.

Gollapudi, Aparna. "Virtuous Voyages in Penelope Aubin's Fiction." *Studies in English Literature* 45, no. 3 (Summer 2005): 669–690.

Goudie, Sean. *Creole America: The West Indies and the Formation of Literature and Culture in the New Republic.* Philadelphia: University of Pennsylvania Press, 2006.

Gqola, Pumla Dineo. "'Where There Is No Novelty, There Can Be No Curiosity': Reading Imoinda's Body in Aphra Behn's *Oroonoko or, the Royal Slave.*" *English in Africa* 28, no. 1 (2001): 105–117.

Greenblatt, Stephen. *Marvelous Possessions: The Wonder of the New World.* Chicago: University of Chicago Press, 1991.

Grove, Richard. *Green Imperialism: Colonial Expansion, Tropical Island Edens, and the Origins of Environmentalism, 1600–1860.* Cambridge: Cambridge University Press, 1995.

Gundersen, Joan R. *To Be Useful to the World: Women in Revolutionary America, 1740–1790.* Rev. ed. Chapel Hill: University of North Carolina Press, 2006.

Hagemann, Karen, Gisela Mettele, and Jane Rendall, eds. *Gender, War and Politics: Transatlantic Perspectives, 1775–1830.* Basingstoke: Palgrave Macmillan, 2010.

Hahner, June E. *Women through Women's Eyes: Latin American Women in Nineteenth-Century Travel Accounts.* Wilmington, DE: Scholarly Resources, 1998.

"Haitian Constitution of 1801." The Louverture Project, October 10, 2007. Accessed January 21, 2020. https://thelouvertureproject.org/index.php?title=Haitian_Constitution_of_1801_(English).

Hale, Charles A. Review of *Life in Mexico. The Letters of Fanny Calderón de la Barca,* edited by Howard T. Fisher and Marion Hall Fisher. *Hispanic American Historical Review* 47, no. 4 (1967): 581–583.

Hamilton, Elizabeth. *Translation of the Letters of a Hindoo Rajah.* 2 vols. London: printed for G. G. and J. Robinson, 1796.

Hawkes, Jean. Translator's introduction to *Peregrinations of a Pariah,* by Flora Tristan, x–xi. Translated and edited by Jean Hawkes. London: Virago Press, 1986.

Haywood, Ian. *Bloody Romanticism: Spectacular Violence and the Politics of Representation, 1776–1832.* Basingstoke: Palgrave Macmillan, 2006.

Hemingway, Andrew, and Alan Wallach, eds. *Transatlantic Romanticism: British and American Art and Literature, 1790–1860.* Amherst: University of Massachusetts Press, 2015.

Horrocks, Ingrid. *Women Wanderers and the Writing of Mobility, 1784–1814.* Cambridge: Cambridge University Press, 2017.

Houbraken, Jacobus, after Georg Gsell. *Maria Sibilla Merian 1717.* RCIN 670216. Royal Collection Trust, London. Accessed February 18, 2020. https://www.rct.uk/collection/search#/1/collection/670216/maria-sibilla-merian.

Hume, David. *A Treatise of Human Nature.* London: John Noon, 1739–1740.

Hunter, J. Paul. *The Reluctant Pilgrim: Defoe's Emblematic Method and Quest for Form in "Robinson Crusoe."* Baltimore: Johns Hopkins University Press, 1966.

Hutchings, Kevin, and John Miller, eds. *Transatlantic Literary Ecologies: Nature and Culture in the Nineteenth-Century Anglophone Atlantic World.* London: Routledge, 2017.

Hutchings, Kevin, and Julia M. Wright, eds. *Transatlantic Literary Exchanges, 1790–1870.* Burlington, VT: Ashgate, 2011.

Imbarrato, Susan C. *Traveling Women: Narrative Visions of Early America.* Athens: Ohio University Press, 2006.

Jasanoff, Maya. *Liberty's Exiles.* New York: Vintage Books, 2011.

Johnson, Charles. *A General History of the Robberies and Murders of the Most Notorious Pyrates.* London: T. Warner, 1724.

———. *The History of the Pyrates: Containing the Lives of Captain Misson. Captain Bowen. Captain Kidd. . . . And Their Several Crews.* London: T. Woodward, 1728.

Johnson, Claudia L. *Equivocal Beings: Politics, Gender, and Sentimentality in the 1790s.* Chicago: University of Chicago Press, 1995.

Joyce, James. "Daniel Defoe." Edited and translated by Joseph Prescott. *Buffalo Studies* 1 (December 1964): 24–25.

Kazanjian, David. *The Brink of Freedom: Improvising Life in the Nineteenth-Century Atlantic World.* Durham, NC: Duke University Press, 2016.

Klein, Ula Lukszo. "Eighteenth-Century Female Cross-Dressers and Their Beards." *Journal for Early Modern Cultural Studies* 16, no. 4 (2016): 119–143.

Knott, Sarah. "Sensibility and the American War for Independence." *American Historical Review* 109, no. 1 (February 2004): 19–40.

Korte, Barbara. *English Travel Writing from Pilgrimages to Postcolonial Explorations.* Basingstoke: Palgrave Macmillan, 2000.

Kozaczka, Edward J. "Penelope Aubin and Narratives of Empire." *Eighteenth-Century Fiction* 25, no. 1 (Fall 2012): 199–225.

Kuehn, Julia, and Paul Smethurst, eds. *Travel Writing, Form, and Empire: The Poetics and Politics of Mobility.* London: Routledge, 2009.

Kvande, Marta. "'Had You No Lands of Your Own?': Seeking Justice in *The Female American* (1767)." *Women's Studies* 45, no. 7 (2016): 684–698.

[Lacy, B.]. *Miscellaneous Poems Compos'd at Newfoundland, on Board His Majesty's Ship the* Kinsale. London: printed for the author, 1729.

Lamb, Susan. *Bringing Travel Home to England: Tourism, Gender, and Imaginative Literature in the Eighteenth Century.* Newark: University of Delaware Press, 2009.

Lanser, Susan. *The Sexuality of History: Modernity and the Sapphic, 1565–1830.* Chicago: University of Chicago Press, 2014.

Lapsansky, Phillip S. "Afro-Americana: Rediscovering Leonora Sansay." In *The Annual Report of the Library Company of Philadelphia for the Year 1992*, 29–46. Philadelphia: Library Company of Philadelphia, 1993.

Law-Sullivan, Jennifer. "Liberté, Egalité, Sororité: Flora Tristan and the Contact Zone between Race and Gender." *Nineteenth-Century French Studies* 39, no. 1–2 (2010–2011): 62–76.

Lee, Debbie, and Louis Kirk McAuley. "Romantic Recycling: The Global Economy and Second-hand Language in Equiano's *Interesting Narrative* and the Letters of the Sierra Leone Settlers." In *Global Romanticism: Origins, Orientations, and Engagements, 1760–1820*, edited by Evan Gottlieb, 169–197. Lewisburg, PA: Bucknell University Press, 2015.

Legge, Valerie E. "With 'High Hearts': Women Travelers to Newfoundland and Labrador." In *Pathways of Creativity in Contemporary Newfoundland and Labrador*, edited by Maria Jesús Hernáez Lerena, 51–73. Newcastle upon Tyne: Cambridge Scholars Publishing, 2015.

Lennon, Patrick. "Translation Original Texts *Metamorphosis insectorum Surinamensium*." In *Metamorphosis insectorum Surinamensium*, by Maria Sibylla Merian, 177–186. Facsimile ed., edited by Marieke van Delft and Hans Mulder. Tielt, Belgium: Lannoo Publishers, 2016.

Lerner, Gerda. *The Creation of Patriarchy*. New York: Oxford University Press, 1986.

Linnaeus, Carolus. *A General and Universal System of Natural History, Comprising the Three Kingdoms of Animals, Vegetables, and Minerals, Arranged under Their Respective Classes, Orders, Genera, and Species*. Vol. 12. London: W. Lewis, [18—?].

Liu, Tessie P. "The Secret beyond White Patriarchal Power: Race, Gender, and Freedom in the Last Days of Colonial Saint-Domingue." *French Historical Studies* 33, no. 3 (Summer 2010): 387–416.

Lively, Adam. *Masks: Blackness, Race, and the Imagination*. New York: Oxford University Press, 2000.

London Missionary Society. *Transactions of the Missionary Society in the Years 1803, 1804, 1805, and 1806*. Vol. 2. London, 1806.

Mackenzie, Anna Maria. *Slavery: Or, The Times*. 2 vols. London: G.G.J. and J. Robinsons and J. Dennis, 1792.

MacNeil, Denise Mary. "Empire and the Pan-Atlantic Self in *The Female American; or, The Adventures of Unca Eliza Winkfield*." In *Women's Narratives of the Early Americas and the Formation of Empire*, edited by Mary McAleer Balkun and Susan C. Imbarrato, 109–122. New York: Palgrave Macmillan, 2016.

Macpherson, Heidi Slettedahl. *Transatlantic Women's Literature*. Edinburgh: Edinburgh University Press, 2008.

Mancke, Elizabeth, and Carole Shammas. *The Creation of the British Atlantic World*. Baltimore: Johns Hopkins University Press, 2015.

Manganelli, Kimberly Snyder. *Transatlantic Spectacles of Race: The Tragic Mulatta and the Tragic Muse*. New Brunswick, NJ: Rutgers University Press, 2012.

Manning, Susan. "Characterless Women and Men: A Transatlantic Perspective." *Symbiosis: A Journal of Anglo-American Literary Relations* 10, no. 1 (April 2006): 21–45.

———. *Poetics of Character: Transatlantic Encounters, 1700–1900*. Cambridge: Cambridge University Press, 2013.

Manning, Susan, and Francis D. Cogliano, eds. *The Atlantic Enlightenment*. Burlington, VT: Ashgate, 2008.

Manning, Susan, and Andrew Taylor, eds. *Transatlantic Literary Studies: A Reader*. Baltimore: Johns Hopkins University Press, 2007.

Mayer, Holly A. *Belonging to the Army: Camp Followers and Community during the American Revolution*. Columbia: University of South Carolina Press, 1996.

McKeon, Michael. *The Origins of the English Novel, 1600–1740*. Baltimore: Johns Hopkins University Press, 2002.

McMichael, Trevor. "Gender, Neutrality, and the Nursing Father in Pratt's *Emma Corbett*." *The Eighteenth Century* 56, no. 3 (Fall 2015): 279–295.

McMurran, Mary Helen. "Realism and the Unreal in *The Female American*." *The Eighteenth Century* 52, no. 3–4 (Fall–Winter 2011): 323–342.

Méndez Rodenas, Adriana. *Transatlantic Travels in Nineteenth-Century Latin America: European Women Pilgrims*. Lewisburg, PA: Bucknell University Press, 2014.

Menefee, Samuel Pyeatt. *Wives for Sale: An Ethnographic Study of British Popular Divorce*. Oxford, UK: Basil Blackwell, 1981.

Merchant, Carolyn. *The Death of Nature: Women, Ecology, and the Scientific Revolution*. San Francisco: Harper and Row, 1980.

Merian, Maria Sybilla. *Dissertation sur la generation et les transformations des insectes de Surinam*. Paris: a la Haye, chez Pierre Gosse, 1726. New York Public Library, Rare Book Division, New York Public Library Digital Collection. Accessed May 11, 2020. http://digitalcollections.nypl.org/items/f160db30-ad53-0135-88ba-0f6a25accce9.

Mills, Sara. *Discourses of Difference: An Analysis of Women's Travel Writing and Colonialism*. London: Routledge, 1993.

Monthly Review; or, Literary Journal. Vol. 21 (October 1796): 176–181.

Monthly Review; or, Literary Journal. Vol. 62 (June 1810): 212.

Moore, Lisa L., Joanna Brooks, and Caroline Wigginton, eds. *Transatlantic Feminisms in the Age of Revolutions*. Oxford: Oxford University Press, 2012.

Mullan, John. *Sentiment and Sociability: The Language of Feeling in the Eighteenth Century*. Oxford: Clarendon Press, 1990.

Newman, Lance, Joel Pace, and Chris Koenig-Woodyard, eds. *Transatlantic Romanticism: An Anthology of British, American, and Canadian Literature, 1767–1867*. New York: Pearson Longman, 2006.

Newton, Isaac. Minutes. Journal Book of the Royal Society, vol. 11 (1702–1714), July 14, 1703, 27–28. JBO/11. Royal Society of London, London.

———. Minutes. Journal Book of the Royal Society, vol. 11 (1702–1714), October 27, 1703, 32–33. JBO/11. Royal Society of London, London.

Ney, Eugene. "The English Shore." In *French Visitors to Newfoundland: An Anthology of Nineteenth-Century Travel Writings*, translated and edited by Scott Jamieson and Anne Thareau, 65–69. St. John's, NL: ISER Books, 2013.

Nixon, Rob. *Slow Violence and the Environmentalism of the Poor*. Cambridge, MA: Harvard University Press, 2011.

Nordius, Janina. "'Thus Might I Reason with a Heathen . . .': The Gothic Moment in *The Female American*." *Nordic Journal of English Studies* 7, no. 2 (2008): 1–18.

Novak, Maximillian. *Economics and the Fiction of Daniel Defoe*. Berkeley: University of California Press, 1962.

Nugent, Maria. "Lady Nugent's Journal of Her Residence in Jamaica from 1801 to 1805." In *Travel Writing 1700–1830: An Anthology*, edited by Elizabeth A. Bohls and Ian Duncan, 325–333. Oxford: Oxford University Press, 2008.

Nussbaum, Felicity. *Torrid Zones: Maternity, Sexuality, and Empire in Eighteenth-Century English Narratives*. Baltimore: Johns Hopkins University Press, 1995.

O'Driscoll, Sally. "The Pirate's Breasts: Criminal Women and the Meanings of the Body." *The Eighteenth Century* 53, no. 3 (2012): 357–379.

O'Hanlon, Redmond. "Maria, the Jungle and Bird Eating Spiders." Paper presented at the Maria Sibylla Merian Conference 2017, "Changing the Nature of Art and Science: Intersections with Maria Sibylla Merian," Amsterdam, Netherlands, June 4–7, 2017.

O'Loughlin, Katrina. *Women, Writing, and Travel in the Eighteenth Century*. Cambridge: Cambridge University Press, 2018.

Omiah. *An Historic Epistle, from Omiah, to the Queen of Otaheite; Being His Remarks on the English Nation*. London: T. Evans, 1775.

Paravisini-Gebert, Lizabeth. "Cross-Dressing on the Margins of Empire: Women Pirates and the Narrative of the Caribbean." In *Women at Sea: Travel Writing and the Margins of Caribbean*

Discourse, edited by Lizabeth Paravisini-Gebert and Ivette Romero-Cesareo, 59–97. New York: Palgrave, 2001.

Paravisini-Gebert, Lizabeth, and Ivette Romero-Cesareo. "Introduction: Traveling the Margins of Caribbean Discourse." In *Women at Sea: Travel Writing and the Margins of Caribbean Discourse*, edited by Lizabeth Paravisini-Gebert and Ivette Romero-Cesareo, 1–7. New York: Palgrave, 2001.

———, eds. *Women at Sea: Travel Writing and the Margins of Caribbean Discourse*. New York: Palgrave, 2001.

Parrish, Susan Scott. *American Curiosity: Cultures of Natural History in the Colonial British Atlantic World*. Chapel Hill: University of North Carolina Press, 2006.

Pearsall, Sarah M. S. *Atlantic Families: Lives and Letters in the Later Eighteenth Century*. Oxford: Oxford University Press, 2008.

Perkins, Pam. "A 'Remote and Cheerless Possession': Early Nineteenth-Century Newfoundland in the British Cultural Imagination.'" In *Romantic Norths: Cultural Exchanges 1750–1850*, edited by Cian Duffy, 234–249. London: Palgrave, 2017.

Perkins, Pamela, and Shannon Russell. Introduction to *Translation of the Letters of a Hindoo Rajah*, by Elizabeth Hamilton, 7–45. Edited by Pamela Perkins and Shannon Russell. Reprinted with corrections. Peterborough, ON: Broadview Press, 1999.

Perry, Ruth. "Colonizing the Breast: Sexuality and Maternity in Eighteenth-Century England." In "The State, Society, and the Regulation of Sexuality in Modern Europe," pt. 1. Special issue, *Journal of the History of Sexuality* 2, no. 2 (1991): 204–234.

Phillips, Dana. *The Truth of Ecology: Nature, Culture, and Literature in America*. Oxford: Oxford University Press, 2003.

Phillips, Mark. *Society and Sentiment: Genres of Historical Writing in Britain, 1740–1820*. Princeton, NJ: Princeton University Press, 2000.

Pope, Alexander. *The Twickenham Edition of the Poems of Alexander Pope*. Edited by John Butt. 11 vols. London: Methuen, 1961–1969.

Pratt, Mary Louise. *Imperial Eyes: Travel Writing and Transculturation*. London: Routledge, 1992.

Pratt, Samuel Jackson. *Emma Corbett, or The Miseries of Civil War*. Edited by Eve Tavor Bannet. Peterborough, ON: Broadview Press, 2011.

Prescott, Henrietta. *Poems, Written in Newfoundland*. London: Saunders and Otley, 1839.

Prescott, William H. *History of the Conquest of Mexico*. New York: Harper and Brothers, 1843.

———. Review of *Life in Mexico during a Residence of Two Years in That Country*, by Madame Calderón de la Barca. *North American Review* 56, no. 118 (1843): 137–170.

Price, Richard, and Sally Price. Introduction to *Stedman's Surinam: Life in an Eighteenth-Century Slave Society; An Abridged, Modernized Edition of "Narrative of a Five Years Expedition against the Revolted Negroes of Surinam" by John Gabriel Stedman*, edited by Richard Price and Sally Price, xi–lxxv. Baltimore: Johns Hopkins University Press, 1992.

Prowse, D. W. *A History of Newfoundland*. Portugal Cove, NL: Boulder Publications, 2002.

Public Ledger (St. John's, NL). 1827–1834.

Pybus, Cassandra. *Epic Journeys of Freedom: Runaway Slaves of the American Revolution and Their Global Quest for Freedom*. Boston: Beacon Press, 2006.

Quijano, Anibal. "Coloniality of Power, Eurocentrism, and Latin America." *Nepantla: Views from South* 1, no. 3 (2000): 533–580.

Quirk, Joel. *The Anti-Slavery Project: From the Slave Trade to Human Trafficking*. Philadelphia: University of Pennsylvania Press, 2011.

Raleigh, Sir Walter. *The Discouerie of the Large, Rich, and Beuutiful Empyre of Guiana, with a Relation of the Great and Golden Citie of Manoa (Which the Spanyards Call El Dorado), And of the Prouinces of Emeria, Arromaia, Amapaia, and Other Countries, with Their Riuers Adioyning. Performed in the Year 1595*. London: Robert Robinson, 1596.

The Ranelean Religion Displayed. In a Letter from a Hottentot of Distinction, now in London, to his Friend at the Cape of Good-Hope. Containing the Reasons Assign'd by the Raneleans for Abolishing Christianity. London: W. Webb, 1750.

Rediker, Marcus. *Between the Devil and the Deep Blue Sea.* Cambridge: Cambridge University Press, 1987.

———. "Liberty beneath the Jolly Roger: The Lives of Anne Bonny and Mary Read, Pirates." In *Iron Men, Wooden Women: Gender and Seafaring in the Atlantic World*, edited by Margaret S. Creighton and Lisa Norling, 1–33. Baltimore: Johns Hopkins University Press, 1996.

Reitsma, Ella. "Maria Sibylla Merian: An Exceptional Woman." In *Metamorphosis insectorum Surinamensium*, by Maria Sibylla Merian, 8–18. Facsimile ed., edited by Marieke van Delft and Hans Mulder. Tielt, Belgium: Lannoo Publishers, 2016.

Richardson, Samuel. *Clarissa. Or, The History of a Young Lady.* 3rd ed. 8 vols. London: S. Richardson, 1751.

Romero-Cesareo, Ivette. "Women Adrift: Madwomen, Matriarchs, and the Caribbean." In *Women at Sea: Travel Writing and the Margins of Caribbean Discourse*, edited by Lizabeth Paravisini-Gebert and Ivette Romero-Cesareo, 135–160. New York: Palgrave, 2001.

Royal Gazette and Newfoundland Advertiser (St. John's). June 30, 1814.

R.R. "The Surinam Toad." N.d. Classified Papers on Zoology, 1660–1724. CLP/15i/36. Royal Society of London, London.

Said, Edward W. *Culture and Imperialism.* New York: Alfred A. Knopf, 1993.

Salih, Sara. *Representing Mixed Race in Jamaica and England from the Abolition Era to the Present.* London: Routledge, 2011.

Sansay, Leonora. *Secret History; or, The Horrors of St. Domingo.* Edited by Michael J. Drexler. Peterborough, ON: Broadview Press, 2007.

Schama, Simon. *Rough Crossings.* New York: HarperCollins, 2005.

Schiebinger, Londa. *Nature's Body: Gender in the Making of Modern Science.* Boston: Beacon Press, 1993.

———. *Plants and Empire: Colonial Bioprospecting in the Atlantic World.* Cambridge, MA: Harvard University Press, 2007.

Schlick, Yaël Rachel. *Feminism and the Politics of Travel after the Enlightenment.* Lewisburg, PA: Bucknell University Press, 2012.

Scots Magazine. Vol. 59 (January 1797): 47–48.

Seifert, Marina. *Rewriting Newfoundland Mythology: The Works of Tom Dawe.* Berlin: Galda and Wilch, 2002.

Shakespeare, William. *Royal Shakespeare Company Complete Works.* Edited by Jonathan Bate and Eric Rasmussen. Basingstoke: Macmillan, 2008.

Sharpe, Jenny. "The Violence of Light in the Land of Desire; or, How William Jones Discovered India." *Boundary 2* 20, no. 1 (1993): 26–46.

Shelley, Percy Bysshe. *A Defence of Poetry.* In *Major Works*, edited by Zachary Leader and Michael O'Neill, 674–701. Oxford: Oxford University Press, 2009.

Sher, Richard B. "Transatlantic Books and Literary Culture." In *Transatlantic Literary Studies, 1660–1830*, edited by Eve Tavor Bannet and Susan Manning, 10–27. Cambridge: Cambridge University Press, 2012.

Simon, Edward. "Unca Eliza Winkfield and the Fantasy of Non-Colonial Conversion in *The Female American*." *Women's Studies* 45, no. 7 (2016): 649–659.

Simpson, Frances, Lady. (Journal of a Voyage from Montreal thro' the Interior of Canada to York Factory). D.6/4. Hudson's Bay Company, Winnipeg, MB, 1830.

Smith, Chloe Wigston. "The Empire of Home: Global Domestic Objects and *The Female American* (1767)." *Journal for Eighteenth-Century Studies* 40, no. 1 (2017): 67–87.

Smith-Rosenberg, Carroll. "Black Gothic: The Shadowy Origins of the American Bourgeoisie." In *Possible Pasts: Becoming Colonial in Early America*, edited by Robert Blair St. George, 243–269. Ithaca, NY: Cornell University Press, 2000.

Society for the Propagation of the Gospel. *A Collection of Papers, Printed by Order of the Society for the Propagation of the Gospel in Foreign Parts*. London: Joseph Downing, 1706.

Sorensen, Janet. "Literature of the Ocean." In *Transatlantic Literary Studies, 1660–1830*, edited by Eve Tavor Bannet and Susan Manning, 124–138. Cambridge: Cambridge University Press, 2012.

Sorensen, Lise. "Susanna Rowson and the Transatlantic Captivity Narrative." In *Transatlantic Literary Studies, 1660–1830*, edited by Eve Tavor Bannet and Susan Manning, 169–185. Cambridge: Cambridge University Press, 2012.

Southey, Robert. *Letters from England*. By Don Manuel Alvarez Espriella [Robert Southey]. Edited by Carol Bolton. London: Routledge, 2016.

Spence, Caroline. "Ameliorating Empire: Slavery and Protection in the British Colonies, 1783–1865." PhD diss., Harvard University, 2014.

Spivak, Gayatri Chakravorty. "Can the Subaltern Speak?" In *The Post-Colonial Studies Reader*, edited by Bill Ashcroft, Gareth Griffiths, and Helen Tiffin, 28–37. 2nd ed. London: Routledge, 2006.

Stark, Suzanne. *Female Tars: Women aboard Ship in the Age of Sail*. Annapolis, MD: Naval Institute Press, 1996.

Stedman, John Gabriel. *Narrative of a Five Years Expedition against the Revolted Negroes of Surinam, Transcribed for the First Time from the Original 1790 Manuscript*. Edited by Richard Price and Sally Price. Baltimore: Johns Hopkins University Press, 1988.

Steele, Robert. *A Tour through Part of the Atlantic; or, Recollections from Madeira, the Azores (or Western Isles) and Newfoundland*. London: J. J. Stockdale, 1810.

Stone, Lawrence. *The Family, Sex, and Marriage in England, 1500–1800*. New York: Harper, 1977.

Thomas, Helen. *Romanticism and Slave Narratives: Transatlantic Testimonies*. Cambridge: Cambridge University Press, 2000.

Thompson, Carl. *Travel Writing*. London: Routledge, 2011.

Thompson, E. P. *Customs in Common: Studies in Traditional Popular Culture*. New York: New Press, 1991.

Todd, Janet. *Sensibility: An Introduction*. London: Routledge, 1986.

Todd, Kim. *Chrysalis: Maria Sibylla Merian and the Secrets of Metamorphosis*. New York: Harcourt, 2007.

Tristan, Flora. *Pérégrinations d'une paria (1833–1834)*. 2 tomes. Paris: Arthus Bertrand, 1838.

———. *Peregrinations of a Pariah*. Translated and edited by Jean Hawkes. London: Virago Press, 1986.

Tsing, Anna Lowenhaupt. *The Mushroom at the End of the World*. Princeton, NJ: Princeton University Press, 2017.

Turley, Hans. *Rum, Sodomy, and the Lash: Piracy, Sexuality, and Masculine Identity*. New York: New York University Press, 1999.

Ubisoft. *Assassin's Creed IV: Black Flag*. Montreal, 2013.

Usherwood, Stephen. "The Black Must Be Discharged—the Abolitionists' Debt to Lord Mansfield." *History Today* 31, no. 3 (March 1981): 40–45.

Vaccaro, Kristianne Kalata. "'Recollection . . . Sets My Busy Imagination to Work': Transatlantic Self-Narration, Performance, and Reception in *The Female American*." *Eighteenth-Century Fiction* 20, no. 2 (Winter 2007–2008): 127–150.

Van Renen, Denys. "'The Temple of Folly': Transatlantic 'Nature,' Nabobs, and Environmental Degradation in *The Woman of Colour*." In *Romantic Sustainability: Endurance and the*

Natural World, 1780–1830, edited by Ben P. Robertson, 147–168. Lanham, MD: Lexington Books, 2016.

Voltaire. *Le Huron, ou L'ingénu*. 2 vols. Lausanne, 1767.

Wahrman, Dror. "The English Problem of Identity in the American Revolution." *American Historical Review* 106, no. 4 (October 2001): 1236–1262.

Walker, James W. St. G. *The Black Loyalists*. Toronto: University of Toronto Press, 1976.

Walls, Laura Dassow. *The Passage to Cosmos: Alexander von Humboldt and the Shaping of America*. Chicago: University of Chicago Press, 2009.

Wandless, Bill. "Narrative Pain and the Moral Sense: Towards an Ethics of Suffering in the Long Eighteenth Century." *Literature and Medicine* 24, no. 1 (2005): 51–69.

Watt, Ian. *The Rise of the Novel: Studies in Defoe, Richardson, and Fielding*. Berkeley: University of California Press, 2000.

Watts, Isaac. *Logick: Or, The Right Use of Reason in the Enquiry after Truth*. 2nd ed. London: John Clarke et al., 1725.

Weekly Herald and Conception Bay General Advertiser (Harbour Grace, NL). May 14, 1851.

Wheelwright, Julie. *Amazons and Military Maids: Women Who Dressed as Men in the Pursuit of Life, Liberty and Happiness*. London: Pandora, 1989.

White, Gabrielle. *Jane Austen in the Context of Abolition: "A Fling at the Slave Trade."* Basingstoke: Palgrave Macmillan, 2006.

Williams, Helen Maria. *Letters Written in France, in the Summer 1790*. Edited by Neil Fraistat and Susan Lanser. Peterborough, ON: Broadview Press, 2001.

Wilson, Kathleen. *The Island Race: Englishness, Empire, and Gender in the Eighteenth Century*. New York: Routledge, 2003.

Winkfield, Unca Eliza [pseud.]. *The Female American; or, The Adventures of Unca Eliza Winkfield*. Edited by Michelle Burnham and James Freitas. 2nd ed. Peterborough, ON: Broadview Press, 2014.

Woertendyke, Gretchen J. "Geography, Genre, and Hemispheric Regionalism." *Atlantic Studies* 10, no. 2 (2013): 211–227.

Wollstonecraft, Mary. *Analytical Review, IV*. In *The Works of Mary Wollstonecraft*, edited by Janet Todd and Marilyn Butler, vol. 7. London: Pickering and Chatto, 1989.

The Woman of Colour, A Tale. London: Black, Parry and Kingsbury, 1808.

The Woman of Colour: A Tale. Edited by Lyndon J. Dominique. Peterborough, ON: Broadview Press, 2008.

Wordsworth, William. *Descriptive Sketches. In Verse. Taken during a Pedestrian Tour in the Italian, Grison, Swiss, and Savoyard Alps*. London: printed for J. Johnson, 1793.

Youngs, Tim, ed. *The Cambridge Introduction to Travel Writing*. Cambridge: Cambridge University Press, 2013.

Zelica, the Creole; A Novel, by an American. 3 vols. London: William Fearman, 1820.

Zuck, Rochelle Raineri. "New World Roots: Transatlantic Fictions, Creole Marriages, and Women's Cultivation of Empire in the Americas." In *Women's Narratives of the Early Americas and the Formation of Empire*, edited by Mary McAleer Balkun and Susan C. Imbarrato, 187–199. New York: Palgrave Macmillan, 2016.

NOTES ON CONTRIBUTORS

EVE TAVOR BANNET is George Lynn Cross Professor Emeritus at the University of Oklahoma. Her monographs include *Empire of Letters*, *Transatlantic Stories and the History of Reading*, and *Eighteenth-Century Manners of Reading*. She is completing a book, "The Letters in the Story," and acting as series editor for Eighteenth-Century Connections, an online series of short books.

VICTORIA BARNETT-WOODS is a visiting assistant professor at Loyola University Maryland and the editor of *Cultural Economies of the Atlantic World*, a collection that considers the intersection of material culture and the eighteenth-century Atlantic. Her research explores the cross-pollination of imperial history in the British Caribbean and the "rise of the novel" in the eighteenth and nineteenth centuries.

OCTAVIA COX teaches and researches at the University of Nottingham. She has published on women's writing in the *Lady's Poetical Magazine* and on opium imagery in eighteenth-century culture. She is currently writing her first monograph, "Alexander Pope in Romantic Culture."

DIANA EPELBAUM is an assistant professor and director of the Academic Writing Program at Marymount Manhattan College. Her scholarship bridges eighteenth-century studies, history of science, early American literature, and writing studies. Her book project, "Genre of Empire: Gender and Place in Women's Natural Histories of the Americas, 1688–1808," argues for a remapping of the natural history genre's historiography.

JENNIFER GOLIGHTLY is an academic applications specialist at Colorado College and an instructor at the University of Denver. Her research focuses on the novels of the late eighteenth century. She is the author of *The Family, Marriage, and Radicalism in British Women's Novels of the 1790s* and an essay on reproduction in the novels of the 1790s.

GRACE A. GOMASHIE is a doctoral candidate in Hispanic studies at the University of Western Ontario. Her thesis focuses on the language maintenance of Nahuatl in Mexico. She has published on the Equatorial Guinean variety of Spanish,

Mohawk language revitalization in Canada, translations of travel accounts, and the role of community in Latin American novels.

SHELBY JOHNSON is an assistant professor of English at Florida Atlantic University, where she researches and teaches early American literature and sexuality, long eighteenth-century race and ecocriticism, and Indigenous studies. She is completing a book project on iterations of an "earth given to the children of men" in early Caribbean and Native texts.

ULA LUKSZO KLEIN is the director of Women's and Gender Studies at the University of Wisconsin–Oshkosh. Her book *Sapphic Crossings: Cross-Dressing Women in Eighteenth-Century Literature* is forthcoming, and she recently co-edited a special issue of *ABO: Interactive Journal for Women in the Arts, 1640–1830* on "eighteenth-century camp." Her recent article "Dildos and Material Sapphism in the Eighteenth Century" appeared in *Eighteenth-Century Fiction*.

MISTY KRUEGER is an assistant professor of English at the University of Maine at Farmington. She is the editor of *Transatlantic Women Travelers*, and she also co-edited an issue for the Jane Austen Society of North America (JASNA) journal *Persuasions On-Line*. She was the 2017 JASNA International Visitor and has published on Austen's juvenilia, three of her novels, and Austen-related adaptation, pedagogy, popular culture, and social media, as well as long eighteenth-century drama.

ALEXIS MCQUIGGE is the Student Success Centre writing coordinator and an adjunct professor in the University of Regina's Department of English. Her research and teaching interests are in eighteenth-century women's writing, including travel literature and the novel. She is the author of "'They Give No Cordials to Heighten the Fever': Lady Mary, Corruption, and the Problem of Royal Influence."

KATHLEEN MORRISSEY is an English lecturer at Anna Maria College, and she teaches in a summer program at the Massachusetts Institute of Technology. Her interests include gender, disability, and game studies. She has essays in two forthcoming collections: one in *Joyce Writing Disability* and another in *Final Fantasy VII: Critical Essays*, for a gaming series.

PAM PERKINS is Distinguished Professor of English at the University of Manitoba, specializing in eighteenth-century and Romantic literature. She has edited a number of late eighteenth- and early nineteenth-century works of fictional and nonfictional travels, including excerpts from Sir Thomas Cochrane's Newfoundland journals. Her current research focuses on turn-of-the-nineteenth-century British travels along the North Atlantic rim.

INDEX

Page references in *italics* indicate illustrative material.